Hannah Arendt and Politics

THINKING POLITICS

Series Editors: Geoff M. Boucher and Matthew Sharpe

Published titles

Agamben and Politics: A Critical Introduction
Sergei Prozorov

Foucault and Politics: A Critical Introduction
Mark G. E. Kelly

Taylor and Politics: A Critical Introduction
Craig Browne and Andrew P. Lynch

Habermas and Politics: A Critical Introduction
Matheson Russell

Irigaray and Politics: A Critical Introduction
Laura Roberts

Lyotard and Politics: A Critical Introduction
Stuart Sim

Hannah Arendt and Politics
Maria Robaszkiewicz and Michael Weinman

Forthcoming titles

Nancy Fraser and Politics
Marjan Ivković and Zona Zarić

Nussbaum and Politics
Brandon Robshaw

Judith Butler and Politics
Adriana Zaharijević

HANNAH ARENDT AND POLITICS

∞

Maria Robaszkiewicz and Michael D. Weinman

EDINBURGH
University Press

Edinburgh University Press is one of the leading university presses in the UK. We publish academic books and journals in our selected subject areas across the humanities and social sciences, combining cutting-edge scholarship with high editorial and production values to produce academic works of lasting importance. For more information visit our website: edinburghuniversitypress.com

Edinburgh University Press Ltd
The Tun—Holyrood Road
12(2f) Jackson's Entry
Edinburgh EH8 8PJ

Typeset in 11/13pt Adobe Sabon LT Pro
by Cheshire Typesetting Ltd, Cuddington, Cheshire, and
printed and bound in Great Britain

A CIP record for this book is available from the British Library

ISBN 978 1 4744 9722 0 (hardback)
ISBN 978 1 4744 9724 4 (webready PDF)
ISBN 978 1 4744 9725 1 (epub)

Contents

Acknowledgments

Hannah Arendt and Politics has come to see the light of day thanks to the collaborative effort of many people over a number of years. It is our duty, and a privilege, to share our sincere thanks to all of those whose work and whose encouragement made this project possible. First, we would like to thank Geoff M. Boucher and Matthew Sharpe, editors of the *Thinking Politics* series, for giving us the opportunity to shape the presentation of this central thinker for this audience. We also extend our gratitude to everyone at Edinburgh University Press who has been involved in contracting, completing, and publishing this book, especially Ersev Ersoy for her excellent advice and professionalism throughout the late stages of bringing this project to completion.

Maria Robaszkiewicz would like to thank Marieke Borren, Antonio Calcagno, Katja Čičigoj, Marta Famula, Ruth Hagengruber, Wolfgang Heuer, Andrea Karsten, and Ursula Ludz for their helpful suggestions and their friendship. She very much appreciates the support of her student assistants, Simge Altunbüken and Aleksandar Cvetkovic, during the work on this book. She would like especially to thank her mother, Anna Pikulska-Radomska, who never stops believing in her. Michael Weinman wishes to thank Sabrina Slipchenko for research assistance and substantial practical contributions of numerous kinds. He also gratefully acknowledges his debt to his friends and colleagues in the Hannah Arendt Working Group in Critical Theories of Modernity at the Institute for Advanced Studies in Culture, and in particular the co-convenor of that group, Isaac Ariail Reed, for years of stimulating interdisciplinary dialogue without which his contributions to this volume would not have been possible.

Portions of Chapter 8 have appeared previously, in different form, as: Michael Weinman (2020), "Arendt and the Return of Ethnonationalism," Demos vs. Polis: The New Populism, *Liberal Herald* 4: 42–8; Michael Weinman (2018), "Arendt and the Legitimate Expectation for Hospitality and Membership Today," *Moral Philosophy and Politics* 5 (1): 127–50. Both authors gratefully acknowledge the editors and publishers of those publications for permission to present reworked versions of these excerpts.

Last but not least, our deepest gratitude to our first readers for their intellectual inspiration and generous responses to drafts of some or all of what follows: Marieke Borren, Irit Dekel; David Kretz; Isaac Ariail Reed. With so many to thank for these various reasons, we alone take responsibility for whatever errors remain.

Abbreviations of Frequently Cited Works by Hannah Arendt

BPF *Between Past and Future*
CC "The Crisis in Culture: Its Social and Its Political Significance"
CE "The Crisis in Education"
CH "The Concept of History: Ancient and Modern"
EJ *Eichmann in Jerusalem*
Ex "What is Existential Philosophy?"
GBPF "The Gap Between Past and Future"
H80 "Heidegger at Eighty"
HC *The Human Condition*
IP "Introduction *into* Politics"
LKPP *Lectures on Kant's Political Philosophy*
LoM I *The Life of the Mind One: Thinking*
LoM II *The Life of the Mind Two: Willing*
MDT *Men in Dark Times*
OR *On Revolution*
OT *The Origins of Totalitarianism*
OV *On Violence*
PP "Philosophy and Politics"
PRD "Personal Responsibility Under Dictatorship"
RLR "Reflections on Little Rock"
SQMP "Some Questions of Moral Philosophy"
TMA "Tradition and the Modern Age"
TP "Truth and Politics"
UP Understanding and Politics
VA *Vita activa*
WA "What is Authority?"
WF "What is Freedom?"
WRLR "What Remains? The Language Remains"

Please note that all citations refer to the editions included in the Bibliography.

There would be much to write about Hannah Arendt's own life story. This has been done in a wonderful way by Elisabeth Young-Bruehl (1982) in her classic *For Love of the World*, and recently taken up from a different angle in Samantha Rose Hill's *Critical Lives* biography (2021), to name just two sources shedding light on her rich life, full of unexpected twists and turns.[1] Arendt herself reveals some autobiographical details in her famous 1964 interview, published as "What Remains? The Language Remains" (1994), and widely available as an online video source. This is why here, we restrict ourselves to a couple of words, marking some points in her life, to which we refer later in this book. Born in a Jewish family in Hanover on October 14, 1906, she lost her father soon after and moved with her mother to Königsberg, where she grew up. Her mother was a communist and a supporter of Rosa Luxemburg. The question of being Jewish was treated in the family as a plain fact, not a political matter. Already as a teenager, Hannah Arendt was fascinated by philosophy; she read Kant and Jaspers, and soon decided to study philosophy. She began her studies in Berlin, then moved to Marburg upon hearing rumors of Martin Heidegger's genius. Heidegger and Arendt engaged in a brief romantic relationship, after which she left Marburg to complete her dissertation about Saint Augustine with Karl Jaspers. In the early 1930s, upon the rise of National Socialist party and antisemitic sentiments in Germany, Arendt discovered her political side and got involved with Zionists, even though she never became a member of any party or organization. After being briefly imprisoned, she fled to Paris, and later, with her husband Heinrich Blücher, to New York, where they arrived in 1940. As a Jewish migrant, Arendt joined the already established Jewish intellectual community. In 1949, she published her voluminous study *The Origins of Totalitarianism*, which made her famous overnight. From there, her career as a political theorist—not a philosopher, as she stressed—developed very dynamically. In 1951, after over a decade of statelessness, she received US citizenship. She published many books (*The Human Condition* is probably the most popular one) and essays, and taught highly regarded courses as a guest lecturer at many leading American universities, including Princeton and the University of Chicago, before taking a permanent position at the New School for Social Research. In 1961, Arendt reported for the *New Yorker* about the trial of Adolf Eichmann. The report, published as a book in 1963, and in particular its subtitle introducing the phrase "banality of evil," sparked a heated debate, which had serious consequences for her, especially regarding conflicts with other Jewish intellectuals. Later in her life, she returned to more philosophical reflections in her trilogy *The Life of the Mind*. She died on December 4, 1975, and the title page of its third part, *Judging*, was found rolled in her typewriter.

Hannah Arendt has been classified as a critical theorist (Habermas 1981), a reluctant modernist (Benhabib 1996), a phenomenologist (Borren 2010; Hinchman and Hinchman 1994; Loidolt 2018), an anti-feminist (Millet 1969; Pitkin 1995, 1998), a feminist ally (Allen 1999b; Borren 2013; Zerilli 2005a), a democratic theorist (Honig 2017; Lederman 2019), a republican theorist (Barbour 2014; Forst 2007), a Heideggerian (Faye 2009; Villa 1996), and a nostalgic or critical Graecophile (Euben 2000; Taminaux 1997; Tsao 2002). This book responds to these perspectives in two ways. First, we recognize that all these positionings can legitimately be derived from one or another of her writings; second, we insist nevertheless and precisely because all these approaches play some role in her work that her readers ought to follow her own claim (WRLR 4) about her political awakening in the 1930s: "I did not belong to a party, nor did I have need to," which, in a more metaphoric way, remained true all her life. Instead, we introduce her works as exercises in political thinking, treating her as a dialogue partner, whose judgments and opinions remain open for reflection and discussion.

Hannah Arendt and Politics thus presents Hannah Arendt from a fresh angle: as a thinker who engages in both word and deed with the practices of the common world, and who invites us to do the same. The essential element of her unique manner of thinking politics, her concept of "exercises in political thinking," remains insufficiently regarded, for all the recent flurry of discussion about her work. Based on this concept, we aim here to uncover the deeply practical aspect of her thinking, including in what is generally taken to be her most abstract and theoretical writings, such as *The Human Condition* and *The Life of the Mind*. Arendt is well known for her accounts of action, totalitarianism, and revolution, alongside her insightful study of lying in politics and the prevalence of prejudice, to name but a few. These aspects of her thought have gained widespread academic, as well as popular, attention in recent years. A growing number of publications on Arendt's political theory, especially those engaging in critical analysis of current political phenomena, amply demonstrates the contemporary relevance of her theoretical concepts. Our book, however, will introduce the reader not only to Hannah Arendt's theory and its current salience but also to her practice of reflective judgment.

Why so? Because, as Arendt stresses more than once, her aim is not to construct a theory that appeals to academics and intellectuals but to understand the phenomena of our common world: in her oft-cited phrase, this means, essentially, "to think what we are doing" (VA 5). This understanding can be interpreted as "a creative process of lending meaning to reality resulting in stories" (Vasterling 2007: 85). As such, it is connected to our ever-changing reality, and must remain open, revisable, and negotiable. While Arendt only explicitly refers to the essays collected in *Between Past and Future* as exercises in political thinking, we show in the following chapters that this moniker can be applied to all her writings. Her main objective, we believe, is to invite her readers to join her in thinking about and judging political categories and issues that we hold in common on this basis of our shared experience of contemporary political life, and not as students of one or another school of thought. As such, Arendt's exercises are truly placed between past and future: in their work as critiques, they offer a critical examination of past traditions; in their work as experiments, they provide a perspective on future possibilities, without trying to define or delimit these possibilities. Embracing these critical and experimental elements, her work demands attending to plurality, the co-presence of multiple perspectives considered in their own right and in juxtaposition to alternatives, which is perhaps the supreme guiding and ungrounded norm of her distinctive way of thinking through politics and thinking politically. For Arendt, this kind of reflexivity is a cornerstone of responsible political action.

We aim here to illuminate this unique potential of Arendt's writings through engagement with some of the most pressing political phenomena of our times, such as: the political and cultural challenges resulting from the renewed upsurge in migration; racism and antisemitism and the perennial appeal of populism, post-truth politics and how and why propaganda works; the continuing social and political inequality of women; the climate crisis and youth activism; and the continuing role of religion in public life notwithstanding the legal separation of church and state in liberal societies. By engaging with Arendt's thinking through and about politics, first as a corpus of work that displays her method of exercises in political thinking and then as a series of further exercises in political thinking that bring her written works into direct contact with the challenges and debates of our moment, we invite readers to think politically with and against Hannah Arendt.

Arendt's method of choice for such a critical dialogue was storytelling, which for her resonates closest with the practice of understanding she mentions in the response to Voegelin. In other words, while Voegelin (1953: 70) criticizes her lack of objectivity, as expected in an academic discourse, Arendt chooses an alternative way of theorizing: instead of designing her writings as a chain of deductive argumentations or trying to decipher the historical truth, she turns to storytelling as one of the essential modes of human communication (Worth 2008: 43). Of course, this does not mean that her writings lack logical consistency, even if she, against the advice of her mentor and friend Karl Jaspers, adhered to her "intuitive-chaotic method" (Vowinckel 2001: 42). Through the use of storytelling, she much more draws our attention to the meaning of human life arising from our experience and the fact that human beings are more than incarnations of the reason, but are also embodied, historical, and—political. This is why she is so fond of the quotation by Isak Dinesen (Karen Blixen), which she recalls several times in her writings: "All sorrows can be borne if you put them into a story or tell a story about them."[2] For Arendt, every life story (to be sure: not only full of sorrows) is radically unique and at the same time interwoven with multiple other life stories. The narrative method allows the freedom of action to be adequately expressed: "each human life tells its story and [. . .] history ultimately becomes the storybook of mankind, with many actors and speakers and yet without any tangible authors" (HC 184). Each of these stories mirrors the actor's decisions for acting along the way, with the simultaneous consideration that at any moment she may have chosen differently. Particular events are then related to each other—according to the rules of storytelling—by the explanatory force. This force, however, does not aim at any unambiguous and definite clarification of these relationship (a specific truth), but is rather of an interpretative nature and points to a possibility of multiple understandings. For Arendt, there is no epistemic difference between the storyteller and the political actors, as "the meaning of events rises from within these events, and is not derived from necessary historical laws" (Schoonheim 2020: 852–3).

Such storytelling is a critical practice of communication resting on human plurality. As a means of critical reflection, storytelling is always simultaneously directed at itself and at others (Heuer 2012:

261). It only makes sense if there are both storyteller(s) and listener(s) who can share an understanding. Through stories of judgments and actions, it becomes vital for the common world, whose relative permanence rests on the transmission of the words and deeds that constitute it. At the same time, as Lisa Disch (1994: 109, 155) emphasizes, storytelling does not merely transmit facts but is also a practice of critical thinking and constructing political knowledge, and hence, as we argue, an apt method for exercising political thinking.

But plurality also manifests in a different way in Arendt's approach to history: inspired by Greek poets and historians, and certainly with Walter Benjamin's concept of history in mind, Arendt emphasizes that history (in traditional terms focusing mainly on the dialectic of war and peace) must not be told from the perspective of the winners only. It must also take into account the voices of the defeated (CH 47–8; Arendt 1953: 77; Herzog 2000: 11), who at times cannot tell their stories themselves, being forgotten, made invisible or dead. These stories are a part of the world and deserve attention for the sake of plurality; as Arendt writes, in "any series of events that together form a story with a unique meaning we can at best isolate the agent who set the whole process into motion" (HC 185).

Importantly, if we do not deal with fictional narratives, which Arendt uses often for exemplary purposes, there are limits to the possible and acceptable interpretation of events. While the storyteller does not seek the rationally ascertainable truth about history, she relies on factual truths, as Arendt notes: "Factual truth [. . .] is always related to other people: it concerns events and circumstances in which many are involved; it is established by witnesses and depends upon testimony [. . .]. It is political by nature" (TP 233–4). Facts, then, are something established, something that we ensure to each other by virtue of sharing the world. As events are only accessible to us in the present, in the very moment they appear, it is only through reifying them in the form of stories that we can keep them and turn them into a part of the web of human relationships. Such stories are interpretations, emphatically plural, but they need to—unconditionally—respect the facts, which are backed up by the worldly experience of people in their plurality. These limitations, as we know, have never been treated with due gravity, and are maybe more in jeopardy today than ever before.

In this book, we emphasize the practical nature of storytelling as a method of exercises in political thinking. In Part I, we introduce Arendt's political vocabulary, which, in certain key respects, differs from the way we use these same notions in political debates and our everyday language. We start, in Chapter 1, with her account of action, in combination with other concepts that situate it in her theory. Chapter 2 explores Arendt's distinction between politics and philosophy and her own connection to the practice of thinking. In Chapter 3, we then outline Arendt's theory of judgment, which she also addresses as political thinking, and turn especially to its practical implementation as exercises in political thinking.

This opens a theoretical perspective for Part II of our book, in which we propose six such exercises, all of them illuminating some aspect of Arendt's political theory, and at the same time engaging, through an Arendtian lens, in a discussion of questions and challenges we face today. In Chapter 4 we discuss Arendt's relation to Martin Heidegger, especially in the context of his engagement on the side of the National Socialist regime. We refer centrally to the tension between philosophy and politics, which is one of the ongoing motives in Arendt's thinking, and which leads us to the problem of political and personal responsibility. Our focus in Chapter 5 is Arendt's report on Adolf Eichmann's trial and the controversy it provoked, and takes us subsequently to the current turmoil around the state of Israel, paying special attention to parallels between this controversy and that occasioned by Judith Butler's receipt of the Adorno Prize in 2012. Hannah Arendt's perspective on the earth and nature is our concern in Chapter 6. We link it to Arendt's unique angle not only on civil disobedience but also on education, making the Fridays for Future protests our case study. In Chapter 7, we address the feminist reception of Hannah Arendt's writings, and Chapter 8 offers a view on the role her theory plays in current migration studies, which is (at least partly) rooted in her own experience as a refugee discussed explicitly in more than one of her most impactful written works. Finally, in Chapter 9, we turn to Arendt's engagement with the topic of race and the critical reactions to it, recurring recently in the context of #BlackLivesMatter protests.

Notes

1. The bibliography of biographical writings about Arendt also includes several children's books, which might be a sign of her public popularity.
2. TP 257; MDT 104; HC 175. Arendt does not provide a reference for this quotation. A similar statement can be found in Karen Blixen's telephone interview with the *New York Times Book Review* (November 3, 1957):

"One of my friends said about me that I think all sorrows can be borne if you put them into a story or tell a story about them, and perhaps this is not entirely untrue." The quotation became famous after Arendt used it as an epigraph for the third part of *The Human Condition* (Wilkinson 2004).

Part I

Arendt and Politics:
Thinking About the World as a Public Space

Chapter 1

Action!

The Beginning

Where to begin, when one begins reading, studying, or teaching Hannah Arendt? This question, quite easy to answer in reference to many thinkers we find in the canon of philosophical classics (about which we are not uncritical), proves to be a challenge in the case of Arendt. This is because she is not a systematic thinker, gradually building up her theoretical construction brick by brick. She rather, figuratively speaking, invites her readers to dive right into the deep and rich waters of her thinking. These waters do have a defined geography and once one has recognized how to navigate them, every wave and every sea rock exposes precious elements of her understanding of the world. Since developing, enlarging, and deepening this understanding was Arendt's life-long passion, her thinking moves cyclically, its streams revisiting places they previously sighted, establishing new connections but also strengthening the ones we already know.

The standard—and quite reasonable—way of beginning with Arendt is to read the first chapters of *The Human Condition*, where she lays down the most important distinctions of her theory and introduces most of the central notions which provide a key to her distinctive theory of the world we share as human beings: "fundamental human activities: labor, work and action" (HC 7); plurality and natality; the public, the private, and the social.

Rather than laying out these "key concepts" (Hayden 2014) in this building block format, however, what we do in this chapter is to pave Arendt's conceptual paths in small steps, from one notion to the next, illuminating the fragile framing of her theory. In so doing, we draw from *The Human Condition* but we also go beyond it, to the numerous books and essays where she returns to these abstract concepts to discuss them more thoroughly, add new meanings to them, or put them into different concrete contexts. What we aim at is an introduction to what Lisa Disch (1994: 24) describes as Arendt's new lexicon of politics. Our guideposts will be natality, plurality, action, power, freedom, the private and the public, and the social. These notions are interconnected in Arendt's theory and partly define each other. We need them all to get a grasp of the world as described by Arendt, beginning with

Natality

The world Arendt describes and seeks to understand is almost exclusively an anthropocentric world. Her rare references to nature primarily serve to situate the human being in the world as a whole. The natural world, she writes, is subject to "circular movement of natural life" (HC 19). What we have in common with animals are the natural processes of the body: growth; metabolism; decay. However, in a genealogical gesture, Arendt refers to the difference between human beings and animals as seen by the ancient Greeks and early Christians. Though very different in their cosmology, these traditions had a common understanding of this difference: while animals are specimens of a species and very similar to one another, human beings are individuals, absolutely unique in terms of time and space (HC 7–8). This is where natality comes into play.

Arendt brings up natality as being opposed to mortality (HC 8). To the latter, however, she hardly pays any attention. This is because natality, a category which she meant to be inspired by Augustine and as counterweight to Heidegger's "thrownness" (Marder 2013: 303) and "being-towards-death," entails a significant political potential and constitutes the very first condition of human action. For Arendt, natality is the condition of human uniqueness:

> the new beginning inherent in birth can make itself felt in the world only because the newcomer possesses the capacity of beginning something anew, that is, of acting. In this sense of initiative, an element of action, and therefore of natality, is inherent in all human activities. Moreover, since action is the political activity par excellence, natality, and not mortality, may be the central category of political, as distinguished from metaphysical, thought. (HC 9)

At the same time, every human being, as radically new in the world by virtue of birth, has the potential to make new beginnings. Arendt identifies such new beginnings with acting: the human activity which indeed changes the world. While being thrown into the world in Heideggerian or existentialist sense suggests disorientation of the subject and arbitrariness of life and the world, Arendt draws a different picture. Of course, coming into the world as radically new beings, we know nothing about it and lack orientation. But we are not isolated or alone: as children, Arendt writes, we are introduced into the world as it is by the adults who also assume responsibility for this world (CE 193). The human world is "created by mortal hands to serve mortals for a limited time as home [. . .], it wears out" (CE 189). However, with the continuous birth of the new, the constant renewing of the world becomes possible.

Not only is the fact that the human world is an object of unceasing transformation of anthropological significance, it is first and foremost politically relevant, and this in a twofold sense. First, natality gives us hope, even in a situation of a seemingly insurmountable crisis. Arendt refers to Augustine and his statement about the creation of the human being for the sake of a new beginning to be made at the end of her epochal study *Origins of Totalitarianism*. This book, introducing the reader to the absolute darkness of a totalitarian regime and to the monstrosity of the National Socialist crimes, ends with a gesture of hope: "The beginning is guaranteed by every new birth; it is indeed every man" (OT 479).

Second, crucially, natality is one of two central conditions of the possibility of acting. Action, as Arendt emphasizes, is a new beginning, an insertion into the human world, which is "like a second birth" (HC 176). Therefore, acting as beginning something anew is the very practice of renewing the world. What is important, though, is that this hope and this renewal can never be provided by an individual. It always needs human beings in their

Plurality

From the very first moment when she introduces the notion of plurality in *The Human Condition*, it becomes clear that it is the cornerstone of the meaning of being human. For Arendt, plurality means that "men, not Man, live on the earth and inhabit the world" (HC 7). This seemingly banal presupposition affects her theory as a whole: anywhere one looks, plurality is just around the corner. Action, as we will show, is only possible if people come together. This plurality of acting subjects is the condition for the human world (as opposed to natural world, which supports us as natural beings among others) to emerge. The political, as an aspect of this world, is a space of appearance, and for the appearance of political actors to be meaningful, they need to appear to each other—hence, a plurality of actors is essential. When we make a judgment, we rely on a plurality of opinions, and even Arendtian thinking as an inner dialogue entails an element of plurality.

However, plurality does not only mean that we—human beings—are many. To recall the human condition of natality, each of us is also new and unique. Hence, plurality has two aspects: equality and difference. On the one hand, Arendt argues, we are all equal as human beings. On the other hand, "nobody is ever the same as anyone else who ever lived, lives, or will live" (HC 8). For Arendt, action is always connected to speech, and this twofold character of plurality appears in relation to both these activities:

> If men were not equal, they could neither understand each other and those who came before them nor plan for the future and foresee the needs of those who will come after them. If men were not distinct, each human being distinguished from any other who is, was, or will ever be, they would need neither speech nor action to make themselves understood. Signs and sounds to communicate immediate, identical needs and wants would be enough. (HC 175–6)

Nonetheless, as we are unique beings, the communication and interaction between humans goes beyond these basic modes. As a fact of life, plurality means that we, as individuals, live together with others, with whom we come together, create private relationships, like for example between neighbors, and relationships in the public sphere, like for example political friendship. These relationships produce different kinds of communication and interaction, both affirmative and conflictual. So, in the political sense, plurality can be understood as a plurality of first-person perspectives, which forms an in-between, an assembly of those who act together, which provides a ground for any politics (Loidolt 2018: 153).

However, as a political condition, plurality cannot be taken for granted. In fact, its status is very fragile. In what Arendt, following Bertolt Brecht, calls "dark times," there exists no space for politics. The light of the public dims (MDT viii), human interaction in the political sense of beginning something new becomes inhibited, and what she describes as the "paradoxical plurality of unique beings" (HC 176) has no possibility of actualizing its appearance in public. The paramount example of such an anti-phenomenon in Arendt's work is of course the rise of totalitarianism, but she emphasizes that dark times were not rare in human history, and refuses to equate them with the atrocities of her lifetime (MDT ix). The fragility of plurality manifests itself in Arendt's claim that without it a fully human life, the life of action (HC 176), lacks a proper space to be exercised (HC 49). For action to become possible, plurality as the we exceeding the "I," or consisting of multiple, unique "I"s, needs to be actualized (Loidolt 2018: 175). In Part II of this book, we discuss events and situations that exemplify both human action in the light of the public and those moments when the life of action is impossible because the space of appearance is wanting, and things go dark.

As has now become apparent, Arendt's notion of plurality is everything but simple. Apart from its fragility, living together under this paradox condition not only enriches the world but also becomes a source of significant challenges: acting together in spite of our differences, thinking as an inner dialogue with a particularly demanding dialogue partner, judging politically with respect to an ever-changing spectrum of possible standpoints are all challenging practices we confront in the common world. Plurality, in this sense, creates a dynamic of equality and difference, of convergence and retreat, of consensus and dissent. All this is necessary for human beings to engage in acting and speaking.

Arendt's appreciation of plurality is perhaps best expressed in her reference to the notion of human nature. While she rejected fixing the human subject through any notion of human nature—stating that such a thing does not exist (HC 193)—the closest she gets to a definition of the human is when she addresses human existence as endlessly conditioned. Human beings, she states, "are conditioned beings because everything they come in contact with turns immediately into a condition of their existence" (HC 9). This does not only include the conditions under which life on earth is given to us but also human-made conditions: the way we shape our world through work and

Action

With action, we open the first structural frame of Arendt's understanding of the human condition. Action is one of the three fundamental human activities, alongside labor and work. These activities are connected to the meanings of the notion of world in Arendt's writings. The world in which we live has different dimensions, or layers. The first one is the natural world: a planet that supports us and provides us with living conditions. We share this world with

15

other living beings, and we need it to exist: it constitutes a sustaining basis for our living. Arendt refers to the activities we undertake in this sphere of our lives as labor (HC 7). This includes caring for our bodies and nourishing them, reproduction, family relations, and other intimate or close relations. From this perspective, time can be seen as circular, consisting of cycles of generation and corruption, which our short life on earth spans (HC 96–8). This description of labor might seem deflated but we must not forget that human embodiment is one of the central conditions for all activities we ever undertake. Without a body that we take time to nourish, care for, and cultivate, as subjects we would have no worldly reality.

This, however, is not the only way human beings relate to the natural world. We also act *into* it in the sense of violence but also cultivation. Arendt describes these kinds of activities as work (HC 7). Work comprises all the activities through which things not given in the natural world are created by humans. This includes, for example, extra-natural infrastructure, improving our living conditions, technologies—from the wheel to artificial intelligence—or works of art and literature. In this way, human beings emancipate themselves from the natural world, even if only to a certain degree, creating what Arendt refers to as the world of things: an intermediary between people that "is between those who have it in common, as a table is located between those who sit around it; the world, like every in-between, relates and separates men at the same time" (HC 52). The object of this world can be produced through doing violence to nature—as in all fabrication, "as in the case of iron, stone, or marble torn out of the womb of the earth" (HC 139) or when we deforest large surface areas for breeding animals and producing meat. However, Arendt suggests ways of acting into nature, which at least are less violent and expressed as care for the world, of which nature and the earth are the constitutive elements. We address this issue in Chapter 6.

The last dimension of the world to mention, and most important for Arendt, is that it is common to us all, which we explore further in Part II generally and in Chapter 5 particularly. The world is the realm that human beings share and where they act and speak together "without the intermediary of things or matter" (HC 7). It is closely connected not only to plurality—its direct condition—meaning that even if one person can initiate an action, more are needed to perform it, but also to natality, as acting is a practice of beginning something new, which every human being is capable of by virtue of having been born as a unique being. This means that action differs from the natural order of things:

> Yet just as, from the standpoint of nature, the rectilinear movement of man's life-span between birth and death looks like a peculiar deviation from the common natural rule of cyclical movement, thus action, seen from the viewpoint of the automatic processes which seem to determine the course of the world, looks like a miracle. (HC 246; see also WF 168)

It also differs from the human-made world, which we elevate by shaping matter. We could imagine the common world as a web of human relations. These relations run parallel and across, linking very different people and setting the most apparent and the least expected connections. They also have different meanings, but altogether they add up to the reality of our common world. This web exists everywhere where people come to act together (HC 183).

Arendt emphasizes that action consists of deeds and words. Both elements are vital and they correspond respectively to the two central conditions of human life: acting as the beginning of something new corresponds to natality, while speaking is the actualization of plurality in its mode of distinctness—"living as a distinct and unique being among equals" (HC 178). Through action and speech, we disclose who we are, as opposed to what we are in our everyday routines (HC 10–11), even if this "who" is more perceptible than given to expression in language. It is an intersubjective phenomenon, depending on the political actor exposing herself through words and deeds, and her fellow actors and their perception of her performance (HC 181–2). What is important, the appearance Arendt speaks about here, is embodied appearance. The question of the presumed disdain of embodiment in Arendt's work has been an impulse for critique, especially on the part of feminist scholars of the 1970s and '80s, which we address in Chapter 7. And indeed, Arendt refers to embodiment as "mere bodily existence" and stresses that in acting, human beings appear to each other "not indeed as physical objects but qua men" (HC 176); she refers to the Greek philosophers' resentment of the body (HC 16 n.15) and connects the human embodiment closely with labor and the private realm (HC 7, 30), hence framing it as subject to necessity—not freedom. However, she also clearly writes that action as an insertion into the world "is like a second birth, in which we confirm and take upon ourselves the naked fact of our original physical appearance" (HC 176–7). Thus, the role of embodiment in Arendtian action could perhaps be best understood using the metaphor of layers of the world, which we introduced at the beginning of this section. Acting and speaking are far more than an expression of our embodiment, but the physical body is a necessary foundation for any human activity, including speech and action. This issue could be revisited in the context of virtual spaces and digital communication, and we touch upon it in Chapter 6.

Its dependency upon natality and plurality makes action spontaneous and unpredictable. To say that action is spontaneous (HC 231) might seem counterintuitive, as we tend to think of action as a project: following an aim, introducing means that lead us to this end, and eventually succeeding—or not. But we would argue that denying this is not the intention of Arendt's notion of spontaneous action. It does not entail chaos or contingency of random movements. Of course, action can never do without some dose of arrangement and organization, and even then, it remains unpredictable because it involves a plurality of actors, every one of whom is a new and exceptional being by virtue of birth, distinctive from everybody else. When all these unique strains of action meet, converge with, counter, reinforce, and influence each other, and when all the actors reveal their "who"—which, as we already know, is in itself an intersubjective practice with an uncertain outcome—action becomes unforeseeable (HC 192). If Arendt ever speaks of political institutions beyond constitutions, it is this kind of fragile institution enabling action for the many. Hence, action is a process but it is not predetermined by an external logic: there is an intention, toward which action is directed. There is a need to be someone to make a beginning and there must be people who do not merely follow but much more co-act. However, the spontaneity of action results in its unpredictability. So what Arendt, following Edmund Burke (IP 127; Borren 2010: 212), describes as concerted action is not a process running according to a scheme; it is not a project to be managed and implemented. It is rather a fragile but powerful co-performance by political subjects in their equality and difference. Such, certainly experimental, acting in concert produces

Power

Arendt's concept of power differs from what we mostly associate with this notion in political terms: a hierarchical dependency between two parties where one exercises some form of coercion over the other, whether this coercion actually deploys violence or is merely persuasive in its nature. This way of thinking about power is well known in political theory. Just one example is the Weberian understanding of the state as a

> human community that (successfully) claims the monopoly of the legitimate use of physical force within a given territory. [. . .] The state is considered the sole source of the 'right' to use violence. Hence, 'politics' for us means striving to share power or striving to the distribution of power, either among states or among groups within a state. (Weber 2014: 4)

Another example is Foucault's notion of structures of juridical power, where "we suppose that certain persons exercise power over others" (Foucault 1983: 217).

Arendt, on the contrary, does not theorize these notions to be necessarily related and sees power and violence as distinct phenomena. Her aim is rather to clarify what she sees as a misconception of the dependency between the two. From her perspective, "the current equation of violence and power rests on government's being understood as domination of man over man by means of violence" (OV 52). Power and violence are not the same, even if they can coexist in one worldly event, and we might think about wars, conquests, revolution, or some instances of civil disobedience here. However, Arendt says, "not even wars, let alone revolutions are completely determined by violence" (OR 18), and "no government exclusively based on means of violence has ever existed" (OV 50).[1] But if power is not the capacity to exercise violence, what else could it be?

To find out, we need to refer to the connection between power and action in the Arendtian political framework:

> Power corresponds to the human ability not just to act but to act in concert. Power is never a property of an individual; it belongs to a group and remains in existence only so long as the group keeps together. When we say of somebody that he is "in power" we actually refer to him being empowered by a certain number of people to act in their name. The moment the group, from which the power originated to begin with (*potestas en populo*, without a people or group there is no power), disappears, "his power" also disappears. (OV 44)

Power, as we see, is not firmly bound to and dependent on violence but on plurality. Without there being a group, a plurality of people, there can be no power. Power is inherent in the very existence of any political community; it springs up whenever people get together to act. As such, it is legitimized by its beginning, the event of human beings gathering to act for a cause they share (OV 52).

We could imagine that the more people gather together, the more people share commitment to the same political cause, and the more power could be generated—perhaps even a unification for a worthy cause on a global scale. But we must not forget that plurality, crucially, also means difference. Universal consensus can never be a political aim as it leads to conformity and annuls any possibility of disagreement, any option of resistance. Arendt's concept of power cannot be a foundation for a communicative ethics of consent, as Jürgen Habermas (1977) wished, but only for intersubjective, communicative practices also appreciating dissent. Caring for the world entails protecting plurality: there must always be space for more than one position, more than one opinion, more than one way of acting. In other words, the human world in its political guise must be a space of

Freedom

In her discussion of freedom, Arendt continuously contrasts the notion of free will with what she sees as the essence of politics *par excellence*: the experience of being free. Her aim is to show that the former is—from the genealogical point of view—a mere derivative of the latter. In shifting the traditional philosophical focus on freedom as freedom of the will to freedom as practice, she politicizes freedom and turns it into a worldly phenomenon. She then tells a story of the experience of freedom as it existed in its original form before it was transformed by the metaphysical tradition into an attribute of the individual with her sovereignty. When Arendt writes that "the *raison d'être* of politics is freedom, and its field of experience is action" (WF 145), one may wonder how it was possible to say so much within such a short statement. For a better understanding, let us see where, for Arendt, freedom fits into the structure of the common world.

Arendt draws our attention to contradictory ways by which we experience freedom, pointing to the discrepancy between how we feel free and hence responsible in our consciousness and at the same time we experience our everyday life and the outer world as structured by the principle of causality (WF 142). This is one of the paradoxes of the human life and it might also be expressed as a contradiction between awareness of freedom of the will and outer necessity, or between the feeling of inner freedom and political oppression. When we speak about freedom in political terms today, we would probably primarily conceive it either as an attribute of being free (hence, not subject to an overly coercive regime) or as being liberated from a subjugation previously in force. When we speak of freedom in a philosophical or broadly spiritual sense, freedom of the will is the first intuition. However, freedom is not identical with liberation, as

> liberation may be the condition of freedom but by no means leads auto-matically to it; [. . .] the notion of liberty implied in liberation can only be negative, and hence, [. . .] even the intention of liberating is not identical with the desire for freedom. (OR 29)

It is also a worldly phenomenon, as distinguished from any notion of freedom within a human being.

Arendt suggests a look into the past, especially to ancient Greece, for a better understanding of these intuitions. This is a Heideggerian gesture, which Arendt transforms for her political phenomenology (Borren 2010: 25). In what is both an extension and a partial rejection of Heidegger's reconstruction of the history of metaphysics, she frames her reflection with a narrative about the conflict between philosophy and politics that characterizes the Western tradition after Socrates (Villa 1996: 113–17). Accordingly, the concept of inner freedom derives from philosophical thought and is a kind of substitute for political freedom, which is the original mode of experiencing freedom. It was only in late antiquity, when political freedom was severely restricted, that philosophers—including early Christian philosophers—sought a substitute that would make life bearable in the adverse conditions of "dark times" (LoM II 18; WF 156). Freedom, previously considered a worldly phenomenon and accordingly a tangible condition of human coexistence, now became internalized and identified with freedom of the will or thought, and hence attributed to an individual. As we will see, Arendt offers a very different understanding of freedom.

Inner freedom, as Arendt sees it, is an inferior derivative of political freedom (WF 145). She concludes that the philosophical tradition—again, seen through her Socratic lens—has distorted the concept of freedom rather than contributing to its understanding:

> Since the whole problem of freedom arises for us in the horizon of Christian traditions on one hand, and of an originally antipolitical philo-sophical tradition on the other, we find it difficult to realize that there may exist a freedom which is not an attribute of the will but an accessory of doing and acting. (WF 163)

Taking a step back in human history, Arendt discloses freedom as a worldly phenomenon by tracing its original experience in the pre-Platonic Greek polis. She does so not because the polis was an ideal or utopian political sphere, but precisely because "its founding sins afforded [. . .] an unobstructed view on human being expressed purely in terms of labor or work or action" (Marshall 2010: 131). We will return to this issue later in this chapter.

Assuming that the authentic experience of political freedom has been lost because of the traditional separation between *vita contemplativa* and *vita activa*, theory and practice, or thought and action, Arendt makes an attempt to regain its original meaning. She tells a story about the shift of the experience of freedom from the political to the sphere of the mind and draws a line from its origins in ancient Greece to the crisis of freedom under totalitarian rule, for, as she points out, "the elementary problems of politics never come as clearly to light in their immediate and simple urgency as when they are first formulated and when they receive their last challenge" (TMA 17–18). For the Greeks, Arendt says, freedom was experienced in acting (WF 163–4). She reads the polis as a performative space, where political actors appear to each other in their deeds and words, hence a space of appearance (WF 152), in which freedom is experienced out of common action.

Through such an understanding of freedom, Arendt links it to other concepts, organizing her hermeneutics of the world. She recalls Augustine (for her, definitely more a late-Roman than a Christian figure) with his notion of the human being as a new beginning, and equates this capacity for beginning with freedom (WF 166). By virtue of natality, every human being is capable of making new beginnings, and hence of experiencing freedom in action. In this sense, freedom as praxis is also closely connected to plurality, as opposed to inner freedom being an attribute of the individual. It thus acquires a public character and becomes the motive, even if not always the very goal, of action: "freedom, which only seldom—in times of crisis or revolution—become the direct aim of political action, is actually the reason that men live together and act politically. Without it, political life as such would be meaningless" (WF 145).

As the *raison d'être* of action, freedom must be tangible in the political sphere of appearance. Any kind of inner freedom that cannot be exercised, such as freedom of thought under the conditions of a dictatorship, is politically irrelevant. Freedom always requires the society of others and a public space in which it can manifest itself. Without the fulfillment of these conditions, it is not demonstrable as a fact in the world (WF 147, 167).

Freedom appears through genuine action as the beginning of the new. Arendt (LoM II 198) describes free political action as a "gift of spontaneity, of being able to do what could also be left undone," and adds: "men of action [. . .] ought to be committed to freedom because of the very nature of their activity, which consists in 'changing the world,' and not in interpreting or knowing it." Action as a new beginning has miraculous powers: it calls into being what was not present in it before, creates new factual relations, makes possible a dialogue where none has taken place. But it does not adhere to any necessity and is not secured by any obligation. No coercion and no judgment can compel a free agent to act in a particular way. While inner freedom is realized in the I-will, political freedom is expressed through the I-can (SQMP 114). However, the I-must is pre-political in every case and prevents any political action. This is the ultimate reason why the philosopher should hang her coat at the door of the common world: the compelling force of logical thinking that underlies her activity limits her sphere of action to what already exists. Purely logical thinking does not let us see the new, but only what is already given in the premises (Zerilli 2005a: 148). This leads us to the question of meaning of different human activities and through that to Arendt's distinction between

The Private and the Public

In addition to what we referred to as layers of the human world, the fundamental activities of labor, work, and action, Arendt distinguishes between spheres of life that give meaning to the activities conducted within them: the private, the public, and the social, which is in a way a hybrid realm. The second structural frame coincides to a certain degree with the first but they do not overlap. This structure is one of the most significant analytic tools in Arendt's writings but it also invites critique, mainly due to a suspicion that she essentializes both human activities and the realms in which they are to be enacted; critiques perhaps best raised and answered by Bonnie Honig (1988, 2017). Let us take a closer look at what Arendt writes about the private, the public, and the social as well as at the arguments of her critics.

Arendt develops the distinction between the private and the public in the second chapter of *The Human Condition*, building from the topos of the ancient city-state. She then describes the life of the polis as divided between two spheres: the household as the private sphere, where what was not supposed to be publicly visible took place, and the public, where Athenians made their appearance as political beings. And already here, we encounter the first difficulty: What is the significance of this reference for Arendt? Does she really believe the utopian vision of Greek politics she presents? Why is she leaving out or downplaying all the injustices of Athenian life, like slavery, limited freedom of women, and a very rigid concept of citizenship?

To summarize the still ongoing debate about the role of the polis in Arendt's image of politics, her critics accused her of idealizing the polis as a political utopia, while the advocates of her vision of the *vita activa* seek for more constructive interpretations of this topos. Hence, as Frederick Dolan notes,

> for all her glorification of Athenian politics Arendt is maddeningly elusive about what that politics was about. [. . .] This seeming perversity has led even Arendt's sympathetic critics to seek ways of marginalizing or softening her Hellenism, and less sympathetic ones to dismiss her because of her Hellenism and dismiss ancient political thought because of Arendt. (Dolan 2000: 151–2)

So, the critics state that Arendt's separation between the public and the private is "incompatible with democratic ideals" (Wolin 1983: 3), emphasize that "the exclusionary nature of this theory of the polis as action has, at best, been treated with kid gloves by Arendt's commentators" (Lechte 2018: 3), and see her "view of the *polis* as idealized to the point of sheer fantasy," as summarized by Lisa Disch, who does not share this view herself (Disch 1994: 57, 61). And so, Jacques Taminaux (2000: 165) states clearly that he does not believe that "the alleged Graecomania hold[s] up under examination. A careful scrutiny of Arendt's writings shows that [. . .] the Athenian *polis* does not have in her political thought the status of a paradigm," while Josiah Ober (1996: 145) observes what should by now seem clear, that "Arendt's polis was an ahistorical ideal, based in large part on her own reading of Aristotle's *Politics*."

Even though Arendt's appreciation of the Greek culture is definitely a gesture typical of the intellectual atmosphere in Germany at the time of her school and university education—especially in the novel approach to Greek philosophy in Martin Heidegger's lectures—the topos of the polis appears in Arendt's reflections only after the publication of *The Origins of Totalitarianism* and so may be interpreted as a respective countermodel, but, as David Marshall (2010: 128) notes, not only that: "At that time, she was particularly interested in a kind of distinctive individuality that would be capable of combating the rise of mass society—a development that, in her analysis, was a crucial component in the emergence of modern totalitarianism." As we argue in Chapter 3, interpreting the polis as an exemplary political realm can become a valuable exercise in political thinking.

The two distinctive realms of the polis, namely the private and the public, enable its inhabitants to exercise different activities. The private, Arendt notes, is a realm of lack, of *privatio*: a realm in which we are deprived of something: being among others and appearing to them. Arendt goes as far as to claim that were one to be entirely confined to this realm, it would be as if one had not existed at all (HC 58). Here, the activities of labor take place: care for human bodies, satisfying physical needs of all sorts, family life implementing the predefined roles of all members of the household to safeguard its proper functioning. These are private things that should remain unseen from the outside. A household, in this sense, is a natural community, where speaking has a strictly functional role as communication around the task of sustaining life. It is governed by necessity and violence (HC 30; OV 64), which reinforce the structures of the household, making it fit for its purposes.

The counterpart to the private is the realm is the public. Hannah Arendt's account of the public presupposes the existence of a political space of appearance. In this space, women and men appear to each other through acting and speaking. In so doing, they show *who* they are and display their uniqueness. This kind of being-together is constitutive for the common world, where people in their plurality can share a common reality: "Only where things can be seen by many in a variety of aspects without changing their identity, so that those who are gathered around them know they see sameness in utter diversity, can worldly reality truly and reliably appear" (HC 57). It is important that human affairs be visible in the public space and not hidden from the view of others. Only in this way do they invite responses, which are deeds and words themselves, that open a space in the common world, which can support us not as natural creatures but as human beings exercising freedom and power.

The framing Arendt uses may suggest to us that she favors the public space as a way of relating to the world, as it enables people to experience their lives as fully human. At the same time, she seems to deprecate the private as a negative realm of deprivation. This understanding, however, is oversimplified and deceptive, as for

Arendt each of these realms has its flipside. This can be explained with metaphors of darkness and light, which Arendt frequently uses to describe phenomena of the human world (Robaszkiewicz 2021). The public is vividly illuminated and we expose ourselves when entering the public realm. This requires that we step out of our private sphere, where our sheer survival and emotional and corporeal welfare is of major concern. One needs courage, says Arendt, to step into the light of the public because there, not life but the world—the human in-between—is at stake (WF 155). This is challenging due to embodiment being one of the countless conditions of our existence (and one that is existentially vital), and the courage to leave the private sphere behind or to bracket it for a while decisively entails care for the self to be substantially transformed into care for the world.

This already suggests that also the private is significant for the human condition. It is not only a dark and separated realm of necessity but also the realm in which our corporeality is being secured. Here, inside, our basic bodily needs are fulfilled, while we are protected from the light of the public, which illuminates everything that is outside. In the darkness of the private, we are not seen by a broad range of spectators but only by those who are close to us, with whom we relate and communicate, sometimes without words. Although this space with its structures and boundaries does not allow us much freedom, it offers us a possibility of making our own choices, concerning only ourselves, and not being judged for having made them. It also offers space for love, which, as Arendt points out, "by its very nature, is unworldly, and it is for this reason rather than its rarity that it is not only apolitical but antipolitical, perhaps the most powerful of all antipolitical human forces" (HC 242). Clearly, both the public and the private have ambivalent meaning in Arendt's concept of the human condition. In this way, however, they pose a good example of one of the central strengths of Arendt's new political vocabulary: the ambiguity of her central concepts, which may confuse some of her readers, actually fosters a better understanding of respective phenomena, without judging them conclusively. As we will argue in Chapter 3, this makes her writings particularly powerful as exercises in political thinking.

But first, we need to come back to the storyline of *The Human Condition*, and how the distinction between the private and the public has been distorted in the course of the modern age. In other words, we need to discuss

The Social—and How to Make Sense Out of All This

The Human Condition may be read as a story of a gradual decline of the political, between the Greek polis (to be sure: in the sense of a model of an ideal public space, not a historical fact) and the mass society of today. In this story, Arendt uses her ontological framework as an analytic tool to illuminate this transformative process: which activities count as labor, work, and action; what belongs or does not belong to which sphere of human life for people of different epochs, and how these spheres shift and relocate in the course of time. The spheres of the public and the private, in Arendt's model clearly distinguished in the ancient world, began to merge in modern times. The emancipation of economics out of the private realm of *oikos* played a crucial role in this transformation:

> according to ancient thought on these matters, the very term "political economy" would have been a contradiction in terms: whatever was "economic," related to the life of the individual and the survival of the species, was a non-political, household affair by definition. (HC 29)

The introduction of economy into the space of the political disturbed the known order of the human world. It facilitated the emergence of society: a new, hybrid space in which private and political matters intermingle.

This story can be read as a mere description but Arendt suggests a normative reading when she notes that the rise of society meant the destruction of politics proper:

> It is decisive that society, on all its levels, excludes the possibility of action, which formerly was excluded from the household. Instead, society expects from each of its members a certain kind of behavior, imposing innumerable and various rules, all of which tend to "normalize" its members, to make them behave, to exclude spontaneous action or outstanding achievement. [. . .] Society equalizes under all circumstances, and the victory of equality in the modern world is only the political and legal recognition of the fact that society has conquered the public realm, and that distinction and difference have become private matters of the individual. (HC 40–1)

We instantly see that Arendt's perspective on this development is very critical. What she cherished most—free, spontaneous, and outstanding action of unique human beings within the bright illuminated realm of the public—is to be rendered impossible due to the novel sphere of the social expanding, eventually equalizing all people not as human beings but as members of the mass society where everyone behaves the same way, following the same predetermined rules. From a plural, rich community of exceptional beings capable of making new beginnings, we become a colony of ants, at best. Seen from this perspective, the social threatens both privacy and the public, it is a "curiously hybrid realm where private interests assume public significance" (HC 35).

This framing of the social proves to be quite problematic as it seems to essentialize some phenomena of collective living and brand them as "social," and in this sense less worthy than genuinely political issues. It exposed Arendt to critique on the part of authors who found the exact issues which Arendt rendered as "merely" social to be the proper content of politics: from today's perspective, we could say: economic injustice, social exclusion, gender inequality, domestic violence, poverty, and famine, to name but a few. According to Arendt, these "were matters of administration, to be put into the hands of experts, rather than issues which could be settled by the twofold process of decision and persuasion" (OR 91). As Honig (2017) thoroughly discusses in her vindication of Arendt as a normative thinker interested in public matters, there is more than a little justice in the critiques of her work raised by Seyla Benhabib (1996), Mary Dietz (1991), Kathleen Jones (1993), and Hanna Fenichel Pitkin (1995), among others, who have called attention to a fantastic dimension of Arendt's account of "the rise of the social." Pitkin, for example, points out that in

> *The Human Condition* society or the social is variously said to "absorb," "embrace," "devour" people or other entities; to "emerge," "rise," "grow," and "let loose" growth; to "enter," "intrude" upon, [. . .] "pervert" and "transform"; to "impose" rules on people, "demand" certain conduct from them; to "exclude" or "refuse to admit" other conduct, or people; to "try to cheat" people and to act under a "guise." It's like a science-fiction story: an evil monster, a Blob, entirely external to and separate from us, has appeared as if from outer space, intent on taking us over, gobbling up our freedom and our politics. (Pitkin 1995: 53)

This picturesque metaphor notwithstanding, Pitkin and other critics search for a way to overcome the difficulties caused by this concept, mostly referring to Arendt's work about Rahel Varnhagen and the salons of the late eighteenth and early nineteenth centuries as social spaces (Benhabib 1996: 5–14; Pitkin 1995: 58–64). For the past generation, then, Arendt scholars have generally tried to find some kind of solution to Arendt's "social problem," such as Marieke Borren (2013: 208–9), Rahel Jaeggi (2007: 246–8), Ayten Gündoğdu (2015: 55–89), or Bonnie Honig, who states that "it is simply the case that nothing is ontologically protected from politicization, that nothing is necessarily or naturally or ontologically *not* political" (Honig 1995b: 147). It is no accident that these and other scholars working with and against Arendt in this vein are interested in her work in its abrasive relation to feminist theory and practice, a point to which we return in Chapter 7.

In this vein, Sophie Loidolt (2018) examines human conditionality in her extensive phenomenological interpretation of *The Human Condition*, referring to a famous—and as she shows, easy to misinterpret—systematization of human activities that we discussed above. Loidolt emphasizes the enactive character of Arendt's conditions for the space of appearance and the possibility of politicization, developing an original interpretation of Arendt's theory by applying the concept of 'spaces of meaning' on what, at first sight, seems to be a rigid systematization of *condition humaine*. She criticizes approaches that tend to essentialize and solidify different activities and their respective conditions. These are often naively understood analogically to a baby's shape sorter: just as each wooden block fits into a particular hole in a box, each human activity would correlate to one of three categories. Loidolt, on the contrary, presents labor, work, and action as a dynamic structure where all conditions are interconnected:

> Since all conditions are actualized simply by human existence, i.e. by being a living body, by being involved in the world of objects/tools and by existing in the plural, being human means to dwell, however passively, in all of these meaning-spaces at one and the same time. (Loidolt 2018: 116)

These spaces of meaning are dynamic. Every activity that ever takes place develops its particular logic, and so they stand out as worlds with specific temporality, spatiality, a specific form of intersubjectivity, and an inner logic of sequence, rhythm, and modality. For the question of the normative status of the distinction between the social and the political (Bernasconi 1996: 15), this perspective offers an attractive answer. Loidolt proposes adding a transformative dimension: a shift in meaning takes place when an activity and its space part (Loidolt 2018: 126). Similar to Benhabib (1996: 140), Loidolt (2018: 145) assumes that the private, the political, and the social space in Arendt are "attitudinal rather than content-specific." The notion of meaning-spaces prompts a vivid image that helps us to comprehend the structure of human existence as presented by Arendt in a new way and shows us how to avoid interpretative pitfalls resulting from attempts to essentialize human activities and ascribe them to a clear-cut realm, be it the private, the political, or the social, rather than seeing the human world as a dynamic, pulsing, and lively web of relationships, in which the meaning of a certain activity can change depending on where and when, by whom and in relation to whom it takes place.

This short introduction into Hannah Arendt's perspective on action leaves many questions open. We will revisit the notions introduced in this chapter throughout this book, seeing not just how they fit into the broader framework of Arendt's thinking but also how they help us to address more general issues, including some that carry the greatest possible political relevance today.

Note

1. In both cases Arendt argues that not even totalitarianism can do without a power basis.

Chapter 2

Between Human Action and the Life of the Mind

Hannah Arendt was very careful to keep politics and philosophy apart. At first glance, her two (arguably) best-known books seem to reflect this opposition. *The Human Condition* stands for our active, which is to say political, life among others, while *The Life of the Mind* provides its antipole, examining what happens when we leave the company of others to engage with thinking. A closer look at her works and her biography, however, discloses an unbreakable bond between philosophy and politics, threads of this bond woven together throughout her life, partly as a result of her own actions and partly due to actions of others and the unforeseeable paths of human history. She is remembered for her bold denial of being a philosopher, when asked in a television interview with Günter Gaus in 1964:

> I am afraid I have to protest. I do not belong to the circle of philosophers. My profession, if one can even speak of it at all, is political theory. I neither feel like a philosopher, nor do I believe that I have been accepted in the circle of philosophers, as you so kindly suppose. [. . .] I have said good-bye to philosophy once and for all. As you know, I studied philosophy, but that does not mean that I stayed with it. (WRLR 1–2)

While it was rather political theory where she saw herself at this point, there is no doubt that she was intellectually rooted in the European philosophical tradition, which she—already as a young student—confronted with a considerable dose of skepticism. Even though she had already been well acquainted with classic philosophy during her teens, she was first and foremost interested in the critical movements in philosophy, represented by Martin Heidegger and Karl Jaspers (Young-Bruehl 1982: 32, 36). It was Heidegger who first drew her to philosophy in its then rebellious guise, and it was Heidegger who played a major role in her later distancing from philosophy, philosophers, and philosophical thinking altogether. Later, Heidegger's own involvement in the National Socialist regime's apparatus of power and his commitment to its ideology, as we argue in Chapter 4, were decisive for her diagnosis of a *déformation professionelle* of philosophers, which not only made them incapable of responsible political action but also rendered them potentially harmful when entering the public sphere.

This is why the phrase "thinking politics" gains such an exceptional meaning when applied to Arendt's writings, as well as her life story, and her positioning as a theorist. She makes the distinction between the two realms very clear in her 1954 essay "Philosophy and Politics." Here, she develops her argument about philosophers' tyrannical tendencies, caused by their pursuit of the singular truth—a principle, which proves destructive for the political realm, inherently and inescapably grounded on plurality. She reinforces her stance in *The Human Condition* through the very distinction upon which this book is based: *vita activa* and *vita contemplativa*. Finally, when writing *The Life of the Mind* later in her life, she confirms her self-proclaimed aloofness from philosophical thinking, introducing her project with a qualification:

> I feel I should start [. . .] with a justification. No justification, of course, is needed for the topic itself [. . .]. What disturbs me is that *I* try my hand at it, for I have neither claim or ambition to be a "philosopher" or be numbered among what Kant, not without irony, called *Denker von Gewerbe* (professional thinkers). The question then is, should I not have left these problems to experts, and the answer will have to show what prompted me to venture from the relatively safe fields of political science and theory into rather awesome matters, instead of leaving well enough alone. (LoM I 3)

There is no doubt that for Arendt thinking as a faculty of the mind is clearly a very different practice from what we do in *vita activa*, which consists in embodied engagement with the world we share with others, which includes political acting. How then can we think politics from an Arendtian perspective?

Traditional Hierarchy of Thinking and Acting

In the Western philosophical tradition, this pair of concepts corresponds to two separate spheres of life: *vita contemplativa* and *vita activa*: the theoretical and the practical way of life, where the former was seen as the higher and more accomplished of the two. Arendt takes up this distinction and questions the traditional hierarchy of the two ways of life. Her project thus consists in systematizing the activities of the practical way of life, which has hitherto been regarded as subordinate to the theoretical and therefore neglected. She wants to do "nothing more than to think what we are doing" (HC 5).[1] This shift of emphasis, however, is not a simple reversal of the existing hierarchy, which would leave its elements intact. Instead, Arendt proposes questioning the traditional conceptual apparatus and critically examining its now meaningless components after its structures have been irreversibly destabilized, since the work of Marx and Nietzsche (HC 17). This requires a departure from the framing of traditional metaphysics, for so long as we accept this metaphysical frame, critique merely amounts to "turning upside down" the traditional order of things (HC 17, 293). For Arendt, the tension between philosophical thinking and political action or between the philosopher and the political actor, rather than inevitably ending in a hierarchical prioritization of one or other of the traditional categories, actually results in the possibility of establishing a productive link between thinking and acting. Starting from a specific experience of thinking (namely a reinterpretation of Kant's theory of reflective judgment), she rediscovers modes of thinking forgotten by the tradition and comes up with a notion of political thinking, central to her understanding of politics.

Arendt reflects on the separation between the practical and the theoretical way of life genetically, and her point of reference is the philosophy and culture of ancient Greece. This perspective, typical of her epoch, leads her to the story of Socrates' trial and Plato's reaction to it, through which, as she notes, the gap between thinking and acting was opened. Socrates was accused of spoiling the youth through his teaching—a charge we can trace back to personal resentments of some Athenians frequenting the agora and presumably being harassed by Socrates, who, through his dialogical practice, kept exposing their epistemic naivety. This at least is the picture that Plato draws in *The Apology of Socrates*.

Outraged by the unjust treatment of his teacher and friend, Plato opposes the polis to philosophy. In this understanding, acting and thinking are polarized: persuasion and rhetoric on the side of the polis and philosophical wisdom on the side of philosophy. The conflict, which Arendt traces most sharply in "Philosophy and Politics," is ultimately between the two ways of life: that of a philosopher and that of a citizen, and it is reflected in the opposition between two modes of knowledge, namely opinion (*doxa*) and truth seeking (*episteme*). While a politically wise citizen (*phronimos*) expresses opinions, which are subject to possible change and renegotiation, a philosophically wise thinker (*sophos*) strives for immutable truth. This opposition reaches its culmination in Plato's concept of the state ruled by a philosopher-king: the one who can know *the truth*, as opposed to the traditional manner of a Greek statesman who merely expresses opinions (PP 75–6). This allows him to rule the state in a largely tyrannical manner, while staging it as a republic and claiming the legitimacy of justice itself as the principle of rule. Plato, as Arendt reads him, hated democracy because it allowed his teacher to be sentenced to death due to what may have been personal animosity, and thus opts for absolute norms which could prevent such situations (PP 74).

As we have seen, Arendt holds Plato responsible for separating philosophy from politics, and so establishing a standard that would later be adopted in the philosophical tradition (PP, IP 130–3). Accordingly, opinions, inherent in the political way of life, refer to worldly matters as unstable, contingent events, depending upon human free agency and hence not following rigorous patterns of philosophical argument. Since such lively, changeable entanglements can develop one way or another, they are ontologically inferior to the necessary, immutable things about which one can gain true knowledge. Opinions are uncertain and, unlike knowledge, they can turn out to be wrong as they are correlated to the facts of the world and to its ever-changing relationality. The web of human relationships changes with every action arising from human plurality. This means that an opinion, which was once based in worldly reality, might lose its ground. This also means that a person who was once of a right opinion can again adopt a wrong one. Thus, her opinion may be true or false, and on this depends its usefulness as a guideline for action. Knowledge is a different case because whoever once grasped the truth will always orientate herself toward it. This shows why the philosopher remains in eternal conflict with the polis. In her search for truth, she excludes the possibility of a plurality of opinions, and so any philosopher's attempts to shape the political lead to what Arendt calls "tyrannies of 'truth'" (TP 241).

As described above, acting is primarily the occupation of a statesman or a citizen. Thinking, on the contrary, is concerned with objects outside the acting experience, beyond the common world which we share with others, and so it is the domain of philosophers. However, although Arendt exposes the separation between thinking and acting, it soon becomes clear that she does not do so uncritically. We can distinguish two notions of philosophical thinking in her writings:

one that is oriented toward the metaphysical tradition, to which we will accordingly refer as metaphysical thinking, and the second, which we will call dialectical thinking and which Arendt traces back to Socrates. One of Arendt's classic interpreters, Margaret Canovan (1990: 150), already offers a systematics of modes of thinking in Arendt. She distinguishes between two alternative views on thinking itself: one informed by Plato and Heidegger, the other by Socrates and Jaspers. Crucially, whenever

> Arendt is focusing on Plato and Heidegger, she is inclined to fear that philosophy is intrinsically solitary, antipolitical and sympathetic to coercion, whereas when she concentrates on Socrates and Jaspers, she is tempted to believe that true philosophy may be communicative and in harmony with true politics. (Canovan 1990: 150)

While Canovan does consider whether or not Arendt had a notion of true philosophy on the basis of this differentiation, she does not seem to recognize the normative claim behind it, and suggests that Arendt tried to mediate between the two views on thinking, which led her to elaborate a third mode of thinking: enlarged thinking, which she draws from Kant.

We argue, rather, that this enlarged thinking—for Arendt another way of describing reflective judgment—is an altogether different faculty in her framework (discussed in detail in Chapter 3). We also argue that Arendt definitely did make her choice concerning these two modes of philosophical thinking. Her preferred mode was the one that is not potentially harmful to the common world, namely Socratic thinking. She very clearly distances herself from the radical retreat into philosophical solitude. Yet, even so, she positively advocates the Socratic silent dialogue as a form of philosophical thinking insofar as it promises a positive connection to plurality and acting. Let us now take a closer look at these two modes of thinking.

Metaphysical vs. Dialectical Thinking

Arendt's view on philosophical thinking in its metaphysical guise clearly reflects its radical separation from acting. It has three main characteristics. The first is the unambiguous locating of thinking outside of the realm of action: since acting takes place in the common world, it comprises interacting with others or acting in concert. Thinking, on the contrary, requires being alone, that is, withdrawal from the world. Arendt shows how the two spheres can be traced back to the "old metaphysical two-worlds theory," juxtaposing the world of appearance and the sphere of thinking, primarily characterized by invisibility. As she notes (LoM I 13), metaphysics is a discipline that "dealt with matters that were not given to sense-perception, and that their understanding transcended common-sense reasoning, which springs from sense experience and can be validated by empirical tests and means." In contrast to action and speech, which require the space of appearance and are connected with seeing and being seen, the life of the mind (and in particular thinking) takes place "nowhere." Thinking, especially, does not manifest itself externally: "The only outward manifestation of the mind is absent-mindedness, an obvious disregard of the surrounding world, something entirely negative which in no way hints at what is actually happening within us" (LoM I 72). Such a withdrawal from the world means leaving the company of others in favor of the solitary sphere, where, instead of engaging with individual phenomena of the common world, one can attend to the general.

This necessity for solitude reflected in the singularity of the thinking subject cannot be reconciled with the plurality of *vita activa*. When one acts, one cannot engage in solitary thinking because action, by definition, requires multiple agents. In thinking, we are separated from others, we do not dwell among people but retreat, metaphorically speaking, to the kingdom of thought: a metaphysical realm without space and time (LoM I 207). A subject who has withdrawn from the world to enter this solitary space distances herself from the time continuum that defines the world of appearance. In this sense, past and future are equated with present, so that they appear equally strange to the thinking subject's sense of time. As Arendt describes it, the thinking subject stands in the spiritual present, "the quiet Now in the time-pressed, time-tossed existence of man" (LoM I 209). This Now has nothing in common with biographical or historical time, since it is timeless in the sense of the worldly concept of time. Every activity in the proper sense is characterized by a certain dynamic and carries a potential for change and transformation. Thought, as invisible and timeless, does not evoke any perceptible change. It takes place as if in another world, in a *nunc stans* of which metaphysicians have always dreamed (GBPF 11).

Second, thinking focuses on the universals, unlike action, which always focuses on individual events. The object of metaphysical thinking is situated outside of the space of appearance and hence is

36

not immediately present to the senses, which is why it is the most important or even the "only essential precondition" (LoM I 78) of thinking. In the everyday practice of thinking as we know it, the invisible can be memories from the past but also ideas about the future. Instead, philosophical thinking engages with the invisible in the form of general concepts, which has been its essence throughout the history of philosophy, from its beginnings to modern metaphysics today. Crucially for Arendt, thinking remains concerned with the general (LoM I 81) as opposed to the particular, that is, with the absent or the conceptions of the absent. Acting, on the contrary, always engages in the particular, the present, the tangible, and the plural. Its essence is the appearance of acting subjects in the public space (HC 199), where they are visible and audible to each other. Their action is always present: here and now.

Third, philosophical thinking in its metaphysical version means a search for the singular truth. Arendt recalls Pythagoras' statement that life is like a festival, to which some come for glory or gain, but the best come as spectators—these are philosophers seeking truth (LoM II 93). This kind of philosophical pursuit of truth proves critical to Arendt's concept of the world. On the one hand, citizens participate in shaping the common world by expressing and exchanging opinions, thereby enriching the plurality of the public sphere. Philosophers, however, focus on the search for the singular and certain truth: "To the citizen's ever-changing opinions about human affairs [. . .], the philosopher opposed the truth about those things, which in their very nature were everlasting and from which, therefore, principles could be derived to stabilize human affairs" (TP 228). The stability of the world, which in Arendt's perspective philosophers seek, corresponds to the metaphysical assumption of the primacy of the motionless and the immutable over the movable and the changeable. For Arendt, fulfilling this philosophical dream of firm solidification would entail a fatal stagnation for the world, which is only conceivable in its constant renewal (CE 193).

On the other hand, the truth-centered perspective threatens the world as a space of appearance. The metaphysical distinction between being and appearance implies a gradation: while appearance is immediately accessible, it is often under suspicion of being a deception, as for example in Descartes:

At the same time, I must remember that I am a man, and that consequently I am in the habit of sleeping, and in my dreams representing to myself the same things or sometimes even less probable things, than do those who are insane in their waking moments. [. . .] In thinking over this I remind myself that on many occasions I have in sleep been deceived by similar illusions, and in dwelling carefully on this reflection I see so manifestly that there are no certain indications by which we may clearly distinguish wakefulness from sleep that I am lost in astonishment. (Descartes 1641: Meditation I)

Truth, on the contrary, is the hidden, to which actual knowledge applies, and it is what the philosopher strives for, as for example in Locke: "He that would seriously set upon the search of truth ought in the first place to prepare his mind with a love of it" (Locke 1836: 532). Even a philosopher like Kant, who questions the metaphysical tradition, all the same confesses his love of metaphysics, which only rarely bestows its favors on him (LKPP 7; Kant 2011), and remains oriented toward the fundamental epistemological question of the knowability of truth.

Thus, the primacy of being and truth over mere appearance (LoM I 24) correlates with the primacy of the theoretical over the practical way of life. Moreover, the question of communicability determines the incongruence of philosophical truth with the common world, which is reigned by a plurality of opinions. Truth, according to Arendt, cannot be put into words (LoM I 110)—as in the fifth level of knowledge identified in Plato's *Seventh Letter* (342e–344c). The space of practical action is based on communication and verbal exchange between actors. The existence of an opinion is tied to its communicative manifestation, while truth retains its ontic status regardless of whether it has been communicated or even recognized. However, the main problem Arendt sees in the philosophical orientation toward the search for truth is the tyrannical undertones implicit in the very concept of truth, which point to something immutable, eternal, and firm. Unlike political postulates, philosophical truths are not based on consent—as, for instance, the Declaration of Independence is, as opposed to the categorical imperative—and thus include an element of coercion (TP 242). Hence, they pose a peril for the public sphere. Since philosophical thinking in its search for truth is subordinated to the rules of logic, the transfer of its principles to the sphere of action results in an ideological tyranny: "You can't say A without saying B and C and so on, down to the end of the murderous alphabet" (OT 472). Freedom of action, resulting from human spontaneity, is endangered by the necessity of logical thinking. This commitment to logic explains the tendency of philosophers to support tyrannies and underlies Arendt's claim that they had better stay away from the political as they are hardly equipped to act in the public sphere.

Thus, the two worlds—the common world of human affairs and the kingdom of thought—remain fundamentally separate and do not influence each other directly. "Indeed, in our world there is no clearer or more radical opposition than that between thinking and doing," writes Arendt (LoM I 71), emphasizing that thinking as such has little use for the society (Arendt 2006h: 190).[2] Thinking and acting belong to different worlds of experience and do not intersect; the distinction between them, therefore, goes beyond the abstract opposition of theory and practice (Kohn 1990: 129). They are much more concrete, lived experiences that for Arendt do not cohere with each other.

As Arendt describes them, the two experiences are distant from each other. But her starting point for reflecting about thinking is the question of the distinction between good and evil and its potential connection with the faculty of thinking (LoM I 5). Although they happen in different worlds of experience, both acting and thinking are activities, as Arendt states multiple times (e.g. LoM I 72, 75, 167, 185; HC 5, 291). Thus, the life of the mind is not excluded from the active life but is rather a different mode of being active. To illuminate this, Arendt looks further back into the history of philosophy to show that the metaphysical tradition began with Plato, while Socrates, "who knew nothing of Plato's doctrine of Ideas and hence nothing of the axiomatic, nondiscursive self-evidence of things seen with the eye of the mind" (SQMP 89), still represented a different approach to philosophical thinking.

In Arendt's writings, the second, dialectical, conception of philosophical thinking is represented by Socrates. For her, it offers a concept of thinking that could be associated with worldliness (LoM I 185; SQMP 91-2; PRD 18-19). For Socrates, according to Plato's *Theaetetus*, thinking is "the talk which the soul has with itself about any subjects which it considers" (189e). Crucial to this approach is the shift of emphasis from the "what" to the "how" of the thinking activity. Whereas in the case of metaphysical thinking the weight is on the intent of thought, that is, the knowledge of truth, dialectical thinking focuses on the method or phenomenological description of the experience of thinking. This is precisely what Arendt is aiming for: she emphasizes that it is not the concepts or rules of thought produced by *Denker von Gewerbe* (professional thinkers) that are of interest to her but the lived experience of the thinking self (LoM I

166). Thinking thus turns out to be a thoroughly practical activity, even if of a very particular kind.

Arendt emphasizes that her choice of Socrates, with his understanding of thinking being a silent dialogue with oneself, as the figure of a worldly philosopher was not accidental. Socrates, according to Arendt (LoM I 167), is a very unusual philosopher who unites two passions—thinking and acting—in one person, not in the sense that he applies his thoughts or creates standards for action, but because he is at home in both spheres of life. With Socrates and against Platonic elitism, she argues that any person encountered in the agora can engage in the practice of thinking, even if their skillfulness will surely vary. The ability to think is thus given to people in their plurality rather than merely being an occupation of the few. This egalitarian attribution of the capacity to think alongside the capacity to act is reminiscent of Aristotle's dual definition of man as a rational and political being. Similarly, the human is, for Arendt, the thinking being, even as she is defined by her capacity to act.

There are apparent similarities between the two concepts of thinking, at which we shall take a closer look. In particular, the first of the aforementioned conditions of metaphysical thinking, the withdrawal from the world, is repeated in dialectical thinking: Socrates, too, withdraws from the company of others in order to engage in a silent dialogue with himself. We find this, for example, at the beginning of the *Symposium*, when Socrates appears late at the meeting due to a "pause in thinking" (174d–175e). But the nature of this retreat is now quite different. Socrates does not seclude himself in the solipsistic singularity of the metaphysical kingdom outside of space and time; in his thinking he is alone, but not lonely. When he engages in a dialogue with himself, he, strangely, sees himself doubled. Dialectical thinking in the tradition of Socrates is, according to Arendt, reflexive: in thinking, one acts back on oneself (LoM I 74). In the practice of such thinking, the subject herself is in a very particular existential situation: although she remains one as a subject, she doubles herself for herself in order to reflect herself. Arendt sees an exemplary account of this experience in Socrates' critique of self-contradiction while he is in dialogue with Callicles in the *Gorgias*. Here (482a–c), Socrates states that it is better to suffer injustice than to do injustice and claims that anyone who holds a different view must contradict themselves, which is something to be avoided at all costs, asserting that he would rather hold an opinion contradicting the views of all others than be in disharmony with himself and contradict himself. Arendt emphasizes the phrase that Socrates uses at this point (482c) to describe the condition of the thinking I: if "I, I *one*, were not in harmony with myself and contradicted myself." This lends a paradoxical character to his statement, for Socrates, when he thinks, is at once one and doubled. But this paradox is necessary in order to properly understand the experience of thinking: nothing that is identical with itself can be in harmony with itself or not—one always needs at least two tones to produce a harmony (LoM I 180–1).

Thus, the thinking I is always in the company of an interlocutor, and thereby actualizes a dialectical duality instead of a metaphysical singularity. From a political perspective, Arendt argues, the difference between thinking and acting is that acting is based on power—a potency that arises from acting in concert, between people, and can never be brought out by an individual (OV 44)—whereas thinking is characterized by singularity. But thought in its dialectical guise contains "plurality as if in germ, [. . .] insofar, namely, as I can only think by dividing myself, though I am one, into two" (SQMP 107). And even if this duality, as a foreshadowing of plurality, constitutes only a trace of actual togetherness with others, as in the case of a plant, no growth can be expected without a germ.

It is precisely this duality of the thinking experience that enables it to be linked to action with its plurality. The doubling of the I in thinking

> implies, albeit only in passing, the fact that men exist in the plural and not in the singular, that men and not Man inhabit the earth. Even if we are by ourselves, when we articulate or actualize this being-alone we find that we are in company, in the company of ourselves. (SQMP 96)

The contrast between the loneliness of singularity and the implicit duality of being alone makes clear the difference between the solipsism of metaphysical thinking and the withdrawal from the world in dialectical thinking. In both cases, although all activities of the common world are interrupted and the subject withdraws into a quiet sphere where she can engage in the "purest activity" of thinking, in dialectical thinking the main principle of human togetherness is not negated in the process but merely brought to a different level; bracketed, if one likes to use this Husserlian notion here, which seems justifiable in light of Arendt's self-description as "a kind of phenomenologist" (Young-Bruehl 1982: 405)

The second presumable similarity between both modes of thinking we discuss here is that both dialectical and metaphysical thinking are concerned with general concepts. The foci of Socratic dialogues show this clearly: Socrates speaks to his interlocutors about the meaning of bravery, love, prudence, or virtue in general. However, this focus differs from that of metaphysical thought, for

> the objects of this activity [of thinking] are of course by no means restricted to specifically philosophic or, for that matter, scientific topics. Thinking as an activity can arise out of every occurrence; it is present when I, having watched an incident in the street or having become implicated in some occurrence, now start considering what has happened, telling to myself as a kind of story, preparing it in this way for its subsequent communication to others, and so forth. (SQMP 93–4)

As we see, the process of dialectical thinking can be set in motion by any experience, even the most banal. Accordingly, thinking and acting have a reciprocal effect, for thinking can be triggered by the experiences of action and, at the same time, through preparing sensual particulars so that "the mind is able to handle them in their absence" (LoM I 76–7) so that they can be used for judging, which then prepares ground for acting.

In this sense, the aim of dialectical thinking differs radically from that of its metaphysical counterpart. While the latter strives for the knowledge of truth, in dialectical thinking the activity of thinking itself has an intrinsic value. Thinking in an inner dialogue, as Arendt points out, has no end. In aporetic dialogues, Socrates' conversations with his interlocutors produce no measurable results; the arguments (*logoi*) are constantly in motion. Due to the repetitive contradiction (*elenchos*), the whole dialogue moves in circles (or sometime spirals), leading nowhere (LoM I 169–70). This kind of deliberative reflection does not arrive at a definition and, for this reason, has no concrete result in the sense of scientific or metaphysical thinking (LoM I 171). The thinking process seems endless, the activity is autotelic. For this reason, Socratic philosophizing, from Arendt's perspective, must come to terms with the contingency common to the realm of the political and constitutive of free action but foreign to the philosophers' dream of truth. The inner dialogue still needs to follow some logical principles but rather than being a pursuit of truth, it aims at an agreement with oneself (LoM I 185–6).

The last feature shared by metaphysical and dialectical thinking that merits mention here is the destructive potential of thinking, which manifests in different ways in the two cases. Jerome Kohn (1990: 125) argues that "Arendt intends to show that the *realm* of pure thought, the *sky* of ideas, the very notion of another world than *this* world is a 'metaphysical delusion.'" Here we risk the loss of connection to the common world and its inhabitants. The dialectical process of thinking, on the contrary, keeps us in a fragile relationship to the world, while it uses the eliminative power of thinking: Socratic midwifery that works out the consequences of unexamined opinions and thereby destroys them—values, doctrines, theories, and even beliefs (LoM I 192). Dialectical thinking can thus change our view of the world as well as challenge our moral and political convictions. The reason for this is not so much the character of the maieutic skill Socrates discusses in *Theaetetus* (149a–d), the one that helps in the "birth" of correct ideas. It is rather the Socratic *elenchos*, which seeks wisdom by examining and refuting the opinions of others. To actually acquire wisdom, however, turns out to be a divine skill, inaccessible to human beings, as Socrates argues in Plato's *Apology* (23a–c). This is why the scrutinizing power of the circular dialogue is always indirectly political. Through the destruction of unexamined concepts, it relativizes fixed patterns of thought, thus preparing the way for reflective judgment (LoM I 76, 191), which co-constitutes action, as we show in Chapter 3.

"Plurality inherent in every human being"

According to Arendt, it only rarely happens that the practical relevance of thinking reveals itself in the world. Most of the time, "thinking brings little benefit to society" and "does not create values; it does not say once and for all what 'the good' is; it does not confirm accepted rules of conduct, but dissolves them" (LoM I 192). This influence on worldly life that Arendt attributes to thinking is fairly modest. If we take a look at her concept of the human world and take seriously her reference to society in the quote above, we may soon understand why. As mentioned in Chapter 1, action is not the only mode of human activity in the world, and public space is not the only mode of the world in which we become active. While action is rare and does not fill in our worldly lives by a long way, the activity mode that is much more prevalent is behavior (HC 40), and its space is society. Action is free, spontaneous, and brings the new into the world. Human beings, however, also need a certain stability to live their lives as embodied and temporal creatures. If revolutions—one of the most vivid phenomena of action—were happening constantly, these lives would be a series of exhausting and potentially traumatizing disruptions. This is why we spend most of our time on earth not acting but behaving: fulfilling given tasks according to pregiven, common rules and implementing routines of the everyday. While acting is individual and unforeseeable, behavior is quite predictable and can be systematized according to psychological or sociological patterns. The difference between the effects action and behavior have on the world is essential. Even if revolutionary moments cannot and should not constitute our everyday life, the world in which behavior prevails is in danger of "petrifying" (CE 189), while action ensures the constant renewal of the common world. So, if thinking with its destructive power dissolves fixed rules of behavior and by so doing prevents the world from stagnation by actualizing the new, its practical role in the world is anything but marginal. To be sure, no thought can magically transform itself into action, but the role of thinking as the precondition of judgment—and thereby indirectly of action in its opposition to mere behavior—is crucial.

Accordingly, Arendt holds that the practical relevance of thinking only manifests itself in boundary situations, a concept she adopts from Jaspers (2008: 201–54). She recognizes that human life itself is, in a sense, a liminal phenomenon in that it is limited between birth and death, forcing us to always think of the past, in which we have not yet existed, or of the future, in which we will no longer exist. And

> whenever I transcend the limits of my own life span and begin to reflect on this past, judging it, and this future, forming projects of the will, thinking ceases to be a politically marginal activity. And such reflections will inevitably arise in political emergencies. (LoM I 192)

In those moments of crisis, thinking must play an unmistakably political role. Even if action is not a part of our everyday life and always seems like a miracle to us when it actually occurs (HC 246), situations of starting anew—perhaps not always in such a spectacular form as the founding of the city of Rome—must happen often enough to keep our world from becoming a fossil.

We encounter boundary situations again and again in the course of our lives. And even though political emergencies are sometimes their manifestations, thinking understood as a silent dialogue in itself is a boundary situation. The common world is the only space of appearance establishing a common reality, but not the only space of appearance altogether. In thinking we also expose ourselves in a particular, extreme way. In this dialogical situation, one encounters only one dialogue partner, with her undivided attention. Unlike in the case of speech in the public space, where one appears to others from different, partial perspectives, in the inner dialogue one is completely exposed and can hardly conceal anything from the other, understood as the other self. When we act, the distance of the public space, which Arendt compares to a table, connecting and separating us at the same time (HC 52–3), ensures a certain protection. The acting person can affect the way in which she appears in the world through her actions, even if she can never be sure how those will be received. In the inner dialogue, on the contrary, I stand before my other self exactly as I am; I cannot hide from myself. This is why Arendt emphasizes, following Aristotle, that an inner dialogue can only take place between friends, which means that "its basic criterion, its supreme law, as it were, says: Do not contradict yourself" (LoM I 189). To avoid self-contradiction is central because I must live with myself and be in harmony with myself. I need to make decisions which I myself find justifiable. If I became a villain, a murderer perhaps, how could I face myself in the inner dialogue? The only way to do this would be to lie to myself. But in this case, the most important criterion of dialectical thinking remains unfulfilled: I contradict myself and I am not in agreement with myself. This situation of radical exposure is likely to feel uncanny. Socrates confirms this in *Hippias Major* (304e) by describing his inner dialogue partner as a very obnoxious fellow who constantly cross-examines him; a close relative, who lives in the same house (quoted in LoM I 188). Arendt notes:

> The philosopher who [. . .] takes this flight into absolute solitude, is more radically delivered to this plurality inherent in every human being than anybody else, because it is the companion with others which, calling me out of the dialogue of thought, makes me one again—one single, unique human being speaking with but one voice and recognizable as such by others. (PP 86)

The necessary honesty of the thinking dialogue may also be the reason for some to refuse to engage in the activity of thinking at all. The insecurity or fear of exposure to oneself can lead to the "cog in the wheel" syndrome just as much as the inability to self-reflect—a motive of Arendt's critical discussion of totalitarianism and personal responsibility in times of totalitarian rule, to which we return in Chapter 5 with reference to *Eichmann in Jerusalem*.

This brings us to the one sphere of human life in which thinking, Arendt argues, definitely has practical relevance: morality. Here dialectical thinking proves to be not only destructive but also constructive: thinking, "in contrast to contemplation, with which it is too often equated, is indeed an *activity*, and moreover an activity that has certain moral results, namely that he who thinks constitutes himself as a somebody, as a person or a personality" (SQMP 105). That thinking, Arendt continues, is an activity does not entail that it is in and of itself action; rather, the formation of the person in the sense of the moral I responsible for her deeds and words is something of an ongoing by-product of the activity of thinking itself (SQMP 106). The constituting of the person in an inner dialogue is a *conditio sine qua non* of morality. Without the presence of someone who can be held responsible for an act (good or evil), no common world could emerge between human beings inhabiting the same space. This shows clearly in Arendt's take on the case of Adolf Eichmann: through his inability to think, he refuses to be a somebody, which makes his responsibility for the crimes he enabled appear as diffuse (LoM I 33–4). Since it is where the moral person comes to be, the thinking dialogue between I and myself must be understood as the source of moral action. We may see the relation between them as an instance of the butterfly effect: as a by-product of thinking, the constitution of the person influences all her actions. Since action takes place between people, it always has a moral dimension.

Arendt herself sees this connection as somewhat ephemeral. Because of the value she places on plurality in the public sphere, she denies political relevance to this ethical foundation. Similar to any other field of philosophy, moral philosophy must remain separate from the public sphere. Indeed, its subject is the human being in the singular: my ethical stance remains of relevance to my conscience but not to the community: "in politics not [individual] life, but the world is at stake" (WF 155). Nevertheless, Arendt refers to moral questions in numerous explicitly political cases. Like all her works, the essays in which she takes up the question of evil and its connection to thinking are rooted in the political experiences of her age. Arendt rather reflects on the ethical problems that have relevance for the public instead of developing a purely speculative discourse, as a moral philosopher would. Like Socrates, she is at home in the agora rather than in the sky of ideas.

While the creation of the moral I in inner dialogue is the necessary condition of moral action, the question now is whether it could also be its sufficient condition. With the exposition of the I to my other self in the thinking dialogue in mind, Arendt claims that no one could ever want to live together with a murderer (SQMP 165), which leads her to elevate the practice of thinking as a silent dialogue to the alternative grounding of morality. This claim, however, has been questioned from the very beginning. The first critic was her friend Mary McCarthy, who argued, "The modern person I posit would say to Socrates, with a shrug, 'Why not? What's wrong with a murderer?' And Socrates would be back where he started" (Arendt and McCarthy 1995: 22). Indeed, Arendt starts from the ideal of a rational subject and follows the Socratic conviction: she who has understood what the good is will also do good. The impossibility of self-contradiction, the force of which mainly operates in the sense that one ought not to act in such a way that one is no longer in harmony with oneself (Assy 2005: 15), can certainly be questioned in the face of moral indifference. In the case of people who refuse or are unable to engage in inner dialogue, the necessary condition of moral sense is not given. The moral potential then can only be realized by rational, autonomous persons who refuse to contradict themselves.

For Arendt, the duality of thinking being is prior to the plurality of action. Her faith in the possibility of a new beginning, which she expresses so clearly in the famous last sentences of *The Origins of Totalitarianism*, does not allow her to give up hope in the future of the common world: "*Initium ut esset, creatus est homo*—'that a beginning be made, man was created', said Augustine. This beginning is guaranteed by each new birth; it is indeed every man" (OT 479). The foundation for this hope—the need for inner harmony—cannot function as a universal cure for moral or political ignorance. However, Arendt's primary concern is not to elaborate a normative moral philosophy but to capture evil in political-phenomenological terms. She is not trying to tell her readers how this should be done. Arendt's own need was to understand political phenomena, and her interest was to invite us to join her in this endeavor. However, her depiction of dialectical thinking can become the basis of an educational approach, promising to improve both the moral and the political competence of democratic citizens. Such education would not follow an isolated intellectualist-theoretical principle but focus on the practice of thinking in public: an extended mode of thinking, which originates in the inner dialogue of the I with myself.

Was Arendt a Philosopher After All?

Arendt's claim that she was not a philosopher but rather a political theorist has been an issue of scholarly debate. It often happens that the interpreters try to turn her black-and-white logic around and prove that, eventually, she was not a political theorist but a philosopher. Dolf Sternberger, for example, writes about her political project:

> However vigorously we rehabilitate action in its peculiarity, however defiantly we reverse the ranks of thought and action as of solitude and publicity, however urgently we conjure freedom so as to realize it solely as a practical, that is to say, a political matter within the bounds of the polis—all of this will inevitably remain a philosophical effort. (Sternberger 1977: 132–3)

Margaret Canovan goes even further and argues at length that Arendt was a crypto-philosopher. In her old age, she is said to have admitted that she was not a political animal (Canovan 1990: 136). Moreover, according to Canovan (1990: 163), Arendt experienced the loneliness of the thinking business first-hand, which is supposed to speak for the actually philosophical character of her works: "she herself in her published works did not in general engage in dialogue with anyone except herself." We find this to be a misjudgment. First, because Arendt repeatedly engaged in debates on current political issues and illustrated her theoretical statements with examples of concrete political events, so that they can be read, until this day, also as commentaries. Second, she cultivated public exchanges of ideas with her critics, for example with Eric Voegelin in the case of *The Origins of Totalitarianism*, mentioned in Chapter 1, or, as will be discussed in detail in Chapter 5, with Gershom Scholem in the midst of the controversy over *Eichmann in Jerusalem*. What is more, she wrote reviews and critiques of other authors' publications; she was quite active in the New York intellectual milieu, writing for the *New Yorker* and engaging in polemics in the *New York Review of Books*. In her writings, a dialogue with the thinkers of the past is always present since she was, at bottom, not a theorist but a student and a teacher of her inherited tradition of political and philosophical thinking (Young-Bruehl and Kohn 2001). It is indeed hard to argue, as Canovan does, that the element of plurality disappears from Arendt's works. Her expressed doubt about not being a "political animal" does not seem decisive here. Perhaps this is best understood as a matter of sentimentality, an expression of unfulfilled ambitions, or the question of a life well lived and time well spent. Be that as it may, the dialectical rather than metaphysical character of her oeuvre and the direct involvement in pressing political matters throughout her writing career predominantly outweigh this retrospective comment about her salience as a political being.

Finally, if one interprets Arendt's writings as exercises in political thinking, as we do in this book, one finds an implicit invitation to engage with them. They presuppose a dialogue partner or a listener to the stories Arendt tells. They are thus not transcripts of philosophical thinking in the solitude of the metaphysical kingdom of thought but living dialogues, not only taking the common world as their subject but also directed toward the growth and change of that world. Arendt's writings contain an element of plurality, as does her preferred form of philosophical thinking: the Socratic dialogue of the I with myself. As a thinker (and writer), Arendt is never alone, she never withdraws completely from the world. She always considers her readers as fellow citizens in the common world and her partners in thinking. Therefore, the attempt to classify Arendt clearly as a philosopher or a political theorist is misguided and we reject this binary logic. Seyla Benhabib, for example, opts for such an open interpretation, emphasizing that the recovery of the public sphere postulated by Arendt is not only a political but also a philosophical project, although Arendt herself failed to recognize its philosophical significance (Benhabib 1996: 50). This intuition becomes especially clear in her recourse to Socrates, with whom she looks back to the times when the linking of thinking and doing was still possible. As Arendt notes, the root of the conflict between the philosopher and the polis is to be found in Socrates' wanting to make philosophy useful for the polis (PP 91), thus trying to bring the two opposing elements together. Hence, the bridge-building solution to the problem of whether Arendt should be read as a philosopher, a political theorist, or both, rests upon her fascination with Socrates, whose thinking remains philosophical without renouncing plurality and worldly reference.

For Arendt, the separation between the practical and the theoretical way of life is a fact of tradition. Thus, as long as one remains within the traditional framework, it cannot be disputed. After the breach of tradition, however, the relationship between thinking and acting needs to be determined anew, and the means of this determination are to be sought outside the traditional, metaphysical scheme. In the person of Socrates, Arendt finds a desirable union of two worlds of experience that makes it possible to connect the practice of action to the practice of thinking in a constructive way. For action, it would only be harmful to be affected by the unworldly processes of the theoretical way of life that seek a single, unchangeable truth, as the examples of Plato and Heidegger clearly prove. On the contrary, the opening between thought and action that Arendt points to reveals a mode in which thinking is not only useful for active life but even indispensable for its best practice. Arendt's writings point to the dialogical structure of her own thinking and the need for us, continuously, to restart the process of meaning formation, to redefine and rethink the categories of our political language when familiar categories of traditional thinking about politics cease to offer a reliable reference point.

Notes

1. The German version of this passage makes it even clearer: "dem nach-zudenken, was wir eigentlich tun, wenn wir tätig sind," meaning to think about what we are actually doing when we are active (VA 13).
2. Arendt's statement that thinking as such has little use for the society is included in the German edition, *Vom Leben des Geistes*, but not in the American edition of the book.

Chapter 3

Exercises in Political Thinking

Arendt's point of departure is the situation of the breach of tradition, which had already started with Marx and became a fact with the rise of totalitarianism (TMA; Arendt 2002: 300). For Arendt, this means that, in politics, we cannot rely on the authority of the past or appeal to general rules that seem to have governed politics in the past. What, then, should we do? In this situation, Arendt suggests, reflective judgment needs to stand in for any firm orientation in political practices. Judgment is a particular activity of the mind, political thinking, situated between the past that cannot guide us anymore and the future that we cannot foresee. And so, the relevance of judging is universal as "each new generation, indeed every new human being as he inserts himself between an infinite past and an infinite future, must discover and ploddingly pave it anew" (GBPF 13). This chapter will engage with the practice of reflective judgment and Arendt's suggestion on how to acquire, improve, and exercise one's ability to judge.

The difficulty with Arendt's theory of judgment is that she could not complete the respective study during her lifetime. After her death, a page with the headline of the third volume of *The Life of the Mind: Judging* was found in her typewriter (Young-Bruehl 1982: 467). The manuscript was likely to be based on Arendt's *Lectures on Kant's Political Theory*, which Arendt gave in 1964 at the University of Chicago and then in 1970 at the New School for Social Research. Based on notes of these lectures, Ronald Beiner published an interpretative reconstruction of Arendt's theory of judgment, expressing hope that this reconstruction, together with other references to judgment throughout her work, "can offer clues to the likely direction Hannah Arendt's thinking would have taken in this area" (Beiner 1992: vii). As Arendt had already written about judging in numerous essays, such as "Personal Responsibility Under Dictatorship" (published in 1964), "Some Questions of Moral Philosophy" (1965/6), and "Thinking and Moral Considerations" (1971), traces of her reflections on this topic can be found in her essay "Philosophy and Politics" (a fragment of the lectures at Notre Dame University, which she was preparing in 1954), and she even mentions it in her "A Reply to Eric Voegelin: The Origins of Totalitarianism" (1953), the material at our disposal is relatively broad. And as we already know that Arendt's approach to politics emphatically includes thinking about and rethinking political questions, the fact of her theory of judgment's being unfinished is less a problem than an invitation to continue practicing reflective judgment as she outlined it and beyond (recent examples are Zerilli 2016 and Villa 2021, especially chapter 6). This is exactly what we attempt to do in the second part of this book. But first, let us take a look at what Arendt herself tells us about the practice of reflective judgment.

What is Political Thinking?

In her concept of judgment, Arendt was inspired by Immanuel Kant's Third Critique. Her reading of Kant, however, was without a doubt idiosyncratic. She states several times that Kant never wrote a political philosophy (LKPP 7, 9, 31, 61). Her reasons for making this claim, notwithstanding what tradition generally considers "Kant's political writings" in the sense of the Cambridge History of Political Thought volume under this title (Kant 1991a), spring from her own idea of the political. Kant's *Critique of Judgment*, Arendt says, is the only occasion on which Kant deals with people in the plural, while in all of his other writings, especially in his moral philosophy, the human being appears in the singular, as an individual moral subject. For Arendt, however, plurality is the *sine qua non* of all political thinking and acting.

Judging, much more than thinking, correlates with this central condition of the human life. This is because while thinking, as we have shown, attends to the general even in its dialectic mode, "the faculty of judgment deals with particulars, which 'as such, contain something contingent in respect of the universal,' which normally is what thought is dealing with" (LKPP 13). Since particulars are what we experience (even though, as we discuss later in this chapter, judgment is not concerned with objects of our direct perception but precisely with things and events we do not perceive at the moment when we judge), judgement is closer to our worldly living practices. The relevance of this faculty for public life is then clearly visible, and in Part II of this book we engage with practice of judgment, with and against Arendt.

Further, the recourse to Kant allows Arendt to emphasize the intellectual attitude of critique, that is, of thinking that makes distinctions and sets limits. Arendt spans this concept between two figures: Kant and Socrates, the former implementing critical thinking on the theoretical level, the latter also on the practical level. For Kant, critique is an expression of doubt about traditional metaphysics. It presents an attempt to discover the sources and limits of reason. Kant speaks out against dogmatism but also against indifference, which has been favored by many as the reaction to the crisis of metaphysics:

> [This indifference] is clearly the result, not of the carelessness, but of the matured judgment of our age, which will no longer rest satisfied with the mere appearance of knowledge. It is, at the same time, a powerful appeal to reason to undertake anew the most difficult of its duties, namely, self-knowledge [. . .]. (Kant, KRV A XI [Guyer and Wood 1998: 111–12]; LKPP 39–40)

For Arendt, it is thus not a preparation for a new doctrine, in the sense that a (seemingly negative) critique should lead exclusively to a (seemingly positive) system formation. Rather, critique should promote 'thinking for oneself', or enable one to 'make use of one's own reason' (LKPP 32). Such a public use of reason, as described by Kant (2012) in "What is Enlightenment?," is the condition of the relevance of judgment to political action.

Arendt believes that the public impact critical thinking can have is demonstrated by Socrates' practice of philosophizing: "To think critically, to blaze the trail of thought through prejudices, through unexamined opinions and beliefs, is an old concern of philosophy, which we may date, insofar as it is a conscious enterprise, to the Socratic midwifery in Athens" (LKPP 36). Through his method, Socrates performs a "free and public" examination of opinions, both those of his interlocutors and his own. As a critical thinker, he thus interacts with the polis.

The hostile reaction of the state with its established structures against a critical thinker, exemplified by Socrates' trial, results from fear: critical thinking always has political implications because, unlike dogmatic truths and pure speculation, it is basically anti-authoritarian. Therefore, those who think critically appear as dangerous to the status quo. Arendt advocates this critical practice and sees in it the force that keeps the common world alive. The ossification of the state apparatus with its institutions, bureaucracy, and established norms means a restriction of the freedom of action in its everyday performance and in consequence the paralysis of the public space. For its continued existence and development, the public sphere requires critical thinkers who, as Socrates did, irritate and stimulate the body of the political community like a gadfly.

Arendt was attracted to this way of thinking because in place of an all-encompassing doctrine, it offered a plurality of critical voices. In this way, the condition of plurality is present in her concept of judgment as well as that of action (discussed in Chapter 1). In the common world, the *doxai* (opinions) are conceivable only in the plural. No judgment can be objective, because everyone remains bound to the world and this world opens itself to each person in a different way. A universally valid judgment would either have to bring this infinite multiplicity of perspectives down to the common denominator or be made from an immaterial position of a nobody, detached from the world. In both cases, it would be invalid for the public. At the same time, judgment must not be confused with subjective pleasure. For Kant, aesthetic judgments concern taste, which human beings share to a certain extent, and we can certainly communicate about them in a way that is understandable to others. This understanding is enabled by the *sensus communis*: a sense common to all human beings, a sense that fits us into community (LKPP 70). Hence, a judgment is not subjective, Kant argues (*Critique of Judgment* §40 [Pluhar 1987: 160]), for it "in reflecting takes account (a priori), in our thought, of everyone else's way of presenting [something], in order *as it were* to compare our own judgment with human reason in general."

Arendt projects this concept to the realm of the public, emphasizing that judgment presupposes a plurality of perspectives. In this way she moves from the duality of the dialectical situatedness of thinking toward the plurality of the political sphere. However, the implied plurality of judgment is not, as in the case of action, given in the world but is a speculative one (LKPP 71) in which

> we compare our judgment not so much with the actual as rather with the merely possible judgments of others, and [. . .] put ourselves in the position of everyone else, merely by abstracting from the limitations that [may] happen to attach to our own judging. (Kant, *Critique of Judgment* §40 [Pluhar 1987: 160])

By referring to the *possible* judgments of others, this "enlarged mentality" enables the emergence of a speculative community, which is the condition of exercising the ability to judge, as it makes consideration of multiple perspectives possible. What is more, my judgment is all the more representative the more possible points of view I consider (SQMP 141). In this way, my position is critical, in that 'the judging I' seeks the greatest possible representativeness of my judgment through free and public examination of its elements.

Of course, this account of judgment prompts questions, one of which is quite apparent: Can we really think in place of someone else, let alone everyone else? Arendt herself does not make answering this question easier, since the example she uses to clarify the process of making a judgment clearly misfires: she suggests a thought experiment, in which she imagines how she would feel living in a slum from the perspective of a slum dweller (SQMP 140), and she frames this example as if it was not a problem whatsoever to do so. The fragility of her concept of judgment paired with this example makes many of her readers suspicious that this kind of judging simply would not work, as we discuss in Chapter 9. How can I put myself in somebody else's shoes and reliably imagine her perspective on a given problem?

The answer, also from Arendt's perspective, is: I cannot. It is not possible to think from someone else's perspective in the sense that we use this expression in everyday communication, saying "if I were you." Rather,

> To think with an enlarged mentality means that one trains one's imagination to go visiting. [. . .] I must warn you here of a very common and easy misunderstanding. The trick of critical thinking does not consist in an enormously enlarged empathy through which one can know what actually goes on in the mind of all others. To think, according to Kant's understanding of enlightenment, means Selbstdenken, to think for oneself, "which is the maxim of a never-passive reason. To be given to such passivity is called prejudice" (*Critique of Judgment*, § 40),[1] and enlightenment is, first of all, liberation from prejudice. To accept what goes on in the minds of those whose "standpoint" (actually, the place where they stand, the conditions they are subject to, which always differ from one individual to the next, from one class or group as compared to another) is not my own would mean no more than passively to accept their thought, that is, to exchange their prejudices for the prejudices proper to my own station. (LKPP 43)

Arendt also notes that

> my judgment of a particular instance does not merely depend upon my perception but upon my representing to myself something which I do not perceive. [. . .] Furthermore, while I take others into account when judging, this does not mean that I conform in my judgment to theirs. I still speak with my own voice and I do not count noses in order to arrive at

what I think is right. But my judgment is no longer subjective either, in the sense that I arrive at my conclusions by taking only myself into account. (SQMP 140–1)

As we see, she is very explicit about the fact that the "enlarged mentality" does not imply an acceptance of another person's standpoint, and there is a difference between claiming the ability to assume the position of another and to think "in the place of another," who I am not. In the former case, one thinks as if one were the other. Arendt does not suggest that such an adoption of another's perspective is possible, simply because of the existential condition of natality. Rather, one can attempt to find a third perspective, in which the judging subject simultaneously remains herself and brackets her own position: the one in which she still judges as herself but, in doing so, she imagines multiple other perspectives, which are not her own, and thinks them through in a critical way. It is clear that in this process we might simply be wrong in our representation of other persons' perspectives. Also, opinion, as opposed to truth, is not firm but can be changed, rethought, inversed, or refined, and this applies to every human being in their plurality. This is why judging is a very fragile practice, in which neither the journey nor the destination is certain. But if we never know if our judgment is right or wrong, what is the use of it?

Judging operates with opinions, not with the truth. We should recall Socrates here, for whom *doxa* (opinion) means the way in which the world reveals itself to one, "what appears to me" (*dokei moi*). This implies many perspectives: to each person the world opens differently and each of these appearances has its validity, although they are not equally truthful. The political relevance of Socrates' philosophical practice is to think together with others. Through his maieutic art, he seeks to make the opinions of other citizens more truthful (PP 80–2). In so doing, he does not strive for the truth. Socrates' dialogues often end inconclusively, which indicates that opinion is much more fragile than truth, and it is good that it is so. Opinions can be rethought, reformulated, and even changed into their opposites on their way to becoming more truthful. Since they, as we show below, have the potential to inform action, this flexibility is a condition of political freedom.

To make my *doxai* more truthful, I orient myself on the plurality of the world. As we have already mentioned at the beginning of this chapter, the number and variety of perspectives I take into consideration will be reflected in the quality of my judgment. This, however, does not yet secure my grasping these perspectives in the "right" way, because the plurality of judgment is a speculative one: the others whose opinions I consider in the act of judging are not immediately present, but the object of my imagination. As Kant puts it, we judge by "comparing our judgment with the possible rather than the actual judgments of others, and by putting ourselves in the place of any other man" (*Critique of Judgment* §40 [Pluhar 1987: 160]). We could say that the more often I engage in the practice of judgment, the better and more truthful my judgment becomes through repetition and exercise—provided that I critically examine my past judgments.

Crucially, although Arendt's judging is a faculty of the mind, the judging subject is neither singular, on her own, like in metaphysical thinking, nor engaged in the duality of an inner dialogue, but is in a multilateral exchange with an imaginary community of judgment (LKPP 75). Hence, judging presupposes plurality, which is not only its condition but also relates to our lived experience in the world. As there apparently needs to be a connection between judging as an activity of the mind and acting as a worldly activity, many scholars tried to establish this link (including Benhabib 1992; Young 1997; Zerilli 2005a, 2016).

Arendt emphasizes, following Kant, that judgments must be communicable but impartial. This impartiality results from the use of critical thinking, which is still "a solitary business" but "by the force of imagination it [critical thinking] makes the others present and thus moves in a space that is potentially public, open to all sides; in other words, it adopts the position of Kant's world citizen" (LKPP 43). It is in this potentially public space, with its speculative plurality, that impartiality becomes the crucial condition of the validity of a judgment. Keeping in mind that Arendt was reluctant to accept uncritically the notion of scientific objectivity (HC 269), this impartial position of a judging subject poses an interpretative difficulty, as will be discussed in Chapter 5. On the one hand, she rejects the view of human affairs from outside as distorted and unworldly; she refuses to speak about the political *sine ira et studio* (Arendt 1953: 78). On the other hand, our opinions, understood as the way in which the world opens to us, should be formed impartially. This problem was classically discussed by Seyla Benhabib (1992) and Iris Marion Young (1997), among others. Benhabib argues for judgment depending upon a symmetrical and universal exchangeability of perspectives, leading, finally, to the establishment of universal, judgment-based morality, while Young, countering this view, points to the asymmetrical reciprocity of judging positions, as those depend upon one's worldly position in terms of temporality (determination based on one's life story, with its historical and cultural particularities, as well as personal experience) and social position (which in itself is located within a fluctuating system). Both authors, however, interpret the enlarged thinking as "adopting one another's standpoint," which Benhabib and Young ultimately attribute to Arendt (Benhabib 1992: 137; Young 1997: 357). We find this problematic and misleading, and in what follows we propose a different answer to the question of how reflective judgment can be both impartial and worldly at the same time.

These two claims can be reconciled if the view that impartiality necessarily includes abstraction is set aside. Arendt shows that the judging subject can adopt a detached position without at the same time having to withdraw from the space of human affairs. She describes judgment as "the political kind of insight par excellence" (PP 84), whose validity is "neither objective and universal nor subjective, depending on personal whim, but intersubjective and representative" (SQMP 141). The judging subject remains an individual within the common world, a person. At the same time, however, through imagination, she extends her thinking to include potential opinions of other members in the speculative community of judgment. This figure of a judging person as a critical observer is a meaningful moment in Arendt's philosophy. It is one of the moments in which plurality comes to light in the most vivid way.

One of the metaphors Arendt uses to describe the practice of reflective judgment (following Kant's [1991b (1795)] *Perpetual Peace*) is a game, in which there are players performing the game and spectators observing the players from a disengaged position. There is a clear difference between the partial, uncritical opinion of the interested citizen and the critical, detached opinion of the judging person as a spectator, but the impartiality of the latter is not to be equated with objectivity. Her attitude needs to be understood as relative impartiality (LKPP 73): it is positioned and critical at the same time, whereas the judging subject strives for the intersubjective validity of her judgment. As we know, the more perspectives different from her own she can take into account, the higher the quality of her judgment. At the same time, she needs to measure her judgment by a high, critical standard, verified by its communicability.

Although judgment formation does not depend on the calculus of voices, its communicability and justifiability to the speculative community of judgment play a crucial role. In this sense, a judging person does not withdraw from the world entirely, so she must orient herself to its plurality. A judgment that does not meet with any approval of the fellow judges alienates the person making the judgment.

Judging is based on a kind of dialogue also in the sense that it is the extended Socratic mode of thinking: a silent dialogue is conducted in this case as a multi-voiced conversation in which I consider both my own and possible judgments of others. Plurality of the world comes into play here in both its unifying and its separating guise: one looks in the public sphere for the others with whom one can identify and form political alliances, a community; at the same time, one also looks for the others from whom one can distinguish and separate oneself. Just as in thinking we decide "with whom we want to live," so too do we in judging, in a slightly less metaphorical way. The criterion of communicability helps the judging person to determine, according to the standard of the criterion of "good society" (SQMP 145–6), with whom she wants to act together and co-create the common world. This reinterpretation of Arendt's account of impartiality as something distinct from the standard notion of scientific objectivity immediately connects with how Arendt tried to think beyond the controversy surrounding *Eichmann in Jerusalem* that we address in Chapter 5.

For now, let us note that judging is not objective knowledge, nor does it prescribe any compelling patterns of action. As Arendt reads Kant, any moral rules or maxims for action do not nullify my judgment, and if I forget my insights as a spectator, I "would [. . .] become what so many good men, involved and engaged in public affairs, tend to be—an idealistic fool" (LKPP 54). Arendt herself offers a clue how to overcome the seeming separation between judging and acting by describing the role of communicability of (aesthetic, but above all political) judgments as follows:

> The condition *sine qua non* for the existence of beautiful objects is communicability; the judgment of the spectator creates the space without which no such objects could appear at all. The public realm is constituted by the critics and the spectators, not by the actors or the makers. And this critic and spectator sits in every actor and fabricator; without this critical, judging faculty the doer or maker would be so isolated from the spectator that he would not even be perceived. (LKPP 63)

For Arendt, the common world, that is, the political space in which action takes place, is a space of appearance in which we see others and expose ourselves to them. It is created by seeing and being seen, and so it requires a spectator, who is present in every actor. On the one hand, in order to appear in the public space at all, each actor needs spectators who perceive her appearing. The spectator, on the other hand, needs the play of the actors to legitimize her task. The interrelation between these two positions indicates a connection between judging and acting.

In order to preserve the advantages of both positions, however, there cannot be a fusion of the spectator and the actor. As Linda Zerilli (2005a: 179) notes, "'Spectator' is not another person, but simply a different mode of relating to, or being in, the common world." Thus, it is rather the case that in practice every person incorporates both roles and fluctuates between the two without abstracting completely from the other. The spectator is not fully separated from the world, and the actor draws on her judgments when co-creating the common world. The political knowledge that the judging subject elaborates through this movement is impartial, in that it is critical; it is positioned, in that it cannot be detached from the judging person; it exists only as partial knowledge, because one cannot take into account all existing perspectives; and through its relation to plurality, it is intrinsically political. Judging as political knowledge is a "world-making practice by which we discover not simply the personal preferences of other people [. . .] but the extent and nature of what we have in common" (Zerilli 2005b: 159), constructing the community and setting its limits. Thus, one outcome of such political insight is a world-opening, involving the complex web of human affairs and the infinite sum of perspectives shedding light on our common world. In this sense, the question of how we make our judgments "more truthful" becomes an issue of first-rate political importance.

Between Critique and Experiment

In the introduction to her *Lectures on Kant's Political Philosophy*, Arendt reminds us that for Kant judgment "emerges as 'a peculiar talent which can be practiced only and cannot be taught'" (LKPP 4). Hence, Arendt's most fully formulated answer to this question ("how can we make our judgments more truthful?") is her concept of exercises in political thinking. She introduces it in the introduction to her essay collection *Between Past and Future: Eight Exercises in Political Thought*. Although announced in the title, its description is fairly brief, as Arendt dedicates merely two pages to it. This may be due to her general aversion to methodological statements (Young-Bruehl 1982: 405), and the conciseness of its exposition should not detract our attention from the significance of the concept itself. Arendt elucidates the context of her exercises through a narrative about the "lost treasure of revolution," which becomes perceptible under conditions of political crisis. As the story goes, the rupture of the Western tradition that occurred with the emergence of a totalitarian regime led to a fundamental transformation of the political space. The boundaries of political participation were shifted, because those who made a decision to act politically under the conditions of the totalitarian non-world, and thus to assume political responsibility in a situation of deepest political crisis, did not necessarily belong to the groups typically engaging in politics. The intellectuals, writers, and artists who joined the French *Résistance* had no preparation for or experience in politics, so they acted under the conditions of a lack of tradition. The lost treasure that they suddenly and unexpectedly got hold of—political freedom in the sense of empowerment for making new beginnings—turned out to be extremely ephemeral:

> The history of revolutions [. . .] which politically spells out the innermost story of the modern age, could be told in parable form as the tale of an age-old treasure which, under the most varied circumstances, appears abruptly, unexpectedly, and disappears again, under different mysterious conditions, as though it were a fata morgana. (GBPF 4)

Thus, the political role of these unlikely revolutionary actors ended as soon as the crisis had been overcome, and the treasure of public freedom had to be given away.

This story provides a backdrop to Arendt's concept of exercises in political thinking, and emphasizes the relevance of political judgment for anyone who conceives of herself as an inhabitant of the common world. While the capacity for spontaneous free action is given to every human being by virtue of birth, in a world no longer held together by tradition it needs a reflexive complement. In this situation, the ability to think politically "became a tangible reality and perplexity for all; that is, it became a fact of political relevance," and it could only, as Arendt notes, be won through practice and exercises (GBPF 13). These exercises are a project of enlightenment and she aims for her readers to engage with her in political thinking, the cornerstone of interaction within the public sphere. Arendt here follows Socrates, whose activity in the agora she sees as political (PP 81), seeking through her writings to encourage her readers in the process of making their opinions more truthful. She does this by engaging in the perpetual practice of enlarged thinking that constitutes political cognition. As we argue in this chapter, with her—more and less voluminous—works, Arendt provides her readers with such exercises in political thinking.

Writing her exercises, Arendt picks up on the tradition of essayistic philosophizing. All her writings, even those monographs that run to several hundred pages in length, follow her call for thinking without a banister. This form of thinking replaces any claim to systematicity, yoking political cognition explicitly with its contingency. The literary form of the essay naturally follows the author's train of thought and in so doing, it invites the reader to think along. Choosing this approach is not merely a question of style; writing exercises, as Arendt (GBPF 14) notes, serve as method of gaining experience in how to think—in opposition to what to think—and they do not intend to convey any particular truths. They show how political thinking works as a specific thinking process, a practice that informs action. The validity of their results is contingent, as the essays do not aim to provide universally valid insights into the political and rather offer examples of political thinking; guidance about how to think politically about any issue to which we ascribe public relevance. Without doubt, Arendt's critique of the lack of meaning of the basic concepts of political language today, her descriptions of people serving as models of political actors, or her outlines of ideal public spaces have validity within her theoretical framework. This validity, however, is only exemplary: Arendt does not intend to persuade readers of certain theoretical solutions' being right or wrong or to preach a truth about the nature of the political. She is not interested in debates, in which she would gain the upper hand, but in understanding (WRLR 3) our common world; a reflection to which she invites her readers.

Arendt's essayistic writings, as a particular and agnostic form of thinking about the world, represent a reaction to the crisis that prevails in it. They emphasize the unattainability of clear and simple answers to questions that arise in the face of this crisis. Under these circumstances, the dynamics of the common world require a reflection on the present political questions that is fueled by genuine care for the world. For Arendt, essay is a literary genre of choice when pursuing this aim: "It seems to me, and I hope the reader will agree, that the essay as the literary form has a natural affinity to the exercises I have in mind" (GBPF 14). As such, an essayistic exercise always presents just one possible perspective on a given problem but it simultaneously implies multiple perspectives in two ways. On the one hand, when judging, we consider a plurality of perspectives, and on the other hand, many judgments can (and should) be passed on any given issue of political relevance. This approach is ubiquitous in Arendt's writings. Her essayistic style, full of digressions and not always easy to follow arguments, sums up to her "intuitive-chaotic method" (Vowinckel 2001: 42), which reflects her attitude toward the common world, acknowledging its processual and unpredictable character and its ambiguities.

As we can see, Arendt's style is in tune with her exercises, which do not follow any predefined scheme or strict rules for a philosophical treatise. They are structured by two moments only: the critical and the experimental. Arendt describes them as follows:

> Since these exercises move between past and future, they contain criticism as well as experiment, but the experiments do not attempt to design some sort of utopian future, and the critique of the past, of traditional concepts, does not intend to "debunk." (GBPF 14)

Though these two elements of an exercise are not strictly separated, Arendt assigns a temporal dimension to both of them, critique being associated with the past and experiment with the future. The practice of reflective judgment is thus temporally located, as the judging subject critically directs her gaze to the past, which offers her a reference to pass an experimental, future-oriented judgment. This does not mean that through such an exercise I could simply reappropriate tradition by critical interpretation of its notions. The traditional concepts lost their original sense, "leaving behind empty shells with which to settle almost all accounts, regardless of their underlying phenomenal reality" (GBPF 14). However, they did not lose their power over us: "On the contrary, it sometimes seems that this power of well-worn notions and categories becomes more tyrannical as the tradition loses its living force and the memory of its beginnings recedes" (TMA 25–6). This is why Arendt's exercises do not aim at inventing "some newfangled surrogates" (GBPF 14) of tradition: it is only from my actual position as situated here and now that I can relate to these concepts and I do this through the experimental element of an exercise with its future orientation. Because political thinking, as actualized in the exercises, "arises out of the actuality of political incidents [. . .] and my [Arendt's] assumption is that thought itself arises out of incidents of living experience and must remain bound to them" (GBPF 14), relating to the past is only possible in the form of experimental practice. What results from it is a model of partial, situated political cognition, the outcomes of which can only be temporary and contingent. From the perspective of such an experiment, the freedom of political thinking correlates with that of political action, with the difference that the judging subject as a spectator maintains a distance from the common world, while the political actor is in its midst.

Yet, as she points out, the element of experiment in Arendt's exercises is not about constructing a utopian future. Rather, it is a model situation for judgment: an example of a subject-action constellation is being reflected upon from the position of an observer and thus becomes material for judgment in its propaedeutic and political function. An exercise in political thinking is hence a kind of thought experiment, in which the exercising person does not create a wishful imagery of the world as it should be but defines herself as an observer of the public sphere that actually appears to her, the "world as it is" (CE 186). She lets her judgment "go visiting," expanding her way of thinking, which lets her improve the quality of her judgment. Such an experimental situation has the advantage that it can be exercised without exerting any direct influence on the public sphere and without any obligation to communicate the result of one's judgment to the world. At the same time, the exercises employ the actual judging competence, not any kind of "pre-competence" only imitating political thinking. In this respect, Arendt's essays are truly exemplary exercises, for they bring to consideration a very broad context, in the philosophical and political sense, which may even overwhelm the person engaging in exercising reflective judgment by the overflow of impulses. Her essays might be denser and more intense than our lived experience of judging, but as they are designed as a showcase, this should make them even more valuable. As every exercise mirrors the pluralistic claim of enlarged thinking, just as in the case of our opinions, the result can only be temporary, conditional, and fragmentary. An exercise is always open to modification. Thus, the task of the practitioner is never completed, just as the web of human relations in our common world can never be completed: it is always changing and we are changing with it as well.

When speaking about the critical element of the exercises in political thinking, Arendt does not intend to "debunk" (GBPF 14) traditional categories. This critique, instead, could be read in two contexts: as critical storytelling and as a project of enlightenment that resists both dogmatism and skepticism. Critical storytelling includes looking into the past in search of the original meaning of political notions, which we can only understand indirectly, from our situated perspective; political spaces offering a historical reference for action; and exemplary political agents—real and fictional—whose stories we may read as the prefiguration of an excellent political subject. Using narrative writing, Arendt points toward possible meanings of the past, at the same time opening a space for judgment. When engaging in the exercises, we may assume the role of a storyteller or of a recipient of such a story; in either case, our task is a critical one insofar as we pursue a narrative description of an aspect of the common world from a distance. The experiences that become the material for each story, direct or indirect, thus become a part of the recipient's world to be included as perspectives in her judgments. They become an object of critical consideration.

Critical thinking is both a means of enlightenment and prerequisite of judgment. Arendt shows how it not only serves as a destructive tool, questioning our use of political categories that today are nothing more than "worn out coins" (Young-Bruehl 1982: 325; Hyvönen 2021: 12–13), but also enables us to establish their meaning anew. This entails a critique of the dogmatic perspective on the political. We need the public sphere to remain free and dynamic if it is not to ossify into an administrative bureaucracy. Thinking critically about the categories of political vocabulary, but also about the real or fictional examples of action, allows us to see the world from a new perspective, away from uncontestable dogmas, and to engage in it in a responsible and constructive way.

Arendt's approach opposes not only dogmatism but also skepticism. Even though the exercises do not aim at inventing any surrogate of tradition, this does not mean that a new connection to political concepts beyond their traditional limitations, reinterpreting and understanding them from where we stand, is not possible. This critical reappraisal of the past and the determination of the meaning of political concepts cannot be done once and for all, though. As Arendt emphasizes, every critical interpretation of the past contains an element of the experimental (GBPF 14). The outcomes are always temporary, providing a new, revised understanding, not infrequently based on actual worldly dialogues, and open to further reflections.

The Exemplary Validity of Exercises in Political Thinking

Judging, for Arendt, is a mental activity separate from thinking. It is no accident, however, that she calls it "political thinking" or "enlarged thinking." The mental movement undertaken with the aid of the two faculties is in a way reversed: while the thinking subject reflects on the general from her own perspective, the judging subject considers possibly many different perspectives to think about the particular. The central question here is how an intellectual activity that does not aim at a generalization but rather concerns particular cases is possible at all. For Kant, judgment was a capacity of the mind operating by subsuming the particular under an appropriate general rule (SQMP 137); Arendt opts for a different interpretation. General rules are not trustworthy in the case of political judgment, she argues. This has aptly been shown by the history of the rise of National Socialism: the seemingly universally valid resolutions of morality, which were thought to be fixed standards of judgment and action, proved to be highly unstable and could be reversed "overnight" (SQMP 50). Instead, the validity of political judgment is exemplary: "Examples are the go-cart of judgment" (KRV B174 [Guyer and Wood 1998: 269]; SQMP 143), says Kant, and Arendt adopts this statement for her own theory.

Following Kant, Arendt writes that there are three ways in which we can judge individual cases: we can take our cue from a schema (to which the imagination of an object must conform in order to be acknowledged as this object), from abstraction (by gathering all possible objects of a sort and reducing their properties to the lowest common denominator), or from an example (by imagining the best possible exemplar of a given object) (SQMP 143–4). For her, it is this last option that provides the model for political judgment. Examples give us orientation; they offer a certain ideal to which a particular judgment can be referred. Exemplary validity is also advantageous because an example is not fixed once and for all—we can always look for a new and better one. This flexibility corresponds to the dynamics of the public sphere. Binding judgment to a predetermined general rule would conflict with the meaning of the political. This is why, as Arendt points out, many concepts of political theory and most political virtues also refer to exemplary models of political practice

(SQMP 144): a story whose protagonist exemplifies a certain virtue may very well serve as an orientation toward a particular disposition.

There is no catalog of exercises in political thinking and no fixed list of topics that should be worked through in order to develop one's competence in reflective judgment. Exercising is a flexible method, which can be adapted according to the political circumstances of a given time and place and to currently relevant issues concerning public togetherness. In Arendt's writings, we may distinguish three modes of exercises, each centered around an example: stories about the central concepts of political vocabulary, stories about exemplary spaces of political action, and stories about exemplary actions of political actors. As examples of such exercises, Arendt's essays serve for further development of the capacity for judgment and provide a stimulus for improving it through continuous practice.

The first mode of exercises is concerned with the study of political concepts and inventing a new political vocabulary. Arendt's approach is a genetic one: she searches for the true origins of the basic terms of political language in order to fill them with meaning again. Her metaphor of empty shells indicates that traditional concepts still hold tyrannical power over our political thinking, even though their genuine meaning is no longer apparent. The critical interpretation of the past, hence, is "an interpretation, whose chief aim is to discover the real origins of traditional concepts in order to distill from them anew their original spirit which has so sadly evaporated from the very key words of political language" (GBPF 14). These exercises consist of a narrative account of how these concepts have been conceived and used throughout centuries. For Arendt, the main reference is Greek antiquity, in which she sees the origin of Western thinking about the political—this corresponded to the *Zeitgeist*, and was certainly inspired by Heidegger's way of philosophizing, as classically discussed by Dana Villa (1996), and recently by Sophie Loidolt (2018) and Villa again (2021). This does not mean that Arendt was looking for some kind of fundamental human experience in the past (Benhabib 1996; Hyvönen 2021). Much more, discovered anew, from our particular position, these concepts become metaphorical protagonists of Arendt's stories. The narrative form of the exercises brings them back to life: instead of being meaningless dogmas, they can again be seen as genuine reference points for the way we think and speak about the political.

Arendt takes up this task under conditions of the breach of tradition, "in a world that is neither structured by authority nor held together by tradition" (CE 191), which makes possible a view of the past with eyes unclouded by traditional categories. She begins by dismantling the metaphysical framework imposed on political thinking over the centuries and limiting it today. This process of critical dismantling is not in itself destructive (LoM I 212). Instead of refuting traditional concepts, it goes beyond the metaphysical framework to open a third, distanced perspective. From this vantage point, a view of the relevant pieces of the fragmented past and their critical examination becomes possible. Arendt's genealogical project consists in opening up the particular experiences, meaning, and phenomenological reality that underlie political concepts (Borren 2010: 28) that offer a (critical) vocabulary to describe our current political experience. For it is always political experience that Arendt has in mind: "For the experiences behind even the most worn-out concept remain valid and must be recaptured and re-actualized if one wishes to escape certain generalizations that have proven pernicious."[2] A critical examination of the history of political concepts, down to their roots, helps the judging person to find her position in the political realm. As long as she keeps a distance from the common world, she uses the position of an observer to make her judgment; as soon as she enters the world as a political actor, the newly acquired political insights offer her some orientation in the practices of common speaking and acting.

The second mode of exercises consists in describing exemplary spaces of action that can be actualized through and for common action. These political spaces emerge between people in their plurality, connecting in action and speech, and existing only as long as action persists. They are not to be understood as mere physical spaces, in which politics is made, but as a figurative sphere of possibility, where political action can unfold, or a space of appearance in which agents expose themselves to each other. To briefly recap the debate already mentioned in Chapter 1, Arendt's paradigmatic example of such space was the polis. Her alleged Graecophilia and unrealistic, romanticized portrayal of the Greek city-state were the subject of debate in early interpretations of her works, with Hannah Pitkin, for example, arguing that with Arendt's imagery of the polis, her "citizens begin to resemble posturing little boys, clamoring for attention" (Pitkin 1981: 338), and Lisa Disch (1994: 59) noting that Arendt had "a view of the *polis* that is idealized to the point of sheer fantasy"; such interpretation has been contested multiple times (Taminaux 2000; Tsao 2002; Loidolt 2018). But even though, as already remarked, Arendt's interest in and appreciation for antiquity results from the general orientation of school and university education in her day (Marshall 2010: 125), she actually does not advocate an idealized image of the polis, and her aim is not a historical reconstruction of the idea of the polis as a space for politics either. It is rather a model of an imaginary public space of appearance, whose purpose is primarily to enable and support political action and speech:

> The polis, properly speaking, is not the city-state in its physical location; it is the organization of the people as it arises out of acting and speaking together, and its true space lies between people living together for this purpose, no matter where they happen to be. (HC 198)

By evoking this exemplary space, Arendt brings her concept of action closer to her readers.

The polis is only one of the models of a space of action that Arendt illuminates. Others include the American Revolution, the Roman Republic, but also, as David Marshall (2010: 134) shows, the Sophists' opening up to a plurality of opinions, Herodotus' cultural history, Homeric poetry, the Greek *nomos*, the councils of the Hungarian Revolution, and the literary salon, such as the one run by Rahel Varnhagen. In all of these cases, Arendt's narrative elucidates the way some elements, in historical terms, crystallize to create conditions for free, spontaneous, plural action. These spaces as outlined by Arendt, even if we could assign them a liminal status between factual truth and fiction, present reference points for our judgment, suggesting different ways of acting and co-acting, the space of action being one of its key conditions.

In addition to the genetic interpretation of the terms of political language and description of political spaces, Arendt's exercises consist in drawing portraits of people whose appearance in the common world can be seen as exemplary for political praxis. These persons, as Arendt points out, do not require heroic qualities, for

> the connotation of courage, which we now feel to be an indispensable quality of the hero, is in fact already present in a willingness to act and speak at all, to insert one's self into the world and begin a story of one's own. (HC 186)

Such fictional and real persons appear again and again in Arendt's writings as examples of political actors, in both a positive and a negative sense, that is, as incarnations of political virtues and vices. The result is usually not a biographical piece in the strict sense. Rather,

Arendt writes essayistic portraits, in which she seeks to capture the essence of a person's life and to retrieve her traces in the world. A good example here is Socrates, who certainly has a special place in her writings, as discussed in Chapter 2. As a model of a philosopher, he unites love of wisdom and passion for thinking with concern for the public and appreciation of political action. Through his specific form of philosophizing, which Arendt opposes to the later, metaphysical model, Socrates becomes an example of a thinker who does not deny his connection to the phenomenal world of experience. The story of his life—and also of his death—fits into the narrative about the gap that opens up between philosophy and politics, eclipsing the original experience of philosophical thinking and its connection to the common world. Arendt's writings are populated by numerous figures whose actions could be seen as exemplary: Adolf Eichmann embodies fatal thoughtlessness; René Char becomes a revolutionary against his will; Plato is presented as a villain, who tore apart the polis and philosophy, and Homer as a prime example of a storyteller. Besides drawing on biographical material, as for instance in *Rahel Varnhagen: The Life of a Jewess*, Arendt also refers to fictional figures introduced by writers such as Sophocles, William Shakespeare, Herman Melville, Franz Kafka, Joseph Conrad, or Isak Dinesen, to name but a few. Both real persons and fictional characters offer reference points for political thinking when formulating a judgment, because they represent a certain politically relevant feature or a certain orientation toward action. What is more,

> our decisions about right and wrong will depend upon our choice of company, of those with whom we wish to spend our lives. And again, this company is chosen by thinking in examples, in examples of persons dead or alive, real or fictitious, and of examples of events, past or present. (SQMP 145–6)

With this in mind, Arendt accepts that the choice of one's company is free and we may only hope for those with whom we co-inhabit the earth to judge wisely and with love of the world in mind. What she fears, though, is rather an indifference toward one's worldly company, or "the widespread tendency to refuse to judge at all" (SQMP 146), which implies the exact opposite of love of the world and it prompts the question of whether and in what way we share this world today.

In the second part of this book, we attempt to relate to these concerns by addressing issues which prompt our response to the best of our judgment. Some of those issues relate to Arendt's biography, others draw on her political phenomenology to address worldly questions we face today. Our choice of topics was motivated by what moves us, both as Arendtian scholars and as politically interested persons, with a look at political situations in the world around us, in its plurality. Our aim is to resist, through engagement with exercises in political thinking, this unwillingness to make a judgment that Arendt finds deeply troubling. In the following chapters, we also express our judgments and we do so in an explicitly Arendtian sense: not trying to tell our readers what they should think, but inviting them as dialogue partners to think and judge together about the world that we share.

Notes

1. "The first is the maxim of a reason that is never *passive*. A propensity to a passive reason, and hence to a heteronomy of reason, is called *prejudice*" (Pluhar 1987: 160).
2. Arendt's letter to Kenneth W. Thompson, Rockefeller Foundation, 7 April 1956. Library of Congress, quoted in Young-Bruehl 1982: 325.

Part II

*Arendt and Political Thinking:
Judging the World(s) We Share*

Chapter 4

The Philosopher and Politics:
The Roots of Arendt's Critique of Philosophy

In this chapter, we return to Arendt's distinction between philosophy and politics by focusing on the figure of an unworldly philosopher. We choose Heidegger as a paradigmatic example to highlight what Arendt meant when she spoke of a *déformation professionelle* of philosophers, unable to engage genuinely in politics due to their profession. Philosophers, Arendt argues, tend to refuse to assume political responsibility and are incapable of judging in political matters, or even abstain from judging. They are egocentric in their singularity and do not care about the common world they share with others. They incline toward narcissism. And when forced to take a political stand, they behave opportunistically.

As is well known, Arendt was influenced by Heidegger and his philosophy during her student years and this influence manifests itself time and again in her work. Her short affair with the philosopher and the impact of his thought on Arendt's writings often become the subject of discussion—especially in the context of Heidegger's engagement with National Socialism. Could it be that Arendt excused him for his involvement as a rector of Freiburg University? Why did she, a Jew, repeatedly present him as a philosophical authority, especially in her later writings, despite these compromising events? Why would she not distance herself from Heidegger forever, as for example Hans Jonas or Herbert Marcuse did? To address these questions, we need to look at her theory, but also into her biography. Like Jaspers in his *Psychology of Worldviews* (1919), Arendt holds "that thought itself arises out of incidents of the living experience and must remain bound to them as the only guideposts by which to take its bearings" (GBPF 14).

To illuminate the complicated and unstable attitude of Arendt toward Heidegger, we choose to not just contrast her well-known Heidegger essays, "What is Existential Philosophy?" (1946)[1] and "Heidegger at Eighty" (1971 [German edition 1969]), which is the default way of shaping this discussion. Our account rests on a deeper reading, considering not only what she wrote for the public but also her private exchanges with her friends. We especially look into her correspondence with Karl Jaspers, her mentor and later close friend, who was involved in a troubled friendship with Heidegger himself. In this way, we hope to come up with a fuller and more convincing depiction of their relationship, which had a considerable influence on Arendt's life and her work. Longer passages from letters between Arendt and Jaspers as well as fragments of Arendt's and Heidegger's correspondence with their families, friends, and—in Heidegger's case—critics help us to outline philosophical portraits of the persons involved. We also choose letters because, although published, they offer more of an informal and personal perspective than any piece of writing prepared specifically for the public. Without overemphasizing the role of Arendt's biography on her theory, we acknowledge that there were some pivotal points in her life that left their trace in her works. Just as the impact of Heidegger's philosophy on Arendt's political thought cannot be isolated from the relationship between the two, his commitment to National Socialism affected her on a personal level and at the same time became a stimulus for some of her theoretical concepts.

Inability to Judge or Political Naivety

July 9, 1946, Hannah Arendt to Karl Jaspers:

> Regarding the Heidegger note, your assumption about the Husserl letter is completely correct. I knew that this letter was circular, and I know that many people have excused it for that reason. It always seemed to me that at the moment Heidegger was obliged to put his name to this document, he should have resigned. However foolish he may have been, he was capable of understanding that. We can hold him responsible for his actions to that extent. He knew very well that that letter would have left Husserl more or less indifferent if someone else had signed it. Now you might say that this happened in the rush of business. And I would probably reply that the truly irreparable things often—and deceptively—happen almost like accidents, that sometimes from an insignificant line that we step across easily, feeling certain that it is of no consequence anymore, that wall rises up that truly divides people. In other words, although I have never had any professional or personal attachment to old Husserl, I mean to maintain solidarity with him in this one case. And because I know that this letter and this signature almost killed him, I can't but regard Heidegger as a potential murderer. (Arendt and Jaspers 1993: 47–8)

The letter to which Arendt referred was the infamous decree A.7642 of April 4, 1933, in which Heidegger, installed as the rector of Freiburg University by means of his engagement with the National Socialist power apparatus, recommended to the deans to grant leave of absence to "threatened colleagues." This leave, in point of fact, meant not only a ban on teaching but also a refusal of entry to Freiburg University for Jewish employees, one of whom was Edmund Husserl. The decree did not refer to Husserl by name, but a rumor spread that Heidegger had explicitly forbidden Husserl to enter the university. After 1945, Heidegger admitted in a letter to his wife, but never publicly, that he had not behaved decently toward his teacher (Zaborowski 2010: 389). After the war, he attempted to justify his compliance with the regime and his interest in serving as rector by claiming that his main intention in taking the rectorship was to reform the university, but Arendt emphasizes that the political circumstances in which he held the office were quite clear. She judges Heidegger's actions unambiguously: he was a "potential murderer," since exclusion from the university was unbearable for Husserl, who suffered from severe depression due to the progressive decline of the political situation. As his former teacher and mentor, Husserl experienced Heidegger's political involvement on the side of the Nazi regime as a bitter disappointment and described it as the "bleakest personal experience" (Martin 1989: 149). One must assume that Heidegger was aware that the decree would affect Husserl as well as all other Jewish members of the university; all the same, this did not prevent him from signing this document.

Heidegger's involvement in National Socialism sparked a controversy that continues until this day, all the more so since the publication of his correspondence with his wife Elfride Heidegger in 2005, and Heidegger's private notes, the so-called Black Notebooks, in 2014. Central to these debates—which partly consist in the meticulous search for ever new compromising details, and which we summarize only briefly—is the question of how to read Heidegger after these revelations, the earlier hand-wringing as to whether or not he was a convinced National Socialist having already been mooted. Extensive source material from Heidegger's rectorate period clearly points to his affinity for National Socialism (Trawny 2016). The language he uses, not only in his discredited rectorate speech but also in other documents, lectures, and various university announcements and decrees, is replete with the jargon of totalitarian ideology (Martin 1989: 165–85). Both in his letters to Elfride and his notebooks, we find statements like the following: "The jewification of our culture & universities is certainly horrifying & I think the German race really should summon up the inner strength to find its feet again" (Heidegger 2010: 28). The archival research of Heidegger's unpublished writings also shows that he apparently made changes in his own texts after 1945 in order to soften or eliminate references to the National Socialist regime and its ideology (Faye 2011).

In practice, while his involvement with the Nazi regime was notorious and scandalous, it did not impair his academic and philosophical standing after the war much (Habermas 1988); nor have recent findings discredited him as a philosopher today. In the postwar period, he was gradually redeemed and even if no one questioned his affinity for National Socialism, the dominant narrative tended to relativize it as an error, naivety, or ignorance. Some contemporaries doubted his antisemitism and National Socialist convictions. In a letter to Arendt, Jaspers denies Heidegger was antisemitic—although he emphasizes that in numerous instances Heidegger behaved as if he were (Arendt and Jaspers 1993: 628). Hans Jonas notes that the circle of "Heidegger worshipers" included numerous young Jews. While this affinity was rather one-sided (Heidegger seemed to find it somewhat uncanny that so many Jewish students were attracted to him), Jonas (2008: 59, 68) insists this was not due to his antisemitism. He certainly made a distinction between Jews and non-Jews, but not in a racial-biological sense. It was more of an us *and* them distinction, but one that was not necessarily disadvantageous to Jewish students *qua* Jews (Zaborowski 2010: 634). Last but not least, Heidegger himself denied being an antisemite in a letter to Arendt (Arendt and Heidegger 2004: 52–3). It is reasonable to assume that his attitude toward Jewish people appeared to many in his circle as rather moderate compared with the rise of aggressive antisemitism in the Germany of that time.

This notwithstanding, although Heidegger did not systematically advocate the biological-racist variant of Jew-hatred, a kind of intellectual antisemitism can be clearly traced in his correspondence, speeches, and philosophical writings, as a number of scholars have argued (e.g. Di Cesare 2018; Knowles 2019; Trawny 2016). Perhaps it was Heidegger's intellectual depth and philosophical brilliance that made it so difficult for people who knew him to identify his words and actions with antisemitic and National Socialist tropes. Despite his involvement in university politics in 1933–4, Heidegger has very often been described as apolitical. According to Jonas (2008: 59), for example, he was not of a political nature and did not consider his own political options, but was simply—here Jonas reiterates Heidegger's own excuse—attracted to the National Socialist spirit of renewal. Jonas states that Heidegger lived in the kingdom of philosophy, and the public sphere, in which human affairs and political action take place, was alien to him. But even if he was incapable of finding his way in the world, he used the opportunity to attempt to project some elements of his philosophy onto the public, for, as he later wrote to Marcuse, he "expected from National Socialism a spiritual renewal of life in its entirety, a reconciliation of social antagonisms and a deliverance of western Dasein from the dangers of communism" (Marcuse 2005).

Arendt also consistently presented Heidegger in this light. It is true that immediately after the war she commented on his political commitment in a critical way. She discusses his philosophy in general with a certain dose of irony in her essay "What is Existential Philosophy?," pointing out his failure to respond his own question in *Being and Time* and deriding his inclusion of notions of folk and earth into his original framework, as these notions bear resemblance to the Nazi jargon (Ex 181). She criticizes his ontology, which puts man in the place of God and declares him the Lord of Being, but at the same time "liberates" him from any spontaneity and makes him function according to strictly prescribed patterns (Ex 178). Yet even at that point, she argues that Heidegger is to be seen as "really (let us hope) the last Romantic" (Ex 187), who does not understand anything about politics. Two decades later, in the address for his eightieth birthday, she compares his attempt at political engagement to Plato's dream of materializing his political utopia in Syracuse. And just like Plato, Arendt says, Heidegger failed (H80 428). From this point of view, Heidegger simply does not belong to this world, which leads to his failure as a political agent, entering the presumably public sphere exactly at the moment when it ceases to function as such. He tries to judge political matters, and judges poorly—not only because he speaks in favor of a tyrannical regime, but especially because he does so without proper political conviction and, as Arendt points out, with complete ignorance of the real conditions of National Socialist rule (H80 428–31). Thus, when she speaks of his folly, she means a political naivety which does not allow him to make competent judgments about the events around him, in the world shared with others. She thus sees his actions as resulting from an inability to find his way in the political sphere.

Here, wanting not to avoid judging the one who wrote on judgment, we may agree or disagree with Arendt's judgment. As we discuss in greater detail in Chapter 9, passing a wrong judgment belongs to the practice of judging all along, and as Arendt's readers exercising political thinking, we are fully entitled to see her opinions critically. What should not be forgotten, though, is that even if historically and in view of the known facts Arendt's assessment of Heidegger's commitment to National Socialism is a very mild one, these events nevertheless had a serious impact on her political theory. His political naivety in forming his judgment was not harmless; his concrete actions following his wrong judgment carried harmful or even tragic consequences. Those who decide to act politically but direct their actions decidedly against the plurality of the public sphere, and against the freedom of action of all involved actors, work explicitly against the renewal of the common world and thus contribute to its destruction. Such failed engagement with political affairs is, according to Arendt, a tendency of philosophers in general; in this sense, Heidegger presents a prime example of the philosopher as not just unworldly but fundamentally anti-worldly: philosophy, as a practice, grounds itself against the common world and its adjudication through the practice of politics.

Egoism

In 1949, when Jaspers (Arendt and Jaspers 1993: 140) notes that Heidegger's new work resembles a "self-interpretation of Being and Time," Arendt responds with a critique of his way of life and his philosophical persona:

> At the same time, he lives in depths and with passionateness that one can't easily forget. The distortion is intolerable, and the very fact that he is arranging everything now to look like an interpretation of Sein und Zeit suggests that it will all come out distorted again [. . .]. This living in Todtnauberg, grumbling about civilization and writing Sein with a "y", is really a kind of mouse hole he has crawled back into because he rightly assumes that the only people he'll have to see there are pilgrims who come full of admiration for him. Nobody is likely to climb 1,200 meters to make a scene. And if somebody did do it, he would lie a blue streak and take for granted that nobody will call him a liar to his face. He probably thought he could buy himself loose from the world this way at the lowest possible price, fast-talk himself out of everything unpleasant, and do nothing but philosophize. And then; of course, this whole intricate and

childish dishonesty has quickly crept into his philosophizing. (Arendt and Jaspers 1993: 142)

For Arendt, Heidegger's life in Todtnauberg is representative of his separation from the world. The hut that offers him a hiding place appears here as a kind of ivory tower in which the philosopher can devote himself to his thoughts, undisturbed by the outside world. In Heidegger's case, the protection of his tower is twofold, for he is shielded not only from the distractions of practical life but also from the consequences of his past engagement with the world. He can thereby count on the fact that only admirers of his philosophy would bother visiting him in the Black Forest; he does not want to know anything about the criticism of his involvement in the National Socialist apparatus in the direct postwar period.

Arendt mentions Heidegger's radical self-focus and his cling-ing to his own thinking again and again. In "What is Existential Philosophy?," she criticizes the philosophical approach Heidegger advocates in *Being and Time*: "the concept of Self is a concept of man that leaves the individual existing independent of humanity and representative of no one but himself"; and "the essential character of the Self is its absolute Self-ness [Selbstischkeit], its radical separa-tion from all his fellows" (Ex 181). This *principium individuationis* results from the demand to put man in the place of God as seen in the metaphysical tradition. But since it is not possible for the Self to retreat from its being-in-the-world (with others) into itself, even if the realization of the *principium individuationis* is not possible, in this context all modes of human existence that suggest coexistence in the world with others appear as falling away from one's being-a-self (Ex 180–1). Under the influence of National Socialist ideology, Heidegger tried to revise his framework by offering a kind of common ground to his isolated selves: "Later [. . .] Heidegger has drawn on mytholo-gizing and muddled concepts like 'folk' and 'earth' [. . .]. But it is obvious that concepts of this kind can only lead us out of philosophy and into some kind of nature-oriented superstition" (Ex 181). All this would lead not to a genuine togetherness in the world but to a mechanical reconciliation of the atomized selves, resulting in their organizing in an Over-self to achieve the transition from "resolutely accepted guilt to action" (Ex 182). The latter figure clearly points to the modes of National Socialist mobilization and organization.

But it is not only in his philosophy that Heidegger focuses on the isolated self. His biography, too, reveals an egoistic, narcissistic man who lives, as it were, in isolation from his fellow human beings. The above-mentioned further development of his own philosophy as a self-interpretation of his earlier work can serve as an example here. This egocentrism is perhaps particularly evident when Arendt sends him the German edition of her successful book, *The Human Condition*, in 1960. This apparently offends Heidegger, who temporarily breaks off contact with Arendt and even tries to turn other intellectuals in his circle away from her:

> I was less amused by the following incident. I had written to Heidegger that I would be in town at such and such times and that he could get in touch with me. He did not call, which didn't strike me as odd, because I didn't even know whether he was in town, and the people I was with didn't know either. But then this happened: Fink was among the people Kaiser invited to his house, because I had told Kaiser I had known Fink from our youth [. . .]. And Kaiser told me that Fink had spoken very "positively" of me, so I said why not invite him, too. So what does Fink do but "brusquely" decline the invitation, saying he did not want to see me and referring explicitly to Heidegger, who apparently forbid him to do so. Why? I have no idea. The only conclusion I can draw from the whole thing is that Fink told Heidegger I was there and that he would see me and that Heidegger then said he didn't like that [. . .]. A year ago Heidegger sent me his recent publications with an inscription. I responded by sending him my *Vita Activa*. C'est tout. (Arendt and Jaspers 1993: 447–8)

For some time, Arendt remains wary about the reasons for his hostility (apparently it was not difficult to bruise the great philosopher) but just a few months later she explains the situation to Jaspers as follows:

> My explanation—putting aside for the moment the possibility of some kind of gossip—is that last winter I sent him one of my books, the *Vita Activa*, for the first time. I know that he finds it intolerable that my name appears in public, that I write books, etc. All my life I've pulled the wool over his eyes, so to speak, always acted as if none of that existed and as if I couldn't count to three, unless it was in the interpretation of his own works. Then he was always very pleased when it turned out that I could count to three and sometimes even to four. (Arendt and Jaspers 1993: 457)

Heidegger wants to be admired, his philosophy should always be in the foreground. It was not for nothing that there existed a Heidegger "cult community" in the 1920s in Marburg. As Jonas notes, students worshipped him almost as an initiator of a new faith, and this community was of a sectarian nature (Jonas 2008: 59). His narcissism also shows in the fact that Heidegger had many affairs with his female students (Grunenberg 2006: 293; Heidegger 2010: 255)—Hannah Arendt was not an exception here—which is to say, with women who were inferior to him in regard to their position in the academic power structure, and from whom he could then expect uncritical admiration.

His marriage to Elfride Heidegger was no different: he was the great thinker, she was the mother and wife who was to secure the conditions for his philosophical work, as he wrote to her shortly before their marriage:

> the quiet ways of your working within our marriage, your womanly existence within the most immediate reality of my creativity, your motherly mission within our metaphysical destiny, these are powers in my existence that cannot now be lost & living—they are the metaphysical-historical element of our life's unity. (Heidegger 2010: 30)

Elfride remained in the background; she was a practical woman who knew how to take care of her family. She tolerated his constant erotic adventures, for which he would always apologize to her. Heidegger seemed to understand that he was following his egoism and hurting his wife:

> Many thanks above all for your love—again & again I encounter its greatness & my smallness in the face of it, but I haven't learnt to see your love fully in your severity & hardness; I suppose because I still see myself too much & fall victim to admiration & that sort of thing. (Heidegger 2010: 127)

Two decades later, in 1950, he explained to his wife that it was Eros who moved him to sensuality, which was inseparably connected with the movements of his thinking (Heidegger 2010: 213). He also thought it right to inform Elfride of his affairs (Grunenberg 2006: 306). Thus, Arendt's perspective seems limited when she was describing Elfride as an excessively jealous and vicious woman (Arendt and Blücher 2000: 129). Over the decades of their marriage, Heidegger had no scruples about remedying with numerous affairs "the terrible solitude of academic research, which only man can endure" (Arendt and Heidegger 2004: 3), while he seemed to be less moved by the "icy loneliness" (letter draft from Elfride Heidegger to her spouse, Heidegger 2010: 255) his wife had to suffer.

From the political perspective, such self-centeredness is not a mere psychological trait. Rather, it has a direct impact on agency as Arendt understands it. Indeed, a subject who turns her eyes away from her fellows encapsulates herself in her own, detached world. Not orienting herself toward interaction and communication with others, she sinks into the solipsism of her own thoughts. She is unlikely to step into the public with the proper consciousness of what acting in concert means, since all she knows are solos. Such participation could only be self-referential and would thereby, of necessity, miss the aims of political action, which consists in the exchange of words and joint engagement in cultivation of the public sphere. Since such egoism results from the extreme focus on the objects of philosophical reflection, it goes hand in hand with the philosopher's unworldliness and is thus not a particular characteristic of Heidegger but represents for Arendt an integral part of the philosophical way of life.

Responsibility for One's Own (Political) Actions

March 9, 1966, Karl Jaspers to Hannah Arendt:

> You ask about the article on Heidegger in *Der Spiegel*.[2] It was in large part a review of a book that seemed to me to ask a very legitimate question: Can the basis for Heidegger's political judgements and actions be found in his philosophy? [. . .] In this case I don't think it desirable to "leave Heidegger in peace." He is a presence, and one that everyone who wants an excuse for his own Nazi past likes to fall back on. The significance of his behavior seems to me of no small consequence for current politics in the Federal Republic.
>
> It's a different story where personal matters are concerned. *Der Spiegel* has not just reviewed the book, but has also passed on some ugly rumors. The claim that Heidegger didn't come to see us anymore because Gertrud was a Jew is pure fabrication [. . .].
>
> That Gertrud was a Jew was surely not the reason for his acting as he did. But when he left after his last visit with us in May 1933, he was extremely impolite to her and hardly said good-bye at all. The reason was that she, as is her way, had spoken her mind very openly and directly, whereas I had spoken cautiously and indirectly, with great mistrust [. . .]. I consider the reason that he gave after 1945, namely, that he was ashamed, an excuse. The fact is that Gertrud and I were simply of no further interest to him [. . .]. I don't think we should read any fundamental meaning into these personal things. They just happen. They have great significance in the private sphere, for me at least, and they have their consequences. But statements such as *Der Spiegel* has made are not just oversimplifications.
>
> I take a different view of what he did objectively. Never an anti-Semite himself, he sometimes behaved very well toward Jews, as he did when he wanted to protect someone like Brock (as, by the way, almost all the old

Nazis did). And sometimes he behaved badly, as in the official letter to Göttingen about the Jew Frankel, when he wrote just as the Nazis did. His behavior toward Husserl was another case of obedience to the Nazis. That all falls under the rubric of a vanishing sense of right and wrong. He probably never possessed such a sense, or, if he did, only by chance, so to speak. (Arendt and Jaspers 1993: 629–30)

In this letter to Arendt, Jaspers writes critically about Heidegger's commitment to National Socialism but also his behavior in private. Jaspers assumes that the motivation for Heidegger's judgment and his actions was different in each case. While he sees Heidegger's behavior and later distancing toward him and his wife as rude, he ascribes these to simple motives: Heidegger was angry, offended, and in consequence gradually became indifferent to them both. At the same time, he speaks of Heidegger's public actions much more harshly. Heidegger behaved like an antisemite; wrote letters like a Nazi. Yet, less than two decades after the end of the war, and despite his misdeeds, Heidegger had been largely rehabilitated in the academic milieu and enjoyed great authority. Hence, Jaspers says, Heidegger should not be left in peace. For his past actions show opportunism, obedience to a criminal regime, and the lack of any sense of right and wrong.

Now, the fact that Heidegger—an intellectual, a philosopher, and for many an authority—went with the National Socialist flow is the first part of the problem. The second part, no less grave, is that he never apologized for his political involvement and showed absolutely no remorse. Jaspers, for example, judges Heidegger's few attempts to explain himself as superficial or dubious (Arendt and Jaspers 1993: 161–2). Numerous former colleagues and students would demand that he take a stance on his past involvement with the Nazi regime, among them Karl Jaspers (Heidegger and Jaspers 1990: 169), Herbert Marcuse,[3] and Rudolf Bultmann.[4] But it was all in vain: around 1970 Hannah Arendt (LoM II 188) wrote of an "interruption" in Heidegger's life and thought that coincided with National Socialism and to which no one, including Heidegger himself, had yet paid public attention.

Heidegger's silence was probably not (only) about the lack of civil courage. The dishonesty and superficiality of his statements mirror his vague assessment of his own engagement. For example, he does not seem to understand why he was treated with distrust after 1945 and appears to be stunned by the fact that he was expelled from the university and treated "like a dead dog" (Zaborowski 2010: 670).[5] Moreover, Heidegger doubted, at least in the period immediately after the war's end, that his exclusion was directly related to his political commitment with the National Socialist regime:

> That I have been ostracized has actually nothing to do with Nazism. One senses in my thinking something inconvenient, perhaps even sinister, which one would like to have done; that one is, at the same time, interested in it is only proof of that.[6]

Heidegger's handling of the subject of Nazism after 1945 is revealed as a series of faux pas. Arendt reports:

> Sartre told me later than four weeks (or six weeks) after Germany's defeat, Heidegger wrote to a professor at the Sorbonne (I've forgotten his name), talked about a "misunderstanding" between Germany and France, and offered his hand at German–French "reconciliation." He received no reply, of course. Then, later, he wrote to Sartre. (Arendt and Jaspers 1993: 48)

Heidegger also attempted to relativize the events of Nazi time, both shortly after the war and much later, through various comparisons and metaphors. For example, in a 1948 letter to Marcuse, he equates the extermination of Jews in concentration camps with the expulsion of East Germans (meaning Germans then living in Eastern Europe) by the Allies (Marcuse 2005). Marcuse replies: "From a contemporary perspective, there seems already to be a complete difference in humanity and inhumanity in the difference between Nazi concentration camps and the deportations and internments of the postwar years" (Marcuse 2005). Another instance of such relativizing are Heidegger's Bremen lectures in the 1950s, in which he compared modern agriculture with its industrialized food production to the fabrication of corpses in gas chambers:

> Agriculture is now a mechanized food industry, in essence the same [*das Selbe*] as the production of corpses in the gas chambers and extermination camps, the same [*das Selbe*] as the blockading and starving of countries, the same [*das Selbe*] as the production of hydrogen bombs. (Quoted in Di Cesare 2018: 187)

While the publication of Heidegger's Black Notebooks removed any possible remaining doubt concerning his National Socialist convictions, the quoted passages above also give evidence of his ignorance and particular lack of sensitivity.

In short, Heidegger never took responsibility for his National Socialist involvement. The teaching ban and the difficulties with the publication of his writings he faced shortly after the end of the

Second World War might seem a fairly mild punishment; neverthe-less, Heidegger perceived it as unjust. For this reason, in a letter to Arendt written in July 1946, Jaspers rejects Arendt's remark that Heidegger should be left alone when it comes to his involvement in the Nazi regime. Arendt's reaction to the article in *Der Spiegel* about Heidegger's Nazi engagement is surprising in light of the premises of Arendt's political theory. Her reflections regarding personal and political responsibility under a dictatorship (especially in *Eichmann in Jerusalem*, discussed in Chapter 5) make clear that in Heidegger's case especially personal responsibility becomes relevant. In contrast to political responsibility, which should be understood metaphori-cally as responsibility we assume for the actions of our political predecessors or, in other words, of those who inhabited our common world before us, I must assume personal responsibility for my own actions (PRD 27). In postwar Germany, Arendt notes, guilt and innocence, remorse and lack of a sense of responsibility tended to be misplaced. The popular frame of collective guilt resulted in a para-doxical situation, in which the innocent felt guilty while the crimi-nals showed no remorse (PRD 28). Heidegger should have assumed personal responsibility for his engagement with National Socialism and the concrete steps he took in its support. After the war, he com-mented on his rector's address as follows:

> I saw in the movement that had gained power the possibility of an inner recollection and renewal of the people and a path that would allow it to discover its historical vocation in the Western world. I believed that, renewing itself, the university might also be called to contribute to this inner self-collection of the people, providing it with a measure. [. . .] For this reason I saw in the rectorate an opportunity to lead all capable forces—regardless of party membership and party doctrine—back to this process of reflection and renewal and to strengthen and to secure the influence of these forces. (Heidegger 1985: 483–4)

By accepting the post of rector of Freiburg University, Heidegger actively supported the political takeover of the university with his authority: he was a member of NSDAP who explicitly stated his firm belief in Nazi ideology. As his above argument, his notes, and cor-respondence show, this postwar statement might be read as a (poor) attempt to rehabilitate himself but not an act of taking personal responsibility for his deeds or political responsibility for the misdeeds of the regime. He should have taken this responsibility, yet he never did.

Still, instead of publicly criticizing his engagement, Arendt merely expressed relatively mild dismay. In private writings, on the contrary, she frequently criticizes weaknesses of his character, his behavior, which she finds unacceptable, and his way of life. Above all, it is striking that she often accuses Heidegger of lying and hypocrisy. Thus, she writes to Jaspers in 1946 about Heidegger's attitude after the end of the war: "you'll be familiar with the various interviews he gave after that. Nothing but inane lies with what I think is a clearly pathological streak. But that's an old story" (Arendt and Jaspers 1993: 48). In a 1950 letter to her husband Heinrich Blücher, just before she meets Heidegger for the first time since her forced emigration and while she is still uncertain if she will or won't accept his invitation to come see him, she writes that Heidegger has been a notorious liar (Arendt and Blücher 2000: 128).[7] This tension between the professional pursuit of truth and personal mendacity must have tormented Arendt. For it was pretty much the opposite of what her great philosophical role model Socrates believed and lived up to, namely that

> it would be better for me that my lyre or a chorus I directed should be out of tune and loud with discord, and that multitudes of men should disagree with me rather than that I, being one, should be out of harmony with myself and contradict me. (Plato, *Gorgias* 482c; LoM I 181)

Apparently, Heidegger was not equipped with such inner harmony, so crucial to Arendt's approach to thinking and politics.

To investigate the reasons why Arendt criticizes Heidegger predominantly in private communication,[8] while sparing him such condemnation in public, we need to take a look at Arendt's biography and the fluctuations of her relationship with him. Her feelings were undoubtedly ambivalent, especially after their reunion in 1950. As Annette Vowinckel (2004: 120) notes, she must have been inwardly torn, for the relationship with Heidegger, who embodied all that was dear to her intellectually, but who at the same time contributed to the conditions forcing her to leave Germany, brought to light the very contradictoriness of her existence again and again. It is difficult to escape the conclusion that Arendt applies special treatment to Heidegger, violating her general standard of judgment on questions of personal and political responsibility. Was her controversial judgment of his actions inevitably affected by feelings (be they of respect, love, or both)?

Before we address this question, let us conclude what resulted from Arendt's inner dilemma for her theoretical distinction between philosophy and politics and for her personal relationship to both. For more than the obvious biographical reasons that prompted Arendt's interest in politics and action (Young-Bruehl 1982: 92–110), the reconstruction of her critique of the philosophical way of life reveals her turn to politics, and away from philosophy. This turn was, on one hand, a reaction to the metaphysical core of Heidegger's philosophy—being toward death and the de-anthropologization of his ontology (Goldstein 2012: 43–5), which coincided with his personal unworldliness. On the other hand, it resulted from her deep disappointment with the *Gleichschaltung* of German intellectuals,[9] including, above all, Martin Heidegger himself. Heidegger's inability or unwillingness to assume either personal responsibility for his role in the National Socialist regime or political responsibility for the events of this period made him, in her eyes, the example *par excellence* of philosophers' failure to act politically. It was a major impetus for Arendt to distance herself from philosophy in general.

The Case of Heidegger and Arendt's Conclusion: Déformation professionelle

With this critical image in mind Arendt (H80 431) concludes that when it comes to politics, philosophers tend to side with tyranny due to their intellectual preoccupation. Their professional concern is the pursuit of truth; thus, the realm of human action, with its plurality and its appreciation for freedom as opposed to logical necessity, appears to them as sinister and threatening. Arendt (H80 428) recalls Plato and his project to educate the tyrant of Syracuse to rule as a philosopher-king, which was a politically naive endeavor that ended in a spectacular fiasco. She argues that similar tendencies can be found in most great thinkers and that they cannot be traced back to specific historical circumstances or personal traits but rather present a *déformation professionelle*: philosophers in general are fundamentally incapable of political participation based on free action (H80 431). This certainly mirrors her experience of the National Socialist takeover of Germany, her emphasis on the plurality of the common world, and her insistence on free political action as the central human activity. She thus turns away from philosophy in appreciation of politics, and away from the unworldliness of truth-seekers—most clearly exemplified by Heidegger—toward apprehending the world as a phenomenon characterized by plurality and freedom.

Indeed, Heidegger embodies all the qualities that disqualify philosophers as competent political actors: they refuse to judge politically, and when they do, they become victims of their political naivety. They are not willing to take personal or political responsibility for what has been done; instead, they turn to lying to downplay their role in what has happened. They are egoists who live in and for the kingdom of thought, a solipsistic space where they are alone and disconnected from the common world that people share through acting and speaking. What is more, philosophy implies a search for the (by definition singular) truth, which in practice challenges plurality and prompts a thinker to choose singularity or, in political terms, tyranny. In Arendt's view, this philosophical *déformation professionelle* is the underlying cause of philosophers' being at best unfit for, if not actively harmful to, the public sphere.

Explaining Heidegger's engagement on the side of the National Socialist regime through a slightly metaphorical vocational disease, as Arendt does, is a fairly moderate stance in the so-called Heidegger controversy. Even if we have historical sources at our command today that were not available to Arendt, there were always enough indications of the nature of his involvement, of which she did know. In her eyes, Heidegger was in a sense carried away by National Socialism due to his political naivety, and his later relativizations were simply proof of his political immaturity. Writing in 1946, she notes that "In his political behavior [. . .], Heidegger has provided us with more than ample warning that we should take him seriously" (Ex 187). More than two decades later, in her address on the occasion of his eightieth birthday, her judgment is even more apologetic, as she notes that Heidegger may not have understood much of the essence of National Socialism because, instead of *Mein Kampf*, he read less relevant books by Italian futurists that were only loosely tied to the ideology. After the publication of his correspondence, we now know that this is not true. Rather, already in 1931, Heidegger sent his brother Fritz *Mein Kampf* as a Christmas gift, and in his accompanying letter, infused with Christmas spirit, he noted:

> I hope that you will read Hitler's book; its first few autobiographical chapters are weak. This man has a remarkable and sure political instinct, and he had it even while all of us were still in a haze, there is no way of denying that. The National Socialist movement will soon gain a wholly different force. It is not about mere party politics—it's about the redemption or fall of Europe and western civilization. Anyone who does not get it deserves to be crushed by the chaos. Thinking about these things is no

90

hindrance to the spirit of Christmas, but marks our return to the character and task of the Germans, which is to say to the place where this beautiful celebration originates.[10]

Notwithstanding the above circumstances, of which Arendt might not have been aware, shortly before writing the *Festschrift* for Heidegger's eightieth birthday, she describes Heidegger's understanding of National Socialism's being an encounter between global technology and modern man as grotesque in a letter to a friend.[11] The misunderstanding of what it all was about, Arendt argues (H80 429), was minor "when compared with the much more decisive 'error' that consisted in not only ignoring the most relevant 'literature' but in escaping from the reality of the Gestapo cellars and the torture-hells of the early concentration camps into seemingly more significant regions," which brings us back to philosophers chasing truth in the metaphysical non-world. However, by the time she comes to speak about Heidegger in her last book, *The Life of the Mind Two: Willing*, little is left of her originally critical position. Here, she only mentions his commitment to National Socialism in passing: "In Heidegger's understanding the will to rule and to dominate is a kind of original sin, of which he found himself guilty when he tried to come to terms with his brief past in the Nazi movement" (LoM II 173).

Arendt's public statements about Heidegger's National Socialist engagement clearly became milder over time. Some of them, as we can say today, not only appear to be overly well-meaning but were also definitely counterfactual, for which both Margaret Canovan (1990: 137–8) and Abigail Rosenthal (2011: 164–6) criticize Arendt. Overall, one might say that her interpretation works well with Heidegger's self-presentation after the war. Elisabeth Young-Bruehl (1982: 442) notes that Arendt's address certainly omits some criticisms that she might have made regarding his character and judgments. This seems to be an understatement, and the complicated history of the personal relationship between the two thinkers that Young-Bruehl (1982: 305–6) outlines clearly shows that Arendt's loyalty and compassion for Heidegger's personal situation remained unchanged since their reconciliation in the 1950s. All indications are that Arendt forgave Heidegger for his "error," and the remaining question is: Why?

We argue that we can read this question in the context of Arendt's distinction between the private and the public. One possible answer could be elucidated in reference to Arendt's concepts of the human practices of forgiving and understanding. Forgiving is a mode of action which "serves to undo the deeds of the past, whose 'sins' hang like Damocles' sword over every new generation" (HC 237), and the remedy for the irrevocability of what one has done. It is necessary for action to continue, for if an acting agent could not be forgiven, she would have to bear the consequences of her single act all her life and thus would not be capable of a new beginning. Like other modes of action, forgiving requires plurality because no one can forgive herself. However, it is not the deed itself that is central here but the doer. Indeed, not an act but a person is to be forgiven: "Forgiving and the relationship it establishes is always an eminently personal (though not necessarily individual or private) affair in which what was done is forgiven for the sake of who did it" (HC 241). This suggests judging what Heidegger did from the perspective of his being the one who did this, considering his unique Who-ness.

Such an interpretation raises numerous questions. After all, according to Arendt, a person discloses herself in the world through her deeds—that is, in the specific case of Heidegger, among other things through his involvement in the National Socialist regime. On what basis, then, should he be forgiven? Referring to the New Testament tradition, Arendt suggests that love holds the power to forgive (HC 242). Is it love then, that motivates her to forgive Heidegger, as also Jonas (2008: 63) suggests? We may certainly suspect this, when reading her reflection in "Heidegger at Eighty," where she remembers her experience as a student, hearing rumors of a rebellious voice in conservative German philosophy of the inter-war period: "The rumor of Heidegger put it quite simply: Thinking has come to life again, the cultural treasures of the past, believed to be dead are being made to speak [. . .]. There is a teacher; one can perhaps learn to think" (H80 421). Accompanying her in her time travel to the beginnings of her engagement with philosophy and the discovery of new ways of philosophical thinking, so different and so much more exciting than everything one has heard before, we clearly sense her sentiments and her nostalgia for those Weimar days. Thinking back to her youth, she reflects on Heidegger's role as a source of, first, philosophical fascination and later—obviously not addressed in "Heidegger at Eighty," but certainly perceptible between the lines—erotic relationship. These passages tell a story of love for thinking and imply a story of love for the thinker. And they are written as if without any concern for the future to come which cannot but retrospectively obscure these youthful emotions, which, all her criticism of Heidegger notwithstanding, did not fade away throughout her life.

So, if we forgive out of love, the act of forgiveness is personal. Arendt (HC 241) writes: "not necessarily [. . .] private" but certainly gravitating toward privacy, since—even if forgiving always implies plurality—it is an act of a particular subject, not embedded in the political kind of plurality. The deed, of course, remains reprehensible, even if the doer has been forgiven. In this sense, if we take Arendt's argument to its conclusion, motivating one's forgiveness with love means that it has no political power and no meaning for the public. For love implies unworldliness: due to its emotional power, the in-between which relates us to others and separates us from them disappears between lovers. Without this in-between, a world cannot exist. In this respect, "Love, by its very nature, is unworldly, and it is for this reason rather than its rarity that it is not only apolitical but antipolitical, perhaps the most powerful of all anti-political human forces" (HC 242).

If forgiveness is to have a worldly, and hence public, significance, it involves understanding, that is, the "unending activity by which, in constant change and variation, we come to terms with and reconcile ourselves to reality, that is, try to be at home in the world" (UP 308). One can only understand a phenomenon when it has come to an end, just as one can only truly understand who a person has been after they have died (UP 309). In her reflections on Heidegger's complicity with National Socialism, however, Arendt is dealing with a situation that is not concluded in this sense: neither has National Socialism been eliminated once and for all, nor is the wrongdoer dead. As Serena Parekh (2013: 891) suggests, "It really seems that Arendt spent a good part of her life trying to understand how someone so knowledgeable, and in many ways so thoughtful, could have failed so profoundly when it came to moral judgment."

However, Arendt, when writing about forgiving, does not mention a need for apology, changing one's presumably wrong judgment, or regretting the respective deed as a condition to be forgiven. Quite the opposite, forgiving seems to be an unconditional practice in which we engage for love of the world: as Arendt (HC 240) writes, the "willingness to change their minds" is the only presupposition for human beings to be released from what they did, "remain free agents," and "be trusted with so great a power as that to begin something new." So even if Arendt could fully understand neither the political phenomenon nor the doer of the deeds, she did not need this to forgive

Heidegger in political sense, by trying to understand the person who committed the acts. Like every other human being, however great or small, Heidegger was unique, and his being a philosopher was an integral part of this uniqueness. From Arendt's perspective, such an unworldly philosopher whose "'abode' where he [felt] at home [was] the residence of thinking" (H80 427) was unlikely to have much understanding of the sphere of practical human affairs. Who Heidegger was as doer of these particular deeds and as a subject making these particular judgments would open a way to forgiving him: specifically as an unworldly philosopher.

This is telling not only for the question of Arendt's multifaceted place in the Heidegger controversy but also for the question of the role of political thinking for our worldly practices altogether. Judging is processual, temporary, open to change, but also prone to ambiguities. In this respect, the ambiguities of Arendt's judgment of Heidegger, and the tension between the opinions she expressed in public and private, changing over time, are a good example of such processuality and the impossibility of reconciling incommensurable values or ideas—being a part of the human condition—which also drives not only her response to the calamities of the twentieth century, to which we turn now, but also our responses, with decades of hindsight on the judgments she reached. Judgments, to be sure, regarding Heidegger, and Adolf Eichmann, both as individuals and as Germans who played their parts in the National Socialist regime, but also regarding personal and political responsibility as they are inflected by the regime under which one lives generally.

Notes

1. First published in 1946 as "What is Existenz Philosophy?," *Partisan Review* 8 (1): 34–56.
2. Anonymous, "Mitternacht einer Weltmacht," *Der Spiegel* (1966).
3. Marcuse to Heidegger, August 28, 1947: "Many of us have long awaited a statement from you, a statement that would clearly and finally free you from such identification [with the Nazi regime], a statement that honestly expresses your current attitude about the events that have occurred. But you have never uttered such a statement at least it has never emerged beyond your private sphere" (Marcuse 2005).
4. Hans Jonas reports on his conversation with Rudolf Bultmann, who would tell him a story of his encounter with Heidegger in Zurich around 1948–9. Bultmann, friendly, demanded that Heidegger take a public stance on his National Socialist engagement in 1933, as he would

owe this both to his colleagues and to himself. Heidegger promised him to do so but ten years later, Bultmann said, nothing of the like had happened (Jonas 2008: 189).

5. Heidegger's letter to his friend, art historian Kurt Bauch, from 1950. Bauch was a member of NSDAP from 1933 and an officer in the *Wehrmacht* until 1944.

6. A draft of a letter to an unknown person. See Heidegger 2000: 421 (our translation).

7. On January 3, 1950 Arendt writes: "Whether I'm going to see [Heidegger] or not, I don't know yet—I'll leave everything up to fate. His letters to Jaspers, the ones Jaspers showed me, just as they used to be: the same mix of genuineness and mendacity, or better still cowardice, in which both qualities are primary. With Jaspers, I lost a bit of my keenness for Heidegger" (Arendt and Blücher 2000: 115).

8. Also Jaspers first published his *Philosophische Autobiographie* (1956) without the chapter on Heidegger, which he only wanted to be added to the book after his, his wife's, and Heidegger's death. The extended edition was published in 1977.

9. The support of National Socialism by German (and not only) intellectuals was most vigorous, as for example Evans (2005) shows.

10. Heidegger's correspondence with his brother has been a part of Marburg Archives since 2014. Some fragments were published in *Die Zeit* (Sobczynski and Camman 2016). The quoted translation can be found in Zielinski (2016).

11. Hannah Arendt to J. Glenn Grey, 25 March 1967, cited in Young-Bruehl 1982: 443. She reiterates this argument in "Heidegger at Eighty" (H80 429–30), originally only in the British edition.

Chapter 5

Eichmann, Mass Democracy, and Israel

This chapter will describe Arendt's central claims in *Eichmann in Jerusalem* and the very public controversy that the book spurred, noting the emphasis that Arendt herself placed on her ironic tone in the work, rather than the specific claims, as the true source of the tempest. To do so, we will first discuss the famous private, later public, exchange between Arendt and Gershom Scholem, a massively influential scholar of Jewish philosophy and major figure of the Israeli academy and commentator on its politics and culture, as well as Arendt's friend for over twenty-five years. We will then contextualize Arendt's main argument in *Eichmann* by examining related claims she makes in *The Origins of Totalitarianism*, which we will discuss in this chapter and then again more deeply in Chapters 8 and 9, and some of the key essays collected in *Between Past and Future* concerning the chilling similarities between political communication and the erosion of individual responsibility in public life under conditions of totalitarianism and mass democracy. In concluding, we comment on Judith Butler's recent return to Arendt's thinking about Zionism and the modern State of Israel in these works, noting the remarkable similarities between the controversy surrounding Butler's being honored with the Adorno Prize in 2012 and the controversy around Arendt's publication of *Eichmann* almost exactly fifty years earlier.

Before diving into the controversy surrounding Arendt's book, a few words are in order about (a) Adolf Eichmann the man; (b) his capture, kidnapping, and secret extradition from Argentina to Israel by agents of the Israeli intelligence service; and (c) his subsequent trial in Jerusalem and how it came to pass that Arendt was there to report on the trial. Most briefly, and following the account Tuija Parvikko (2021) provides in the Prologue to her discussion of Arendt, Eichmann, and the politics of the past, we can stipulate the following as basic orienting facts about the place of Eichmann and his trial in Arendt's thinking politics. First, that what makes Eichmann remarkable, both for Arendt and for discussions about German guilt and individual and collective responsibility for the crimes committed under National Socialism more generally, is that, as Parvikko (2021: ix) puts it, he was like Heinrich Himmler "a good *pater familias*, with all the outer signs of respectability," with the shocking consequence that "a good family man had become the greatest criminal of the century." In other words, as Parvikko continues, the trouble with Eichmann and other

> Nazi perpetrators and their fellow travelers and followers was that they were not composed of a group of perverted criminals with their heads full of evil motives [but] normal family men who attempted to conform to and obey the rules and practices of the society, to act decently, pursuing a successful career and good standard of living for their families. (Parvikko 2021: ix–x)

Second, we can say that the importance of the trial—generally speaking—is that, on the one hand, with "the capture of Adolf Eichmann [. . .] a new interest in convicting Nazi criminals arose," while at the same time, "the Eichmann trial was the first great public event in which the voices of witnesses and listening to the stories of victims of the Holocaust were given a significant role" (Parvikko 2021: xi). Finally, as regards how it came to pass that Arendt was in Jerusalem as a courtroom reporter for the *New Yorker*, two facts are salient, as Parvikko (2021: x, xii) notes: first, that while "Arendt had formed her view of the character of the Nazi criminal well before Israeli intelligence captured Adolf Eichmann in Argentina in 1960 [. . .] she had not by then seen a Nazi criminal alive. Therefore, she wanted to attend his trial in Jerusalem"; second, that Arendt's "critical Zionist background constituted the most important part of her personal stance on the Eichmann trial." As we will see amply in the rest of this chapter, from our discussion of the original controversy around Arendt's analysis when it was published in five successive issues of the *New Yorker* and right down until the controversy surrounding Judith Butler's being honored with the Adorno Prize exactly fifty years later, it is ultimately what Parvikko aptly describes as Arendt's "critical" Zionism that truly haunts our discussions of Eichmann (the man), and of *Eichmann* (the book), whether explicitly or implicitly.

The Eichmann Controversy

From *Hannah Arendt in Jerusalem* (Aschheim, ed. 2001) to *Hannah Arendt* (Margarethe von Trotta's 2012 feature film), from *Eichmann*

Before Jerusalem (Stangneth 2014) to *The Trial That Never Ends* (Golsan and Misemer, eds. 2017), it is undeniable that Arendt's most salient intervention in public debate remains what it was during her lifetime: her reporting on the trial of Adolf Eichmann, first published in the *New Yorker* and later as *Eichmann in Jerusalem*. In returning to this controversy with the novice reader of Arendt in mind, we provide an overview of it, focusing on what it means to miss Arendt's irony as Scholem did in their exchange and what happens if we actually grasp that irony. For it is only if we attend actively and sympathetically to the rationale behind Arendt's ironic tone that we can, with Susan Neiman (2001: 66), see *Eichmann* as its author did: as a work of theodicy in which "what was on trial was not (only) German war crimes, or Jewish complicity in them, but Creation itself."

In his introduction to an edited volume that surveyed the state of Arendt's comparative reception in the United States, Germany, and Israel, Steven Aschheim (2001: 1–2) notes that *Eichmann* was not even translated into Hebrew for forty years, positing that this silencing of Arendt's judgments there was necessary not so much because the contents of the book were so shocking or unacceptable—which they were—but because it was "her *involvement* in [Jewish affairs and the Zionist movement], her troubling relevance, that rendered her so threatening." The controversy that manifested in the United States (especially New York) was somewhat different to that which emerged in Germany. Robert Kunath (2021: 161) has recently presented a definitive account of how and why recent Holocaust scholarship in these two countries has turned away from Arendt's interpretations as a "result of several factors." First and foremost, there is "the banality of evil," both the concept itself and its application to the case of Adolf Eichmann. This phrase, meant to call attention to how Eichmann is much more a functionary than supervillain or demon, is foregrounded in the infamous subtitle of the book, "A Report on the Banality of Evil." As Susan Neiman (2010: 307) argues, quite contrary to Arendt's actual intent, many believed this "banality" absolved Eichmann of having committed morally culpable acts of actually evil intent; whereas in fact she aimed to describe "the development of an individual who began as a common careerist and ended as an engineer of the Final Solution." To "be an engineer of the Final Solution" is not to not be culpable, and surely not to not be evil; Arendt's point is that nothing worse than that careerism under extreme conditions can suffice to bring the greatest evils into existence.

The second source of controversy is the claim that Arendt innocently accepted Eichmann's equivocations that he was never truly a committed antisemite. Bettina Stangneth (2014) argues that, in his performance in Jerusalem, Eichmann successfully persuaded many—Arendt included—that he was not personally or in principle an antisemite, while in fact the fuller testimony of his recorded words and deeds makes clear that he was very much both. Kunath (2021: 161) acknowledges that "Arendt scholars like Susan Neiman and Seyla Benhabib have conceded that Stangneth's new research requires significant revisions of Arendt's interpretation of Eichmann, and longtime critics of Arendt have embraced it as a damning refutation of her views," but insists nevertheless that Stangneth has not in any way refuted Arendt's claims, especially because "she rarely argues with Arendt and only cites *Eichmann in Jerusalem* five times in more than a hundred pages of endnotes." Indeed, as Kunath (2021: 162) conclusively demonstrates in a close reading of Richard Wolin's review of Stangneth's book, the claim that with this work "Arendt has been refuted" succeeds only because her book is used as an occasion to repeat charges about Arendt's arguments in *Eichmann* that were never actually her arguments in the first place; his main example is Wolin's claim that Stangneth proves that Arendt was wrong to say Eichmann "could best be described as a mere 'functionary,'" which is outrageous because "the word 'functionary' appears four times in *Eichmann*, three times to refer to Jewish officials, and once sharply to reject the idea that a 'mere functionary' is not wholly responsible for his actions."

The third and final central source of the controversy is Arendt's judgment concerning the complicity of some Jews, especially but not only those who held positions in the Jewish Councils that cooperated with the Third Reich in Eichmann's crimes, and in the Nazi genocide more generally. As Peter Walsh (2015: 8) notes, "so much has been written with so much vehemence, on [this] question," and specifically "Leo Baeck, who she referred to in an early addition of the book—subsequently altered—as the Jewish *Führer*," that "any further intervention will be loaded with controversy." Having said this much about the three main foci of the controversy surrounding Arendt's views on and surrounding Adolf Eichmann, we should immediately note, as Arendt (PRD 17) herself does at beginning of the reflection she wrote a year after the publication of *Eichmann*, that this controversy was actually "touched off" by her writing rather than "caused by" it. She means by this that people talked about her analysis not so much as her readers but as her critics and the critics of her critics and then commentators on her critics.

Agreeing with her that to attend to the details of the controversy about the book in this case means to address the core issues of that book all the less, we will not here rehash the details of these debates. Instead, we aim to engage with Arendt's own interventions, public and private, in the debate around these themes in the decades after the publication of *Eichmann* in order to learn what there is still to learn about Arendt's response to the Eichmann trial as an exercise in political thinking, in much the same way that we examined in Chapter 4 what Arendt writes about personal responsibility under dictatorship as she refers there to her judgment of Heidegger's complicity in the Nazi regime. Here, in like fashion, we will discuss how Arendt responded to these three points of controversy about her account of Eichmann's trial and its broader significance for judgment, in both its reflective and introspective aspect and its role in public life.

We will find that, as Roger Berkowitz (2017: 31) concludes, Eichmann's case is paradigmatic for Arendt because the literal incomprehensibility of his actions makes clear that, "In the face of that which is irreconcilable, one can choose to deny reconciliation. This is the choice that Arendt makes in her own judgment of Eichmann: to act beyond the boundary of reconciliation's power to inaugurate a common world." It is then up to us, in sharing our reflective judgment about a catastrophic failure of judgment, such as Eichmann's, to reinaugurate the possibility of constituting a common world with one another; one which cannot but exclude an actor like Eichmann, about whom, as Arendt (*Denktagebuch* I.1.7, quoted in Berkowitz 2017: 31) writes, "one must say: This ought not to have happened." Arendt makes the same point in her famous 1964 interview with Gunther Gaus, later published as "What Remains?" Here, Arendt (WRLR 14) says that before she knew of the mass killings in administrative massacres, she "had the idea that amends could somehow be made for everything else, as amends can be made for just about everything at some point in politics." But the administrative terror and genocide in Auschwitz was something new and different, something that, in her words, "*ought not to have happened.*" What ought never to have been is not just the number of victims, but the "method, the fabrication of corpses and so on."

As Berkowitz (2011: 6) concludes, the deep and lasting importance of Arendt's judgment of Eichmann, whatever one makes of

Eichmann as a book, is that "the irreconcilable nature of simply inhuman and unbelievable crimes that, for Arendt, is the lesson she takes from the holocaust. And it is this irreconcilability to the crimes that underlies Arendt's judgment of Adolf Eichmann." If this is truly how Arendt meant to judge Eichmann, why has she been so drastically and massively misread? For this we must consider *how* she wrote (and spoke) even more than *what* she did in judging Eichmann.

Missing Arendt's Irony: Scholem's Influential Critique

At the heart of the Eichmann controversy is a comment Arendt makes in the Gaus interview:

> People are irritated with me for one thing—and I can understand that to some extent, outwardly—namely that I can still laugh [about it], right? [. . .] This reaction is what people blame me for. I can't do anything against that. But I know one thing. I would probably still laugh three minutes before [certain death]. (WRLR 15–16)

The crucial point is that she is laughing, even in the face of death she goes on laughing; indeed, she reads Eichmann's testimony and the depositions and she laughs. As she continues her response to Gaus, it becomes clear that Arendt has, perhaps, many critics in mind but none more so than Gershom Scholem:

> That the tone of voice is predominantly ironic is completely true. The tone of voice in this case is really the person. When people reproach me with accusing the Jewish people, that is a malignant lie and propaganda and nothing else. The tone of voice, however, is an objection against me personally. And I cannot do anything about that. (WRLR 16)

The objection to *Eichmann*, Arendt is saying, is actually an objection to her subjectivity: not really the particular content of her judgments, but the personality that comes across in her manner of expressing that content. The objection, in short, is to her irony; her tone, she acknowledges, is "wildly ironic." Immediately after this, Arendt argues that the irony Scholem describes as her private fault is actually a public act with a specific political intent, and for this reason, "love," whether of the Jewish people or whatever, has no place in their debate about her judgment of Eichmann.

This is the source of Scholem's critique of, or one might say "attack" on, Arendt, in an open letter dated June 23, 1963:

There is in the Jewish language something that can in no way be defined and is entirely concrete, which the Jews call Ahabath Israel, love for the Jews. Of that, dear Hannah, nothing is noticeable, like with so many intellectuals who have emerged from the German left. [. . .] I don't have sympathy for the style of lightheartedness, I mean the English "flippancy," which you muster all too often [. . .] in your book. It is unimaginably unbefitting for the matter of which you speak. Was there really no place, at such an occasion, for what one might name with the modest German word *Herzenstakt*? (Knott 2017: 203–4)

When Arendt replies a month later, on July 20, 1963 (Knott 2017: 207), she suggests that Scholem failed to get the irony in her writing: "I never made Eichmann out to be a 'Zionist.' If you missed the irony of the sentence—which was plainly in *oratio obliqua*, reporting Eichmann's own words—I really can't help it." What matters most here is not that Scholem missed the irony in this particular instance but that her ironic tone is for Scholem "unimaginably unbefitting"; for, as Michael Bot (2013) argues, Arendt's irony was precisely the most "befitting" response to the *Sache* or subject matter, which Arendt analyzes as Eichmann's thoughtlessness.

Why so? Because as Arendt states in her reply, what "threw [Scholem] off" was

> my independence. I mean on the one hand that I do not belong to any organization and speak only in my own name, and on the other that a person must think for himself and, whatever you may have against my results, you won't understand them unless you know that they are my results and no one else's. (Knott 2017: 209)

As we saw in Chapter 2, for Arendt such "thinking for oneself" is never to think alone; thinking never happens in complete isolation. According to Bot (2013), this is the reason why a proper understanding of Arendt's ironic tone would see that Arendt attempts to position herself, through irony, as a person *in public*. In short, there is no way that Scholem's proposed *Herzenstakt* can possibly remedy the problem of thoughtlessness. Arendt's irony, however, just might be such a remedy, for by summoning a public into existence by creating the space of debate about how and where to judge Eichmann, Arendt makes thinking possible again.

Getting Arendt's Irony: Eichmann as Theodicy

The chasm that separates Scholem's misapprehension from Arendt's actual intent in *Eichmann* is immediately evident if we begin, unlike him, with its opening chapter. Its title, "The House of Justice," is already ironic given her underlying concerns about both the legitimacy of holding the tribunal in Jerusalem, under Israeli law, rather than in an international tribunal and about the Israeli legal order in the first place, specifically its lack of a constitution. Right at the outset of her report on the trial, Arendt calls attention to what is in her eyes an inexcusable failure of Israeli law and policy in which marriage and family life generally is placed under religious, rather than civil, law, and a corresponding ban on mixed marriages between Jewish and Arab Israelis. Arendt writes:

> Israeli citizens, religious and nonreligious, seem agreed upon the desirability of having a law that prohibits intermarriage, and it is chiefly for this reason [. . .] that they are also agreed upon the undesirability of a written constitution in which such a law would embarrassingly have to be spelled out. (EJ 7)

Indeed, for Arendt, what is noteworthy is not only that there is such a ban but also that the felt need for it justifies the lack of a formal institutionalization of the legal regime of the modern Israeli state under a constitution, itself something that should be—Arendt is suggesting—a shock and shame to the conscience of citizens of a modern, democratic state.

Still more disturbing is how obvious an echo this legally enshrined inequality on the basis of ethnic/religious identity is to the very sort of persecution to which the Jews of Germany had themselves been subjected, as Arendt insists:

> Whatever the reasons, there was certainly something breathtaking in the naiveté with which the prosecution denounced the infamous Nuremburg Laws of 1935, which had prohibited intermarriage and sexual relations between Jews and Germans. The better informed among the correspondents were well aware of the irony, but they did not mention it in their reports. (EJ 7)

Three crucial points demand attention as we reflect on this striking moment in the very early stages of her reporting on the trial.

First and most important is Arendt's very conscious use of the term "irony" in the concluding sentence of this passage, before the entire controversy over her "tone" began. Second is the explicit reference to the Nuremburg Laws and the very clear suggestion that Israel's refusal to recognize civil marriages precisely because it opens the door to public acknowledgment of inter-confessional relationships echoes one of the most infamous legacies of National Socialism, itself obviously connected to the point she wants to make about the complicity of those Jews who used or abused their positions of relative privilege within the Jewish Councils. Third is that Arendt here deigns to provide an account of why it is that Israel lacked—and lacks—a written constitution, and to stress that the ground for this is and ought to be embarrassing to Zionists. As Bernstein (2018: 47) reminds us, Arendt herself was a Zionist, in the sense of supporting a Jewish homeland, though not a Jewish nation-state, in Palestine. In part for this reason her early critiques of Zionism and of the *Realpolitik* of the State of Israel in *Eichmann* have enormous relevance today, as there "will never be anything resembling peace in the Middle East unless there is an attempt to confront honestly the problems that Arendt so brilliantly identified" (Bernstein 2018: 47).

Some readers of Arendt would be surprised to learn that one of the first points she advances regarding the trial of Adolf Eichmann is a commentary on why it is that the Israeli state lacks a written constitution, and why this is problematic. Recalling her choice of title for this opening chapter ("The House of Justice"), the point becomes more explicit: Arendt has chosen to begin her "report" with a sign, in her mind a very jarring and morally outrageous one, of her conclusion, namely that justice has not been done and will not be done in this trial of this man in this place in this way for these reasons. As Idith Zertal (2010: 148–50) argues concerning the reception of Arendt, and *Eichmann* in particular, in her groundbreaking work on "Israel's Holocaust," a central element of the public shunning of her work, in particular but by no means only by Scholem, is precisely that Arendt had the audacity to call attention to Israel's inability to escape the racial thinking that brought the world to the place where a man like Eichmann could be so central a figure in so heinous a crime. Leora Bilsky emphasizes that this controversy by no means ended in the 1960s: when *Eichmann* was finally translated into Hebrew some twenty-five years after Arendt's death, the translation

> replayed the controversy of the 1960s in an entirely new context [where] an intergenerational struggle became interwoven with a very different debate that has emerged in Israel in recent years over the critical interpretations of Israeli history by a new generation of scholars known as the "new historians" or "post-Zionists." (Bilsky 2004: 164–5)

As we will see in this chapter's conclusion, this applies to the German and American reception of *Eichmann* as well, as can be seen in both popular and academic responses to Judith Butler's appropriation of Arendt's thinking about Zionism.

This brings us to the second point: the explicit comparison, which of course does not mean anything like the suggested equivalence, of the prohibition of intermarriage and of sexual relations between Jews and (other) Germans in the Nuremburg Laws with the prohibition of intermarriage between Jewish and Arab Israelis, as well as the refusal to place marriage under civil authority in Israel for the express purpose of preventing intermarriage without having to say so. Arendt is intentionally provocative and somewhat elliptical here, but her point is clear enough: she is not going to spread Attorney General Gideon Hausner's (which, from Arendt's perspective, really means the Israeli Prime Minister David Ben-Gurion's) line about the moral and historical lesson that the trial is supposed to be. Arendt invites us, rather, to judge reflectively for ourselves. Her attention to the silence of the better informed among the correspondents who were aware of the irony is itself the justification of her own ironic stance and her putative lack of "Ahavath Israel." As Bot (2013) suggests, and we insist, "Arendt's irony was the most 'befitting' response to the *Sache*," not because of her lack of love for the Jewish people (or for Israel) but precisely because of her responsibility as a democratic citizen.

Finally, as first comprehensively analyzed by Susan Neiman (2001), Arendt saw *Eichmann* as a theodicy, a vindication of the possibility of goodness in this world as the work of a benign, rational force. Is there truly any conceivable way in which a detailed account of the twisted and vacuous rationalizations of Eichmann, and the uncompelling and self-aggrandizing prosecution carried out by Hausner, could possibly serve as grounds for the vindication of a rational and quasi-theological, or at least cosmological, basis for morality? Yes, as Berkowitz (2017) and Parvikko (2021: xii) note, through irony. Arendt's idea—unmistakably present as well throughout the aforementioned interview with Gaus—seems to be this: to laugh out loud in the company of others who understand one's ground for laughing, when at the same time one is confronted with the most horrible of truths, is the way in which one can restore one's faith in reason and one's love of the world without turning away from the ugliness and the malignancy that perpetuates itself within it.

This is why it is vital for Arendt to effectively begin *Eichmann* with—of all things—a reprimand of Israel and of the Israeli public, and this is what Scholem refuses to see and even less to accept. If there is anything to be learned from the experience of the Shoah, Arendt is saying, it is surely not that a man, however evil or not, however "banal" or not, can be made to pay for his crime. It is that no nation can ever be a force of good and rationality in the world if its legal structures lack a solid foundation, Israel's demerit here being its lack of a constitution. As Bilsky (2010: 203) notes, Arendt was critical of the Israeli tribunal's invocation of "universal jurisdiction" because "the court did not articulate what conditions or limitations (if any), other than the presence of the defendant on trial, are needed in order to establish the competence of the court." It did not do so, Arendt (EJ 9) argues, because Ben-Gurion's underlying rationale for conducting the trial was to teach "'lessons' he thought should be taught to Jews and Gentiles, to Israelis and Arabs, in short to the whole world." The tribunal's competence, its having jurisdiction to hold a trial in the first place, is based on a liberal, internationalist jurisprudence of "universal jurisdiction" that is given the lie, Arendt bravely and forcefully argues, by the particularist and nationalist aims of the Israeli government in conducting the trial.

All the same, Arendt (EJ 9) remains emphatic that "the trial never became a play," and for this reason she takes it very seriously, insisting on calling her audience's attention to the fundamental irony of the situation in "the House of Justice" in Jerusalem. Hausner, the public prosecutor who speaks for the prime minister himself, argues that she is meant to sit back with the other trial correspondents and join in a chorus of praise for the proceedings. From Arendt's perspective (EJ 9–10), the truly unacceptable aspect of this—that she and the other reporters are meant to ignore—is the fact that the court that is establishing its competence to sit in judgment of Eichmann is itself part of a legal system that gives formal legitimacy to the *de facto* enforced inferiority of its non-Jewish minority population. To fail to call attention to that irony, like to fail to notice the very limited but nevertheless historically accurate role that *some* Jews had in the Final Solution, is not to act with *Herzenstakt*, as Scholem would have it; rather, it is to abdicate one's responsibility, precisely, to think—both as a private individual and in Arendt's case as a reporter on the trial and hence a public person.

Arendt's insistence on her ironic tone is absolutely essential to our assessment of *Eichmann* as an exercise in political thinking and an act of judgment. Her irony, itself a response to the deep ironies at work in the very functioning of the trial, sheds light on her role debating the Eichmann controversy privately and publicly—chiefly in her lecture "Personal Responsibility Under Dictatorship" (1964). To see just how and why the ground of this irony runs so deep in her thinking, let us now look into that lecture in detail, reading it together with her main conclusions in *Origins* and the essays collected in *Between Past and Future*, both of which she was editing for republication at the time she wrote "Personal Responsibility" in the wake of the publication of *Eichmann*.

Eichmann, Totalitarianism, and Mass Democracy

Ultimately, the significance of the "ironic tone" Arendt adopted in *Eichmann* is to do with her understanding of thinking and action as inextricably interwoven in judgment as a component of democratic citizenship. In particular, with reference to the comparison between the marriage laws of the modern State of Israel (in 1962) and the Nuremburg Laws of 1935, we saw the public performance of irony as the manner of passing reflective judgment is integral to enacting one's sense of personal responsibility as a democratic citizen. Reflecting on *Eichmann* and the intellectual and ideological background to the controversy it spawned, Arendt (PRD 32) notes: "Totalitarian forms of government and dictatorships in the usual sense are not the same, and most of what I have to say applies to totalitarianism." This rather offhand comment makes clear that if we are to understand the positions that Arendt takes in considering individual human actors caught up in the collective action problems that were endemic to the National Socialist regime as a totalitarian form of government, we must attend to the particularities of such action problems insofar as they uniquely manifest themselves in totalitarian societies, in which action itself is hardly possible.

Considering *Eichmann* thus, we focus not so much on what Arendt says about these issues as on the manner in which she connects thinking and moral responsibility to an analysis of the chilling similarities between totalitarian societies and certain tendencies in modern mass democracies. We confront here the irreducible modernity of our moment, which consists precisely in the *aporia* of how we can employ the dialectical mode of thinking integral to "the tradition" in order to reconcile ourselves with evils that are sadly not "negative externalities" of European modernity, such as social transformations in response to space-age technology (mentioned in Chapter 6) and the dehumanization entailed by race-thinking (discussed in Chapter 9).

107

This connects Arendt's report on the Eichmann trial to her conviction that the task of thinking is a commitment to public and plural deliberation that, as Berkowitz (2017: 30) emphasizes, "can come about only through a dedication to the world as it is." To dedicate oneself to the world *as it is* means that one does not think politics from an abstract perspective but rather that one, in the midst of the flurry of events as they occur, allows one's thinking to be sparked by these events, and reflects on them based on their historical conditions and on the possible futures hidden within them. A comparative account of the interplay between individual responsibility and collective action helps us to see beyond the particular points of controversy in which Arendt's thinking about Eichmann was embroiled, and especially to see why and how the crucial sense in which Arendt is a thinker for the present moment rests not so much in her conclusions about important current issues. Rather, it is much more the way in which she approaches these issues—thinks politically—that makes her writings so inspiring today.

To illustrate this, we sketch out two pairs of questions that present an agenda for thinking through the current crises of democracy together with Arendt's practice of thinking without banisters as reflective judgment, as it manifests both in *Eichmann* and in various lectures and essays delivered and revised around and just after the time of its publication. The first pair is: (1) How, after what Adorno and Arendt identified as twentieth-century barbarism, is it possible to articulate a critical assessment of the Western tradition that does not amount to rejectionism? (2) Why, can it be argued, is it worthwhile or even necessary to do so? The second pair is: (3) When we do engage the tradition in this way, how and where do we find the points of continuity between earlier forms and institutions of late modern civil society not subject to the critique of modern barbarism? (4) On what basis, and through which worldview, is it possible to offer a robust defense of such forms and such institutions?

Reflective judgment is of central importance for Arendt, both as the condition of possibility for a common world and as one way in which that world becomes co-constituted in action. Preserving public life as a space of possibility for such judgments is, as Dana Villa (2021: 324–5) notes, precisely what motivates Arendt when she, in private correspondence with Hans Jonas, rejects the commonly held view that "the whole 'totalitarian business' could have been avoided if only Europeans had remained true to their 'traditional values.'" As Villa (2021: 325) emphasizes, the extreme case presented not by

Eichmann but by "those few who," unlike him, "were still able to tell right from wrong," who "had only their faculty of judgment to fall back on," demonstrates that when we are confronted by something "utterly unprecedented," it is judgment that makes action possible, while action makes judgment actual.

Here we see why, for Arendt in *Eichmann* and the essays collected in *Between Past and Future*, modern mass democracy displays features that alarmingly resemble those in a totalitarian dictatorship. The lynchpin of this resemblance is the role of individual responsibility as both the prerequisite for and the result of reflective judgment, and the endangerment thereof under conditions of bureaucratic rationality in modern mass democracies. This resembles—though surely in much less extreme ways—what happens in totalitarian societies. In both cases, Arendt argues, it becomes more and more difficult to agree about factual knowledge, and for this reason the relationship between truth and opinion and their place in public discourse remains one of Arendt's central concerns.

Among the textual sources concerning the crisis of truth as a matter of singular and objective fact, in distinction to opinions that are always plural and open to revision in public, "Truth and Politics" is the most influential, especially of late as regards our putatively post-truth media and political landscape. Yet, one crucial locus for this discussion remains relatively under-appreciated: the essay "Tradition and the Modern Age." Here, Arendt (TMA 34) turns to a figure who looms large in the debate of the limits of scientism and the dangers of devaluing scientific truth, Friedrich Nietzsche, who "was well aware of the profound nonsense of the new 'value-free' science which was soon to degenerate into scientism and general scientific superstition." The return to Nietzsche is significant for his assault on objectivity. Nietzsche's place is paramount in that his thoroughgoing methodological critique is directed not at the pseudo-scientific nature of the so-called historical sciences but at the very idea of a disinterested science in the first place, very much including putatively exact or natural sciences.

This, Arendt argues in "The Concept of History" and in the "crisis" essays ("The Crisis in Education" and "The Crisis in Culture"), is the deep and often unacknowledged source of the crises of the r/Republic, both in the narrow sense of the schisms within postwar American polity and in the wider sense of what Carl Schmitt (1988 [1923]) infamously diagnosed a decade before the rise of National Socialism as the crisis of parliamentary democracy, or more accurately, the spiritual-historical dimensions of contemporary parliamentarianism.[1] Arendt encapsulates this crisis thus:

> The nineteenth century opposition of the natural and historical sciences, together with the allegedly absolute objectivity of precision of the natural scientists, is today a thing of the past. [. . .] Physics, we know today, is no less a man-centered inquiry into what is than historical research. The old quarrel, therefore, between the "subjectivity" of historiography and the "objectivity" of physics has lost much of its relevance. (CH 48–9)

Underneath the sorest spots in our democratic cultures, Arendt argues in *Between Past and Future*, we find time and again the groundlessness of the sciences and their truth claims.

This does not mean or imply, for Arendt or for us reflecting on this dimension of her work in the midst of the Covid-19 pandemic and the various controversies public policy measures grounded in empirical science have spawned concerning the role of scientific claims in democratic politics, that science lacks—let alone ought to lack—something akin to authority, even if as Arendt (WA 91) argues, a "deepening crisis of authority has accompanied the development of the modern world in our century." What it does mean, however, is that without such a ground, all claims to truth, to universal validity, and to the necessity or even the expedience of one democratically endorsed approach to "the facts of life" remains mired in controversy. It likely need not be mentioned in the context of contemporary American debates about reading lists in literature and science classes at the primary and secondary levels of the education system, which have their echoes (*mutatis mutandis*) in debates about the teaching of history, and of basic STEM subject competence in Britain and the member states of the European Union, that Arendt's point is just as relevant today as it was in the 1960s. Whence this enduring relevance? It arises from the way in which Arendt's exercise in passing judgment on Eichmann (and others) in *Eichmann* underscores her key methodological insight regarding the challenge to preserving the pursuit of truth (which is always singular and universal, if it is to be found at all) as a practice within plural democratic societies which value the freedom of opinion.

How is this even possible? Are not opinion and truth in fundamental opposition? Have we not known this since, at least, Plato? Not necessarily, Arendt argues, because there is a form of objectivity, or something akin to objectivity, that is possible for the sciences—social as well as natural or exact—to aspire to, namely impartiality:

Impartiality, and with it all true historiography, came into the world when Homer decided to sing the deeds of the Trojans no less than those of the Achaeans, and to praise the glory of Hector no less than the greatness of Achilles. This Homeric impartiality [. . .] is still the highest type of objectivity we know. (CH 51)

All along, ever since Homer, there has been this achievable norm for claim-making in public debate about matters of fact that can be established, whether concerning the fabric of the physical world or about the events leading up to a massive armed conflict. Take the question that motivated Thucydides, "Why did the Spartans and their allies find war with the Athenians inevitable?," or the one that motivates Arendt's investigation of the conflict between truth and politics. As Arendt (TP 239) argues, the fact that it is not possible to arrive at a rational consensus concerning "the question of guilt for the outbreak of the First World War" means two things: first, that objectivity as classically defined is impossible when it comes to these matters of fact; second, and nevertheless, that "it would require no less than a power monopoly over the entire civilized world" in order "to eliminate from the record the fact that on the night of August 4, 1914, German troops crossed the frontier into Belgium."

Indeed, Arendt (CH 59) argues, not only may we aspire to impartiality in asking and attempting to answer questions like these, but we must do so, for the "comparatively new social sciences, which so quickly became to history what technology had been to physics" can be restrained from their use of experiment, which they perhaps pursue "in a much cruder and less reliable way than do the natural sciences, but the method is the same: they too prescribe conditions, conditions to human behavior." The sciences, human/historical and exact, are techniques: never content simply to observe "objectively," they are actually forms of human activity that attempt to bring about certain "artificial" conditions. This is why, Arendt concludes, when it comes to questions studied in what we call the social sciences, it

is no longer a question of academic objectivity. It cannot be solved by the reflection that man as a question-asking being naturally can receive only answers to match his own questions. [. . .] What is really undermining the whole modern notion that meaning is contained in the process as a whole [. . .] is that everything is possible not only in the realm of ideas, but in the field of reality itself. (CH 86–7)

This situation "where everything is possible" is, after all, Arendt's diagnosis of what is distinctly totalizing in a totalitarian dictatorship

(OT 459); the world-historically unique manifestation of the human capacity to will a world existing "only in ideas" (ideology) into actual reality. Bearing this in mind, the stakes of finding some democratically salient form of impartiality in claim-making could not be higher.

For, if we fail to achieve this sense of impartiality—what Arendt calls a "common sense"—then what is lost along with the democratic warrant for the pursuit of truth (factual as well as rational) is the common world altogether: this is what Arendt wrote *Eichmann* to avoid. In an echo of the doom foreshadowed and prevailed against in *The Human Condition*, Arendt closes this essay thus:

> In the situation of radical world-alienation, neither history nor nature is at all conceivable. This twofold loss of the world [. . .] has left behind it a society of men who, without a common world which would at once relate and separate them, either live in desperate lonely separation or pressed together in a mass. (CH 89–90)

In "The Crisis in Education" and "The Crisis in Culture," Arendt discusses how the oscillation between lonely isolation and mass movements undermines our trust in public discourse, acting as a conditioning cause of the loss of a common world. Arendt (CE 178) writes that "whenever in political questions sound human reason fails or gives up the attempt to supply answers we are faced by a crisis; for this kind of reason is really that common sense by virtue of which we and our five individual senses are fitted into a single world common to us all and by the aid of which we move around in it"; by this means "a piece of the world, something common to us all, is destroyed." This is Arendt's phenomenological account of crises in politics and political culture, which we could describe in three steps. (1) A common world, as a space of appearance in which citizens can appear together and recognize (in both of the main senses of this term) one another, requires some common sense concerning the basic features of that world as a world, and not just a collection of material and immaterial artifacts. (2) Whenever circumstances arise (as in post-truth politics) where this common sense is impossible to achieve, the assembly of material and immaterial artifacts that would otherwise make up a common world cease to make up anything at all. (3) This disintegration of the common is precisely what we call a crisis, in the original root sense of *krino/krithenai*, which is not to judge/be judged but to distinguish or cut off something from something else.

A crisis, as a moment of decision, entails something as-yet-indeterminate, something that is un-settled. There is, potentially, a positive dimension to this. For in a moment of crisis there is an openness to potential futures, for something truly new. As long as new human beings are being born, you never know; as Arendt (OT 479) famously ends her tireless investigation of all the cruelest elements of imperialism, nationalism, and totalitarianism in *Origins*, "This beginning is guaranteed by each new birth; it is indeed every man." Thus, for Arendt, education requires engagement with a tradition but only as a first step: to understand the world as it is, or at least as it was, considering the breach in tradition, is to construct a foil for our judgments. For this reason, the crisis in education was for Arendt—and remains for us—a chance for something new.

At the same time, we ought not be overconfident that crises are inherently filled with promise for the future. Arendt, thinking about the postwar crisis in education in particular, presents a good reason not to be sanguine, grounded in the larger crisis of authority and the impotence of the tradition in postwar democratic societies:

> A crisis in education would at any time give rise to serious concern even if it did not reflect a more general crisis and instability in modern society. [. . .] The problem of education in the modern world lies in the fact that by its very nature it cannot forgo either authority or tradition, and yet must proceed in a world that is neither structured by authority nor held together by tradition. (CE 185, 195)

Absent some sort of common world, constantly re-envisioned on the basis of a common sense that reconstructs such a world-in-common out of the vestiges of a form of authority and a practice of tradition that no longer "structures" or "holds together" our pluralist societies, a crisis in education is inevitable.

Arendt makes this conclusion—the vital and irreplaceable role of a common sense in order for judgment, and hence democratic culture, to sustain itself—explicit when she turns to the wider "crisis in culture" of which the crisis in education is a symptom:

> Common sense [. . .] discloses to us the nature of the world insofar as it is a common world; we owe it to the fact that our strictly private and "subjective" five senses and their sensory data can adjust themselves to a nonsubjective and "objective" world which we have in common and share with others. Judging is one [. . .] important activity in which this sharing-the-world-with-others comes to pass. (CC 221)

Here, at last, our sojourn through the essays of *Between Past and Future* comes to a positively framed conclusion: there is a possible answer to the mass democratic inclination toward (what we call today) post-truth politics and the loss of the common world; an answer to the opposed tendencies toward loneliness in our (possibly online) silos or aggregation into masses that can easily be mobilized as mobs (Canovan 2002). This answer is, or could be, democratic citizenship as exercising judgment.

The path is narrow, bumpy, and very difficult, however. For, such a practice of exercising judgment requires that common sense upon which a common world is based, and that common sense, in turn, requires a shared understanding of impartiality as the basis of claim-making. And it is precisely this sense of impartiality that seems lost to us as we interminably rehash arguments about the subjectivity and objectivity of knowledge claims. A way out of this crisis, of this moment of disintegration, would require of humanists in particular—with whom Arendt here identifies herself—that we learn to reassert some sense of authority, grounded in the freedom of thought, that is not opposed to political freedom but actually that which alone can safeguard it:

> As humanists, we can rise above these conflicts between the statesman and the artist as we can rise in freedom above the specialties which we all must learn and pursue. [. . .] Then we shall know how to reply to those who so frequently tell us that Plato or some other great author of the past has been superseded. (CC 225)

Here we see what, for Arendt, is required in order for one to judge and to act with authority, and what was entirely absent in the case of the Eichmann trial but also in the controversy about her reporting about that trial. It is disheartening if unsurprising, then, to see Arendt's own attempt to seek this sort of impartiality as an act of trying to maintain the possibility of a common world in the wake of Eichmann's testimony about his role in the active destruction of the same in *Eichmann* fall on such deaf ears. As democratic citizens, it remains for us a permanent possibility to take up the stance Arendt enacts in *Eichmann*, which, as Neiman (2001: 66) notes, "she ascribed to Lessing: not entirely at home in the world, but committed to it." How can this possibility be actualized?

Conclusion

Arendt is a thinker for our times not only in the sense that she inspires arguments and offers a theoretical framework well suited to our most pressing debates, but also, and perhaps mostly, because of her claim to understand; to think about the world and have courage to express judgments among the judgments of others, co-shaping the realm of human affairs. Arendt's way of approaching political thinking and acting, much more than her actual judgments and deeds, many of which we might see as having failed in retrospect, shows us how we ought to think, and act, today. From this perspective, Arendt's report of Eichmann's trial, the controversy it sparked, as well as her own way of dealing with these events serves as an apt example of public judgment and hence as an exercise in political thinking. Its richness in this respect can easily be seen when we turn to a more recent example: the controversy surrounding Judith Butler's receipt of the Adorno Prize in 2012, where public notice of Butler's honor centered on a volatile debate concerning her critique of Zionism, rather than her oeuvre as an extension of the "Frankfurt School" of critical theory (especially Butler 2005), for which she was being honored. That this controversy actually focused on Butler's views about Arendt's discussions of Zionism in "Zionism Reconsidered" and *Eichmann* only intensifies the way in which this event is a literal echo of the original Eichmann controversy.[2]

In reflecting on the salience of the maelstrom around Butler's being honored with the Adorno Prize for our retrospective under-standing of the controversy around the publication of *Eichmann*, it is worth noting that both debates surround the shortcomings and strengths of Arendt's resistance to what she perceives as the reduc-tion of politics to the resolution of social problems. As Butler herself makes clear, both the strengths and weaknesses of Arendt's approach to the politics of identity are integrally connected to the impossibility of separating identity (in all its intersectional dimensions of race, eth-nicity, religion, and gender/sex/sexuality) from the problems posed by nationalism for universal values. Butler (2012: 134) makes this clear while commenting on Arendt's famous exchange with Gershom Scholem about what it means to be "a daughter of the Jewish people," discussed earlier; here, following Arendt in stipulating that "being Jewish" is "an indisputable fact of my life," Butler focuses on Arendt's poetic turn of phrase which is itself an echo of the archaic Greek poet Pindar: "there is such a thing as a basic gratitude for everything that is as it is; for what has been given and is not made; for what is *physei* and not *nomos*."

Butler points us to what might be the most inspired and least impeachable version of Arendt's claim against the reduction of the political to social questions: what is political is that which is made, which is by convention (*nomos*), and which can and must be contested and revised in the public domain. What is social, and for Arendt can never be political in this sense, is that toward which we ought to have an attitude basically opposed to the "no holds barred" agonism that politics both requires and makes possible.

For Butler, following Arendt, political life emanates from a certain "basic gratitude" for the miracle of life—precisely what totalitarianism seeks to abolish. This far Butler follows closely in Arendt's wake. But, as Butler argues:

> it would be hard to read [Arendt's] response to Scholem as something other than an effort to make sense of, or give a particular construction to, the *physei* that she is. And if she is doing that, *physei* is subject to a cultural crafting. (Butler 2012: 134)

For Butler, Arendt's stand against Scholem is a political act focused on the determination of one social question: What does it *mean* to be a woman and a Jew?

That Arendt "naturalized," and thus depoliticized, both her gendered and religious identity in her response to Scholem does not mean that Butler, in seeking to align herself with Arendt on the question of Zionism and its dangers for the full political rights of the non-Jewish minority in the State of Israel, is following Arendt any less. Indeed, it seems likely that a significant factor in Butler's becoming the focus of vituperative attacks in the German media on the occasion of the Adorno Prize is that she remained committed to the same principle that motivated Arendt in her public dispute with Scholem occasioned by her reflection on the Eichmann trial, even as she argued that Arendt's naturalization of identity is wrong. This emphasizes a point that Arendt (PRD 23) had already made when speaking about the unmastered German past, almost exactly fifty years earlier and commenting on the controversy surrounding her Eichmann book: "Well, it looks as though today, after so many years, this German past has turned out to remain somehow unmanageable for a good part of the civilized world." With the raging debates about the BDS movement and the intensifying challenge of making a distinction between anti-Zionism and antisemitism both in Germany and around the world

(Dekel and Özyürek 2021), we can be sure that what Arendt wrote about Zionism and antisemitism in the 1940s through the 1960s will continue to stir debate.

But why, ultimately, does it matter that what Arendt calls "the 'un-mastered past' that concerns us" in her July 20, 1963 letter to Scholem (Knott 2017: 207) continues to be unmanageable for the politics and culture of memory in so many different national contexts? Attention to one of the key conclusions Butler reaches in her discussion of Scholem's open letter helps make this clear:

> Scholem's rebuke is especially problematic here since he is writing from Israel in 1963 and objecting to Arendt's quite merciless account of the Israeli court procedures at the Eichmann trial [with the intended effect of] excluding the diasporic or non-Zionist Jew. (Butler 2012: 136)

This conclusion is telling in multiple respects. First, Butler here names one of the central poles of the controversy around Arendt, in Israel and, more so, in New York: Arendt's focus on the illegitimacy, or incompetence in the technical sense, of the Israeli court system and/or the particular tribunal established for Eichmann, which, in her view, could only have been an international court if it were to be a *legal* proceeding. Second, she calls attention to what is salient about this debate with respect to Arendt's views about popular sovereignty and its inherent, though resistible, tendency toward ethnonationalism and the persecution of minorities. Debates around "the Eichmann controversy" have as much to do with who is entitled to judge in public and how as they have to do with the particular circumstances of democratic societies (like the Federal Republic of Germany and the modern state of Israel) that emerged, or were born/reborn, out of the cataclysm of the Second World War. Finally, we ought to bear in mind that it is sentences such as this one that have made Butler the object of many of the same criticisms leveled at Arendt in the early 1960s.

In this light we can see that Butler's focus on Scholem's intent to delegitimize Arendt as a diasporic Jew who is thus not really part of "the Jewish people"—a body politic that is implicitly identified with those Jews who are either or both (a) citizens of the State of Israel and/or (b) expressly supportive of the state of Israel as a "Jewish and democratic" nation-state—actually doubles back on the present moment. Scholem attacked Arendt, essentially, for advocating against the state of Israel as expressly Jewish and democratic. Here Arendt argues again in the early 1960s, prior to the 1967 war and the beginning of the ongoing occupation of the West Bank, just as she had in the 1940s, before and after the declaration of the existence of the state of Israel in May 1948, that there must be some sort of binational or multicultural democratic state in Israel/Palestine, with equal rights for all citizens, regardless of ethnic or religious identity. Butler, some fifty years later, is attacked, in particular in response to a public debate with Micha Brumlik on the question "Is Zionism an integral part of Judaism?" in 2012, for her public espousal of a post-Zionist position (Weinthal 2012).

Taking into account these three dimensions of Butler's return to Arendt in her public controversy with Scholem, we learn again the importance of Arendt's insight, expressed especially in her major public comments on the controversy around the publication of *Eichmann* in "Personal Responsibility" and "What Remains?," that people's kneejerk condemnation not of the details of her judgment of Eichmann but of the very fact that she dares to pass judgment on him, and on other actors involved in the Final Solution, is indicative of an abdication of reflective judgment on the part of all democratic citizens. Especially because such an abdication is linked, implicitly and explicitly, to the very features of individual decision-making under conditions of totalitarian government that both made it possible for the Nazi genocide to be executed, willingly, by so many citizens of a recently (if imperfectly) democratic state and bears a striking resemblance to what we can count among the imaginable features of modern mass democracy.

Notes

1. In German, *Die geistesgeschichtliche Lage des heutigen Parlamentarismus.*
2. For background on the controversy, see the coverage in *Deutsche Welle* at https://www.dw.com/en/adorno-prize-for-judith-butler-irks-jewish-gr oups/a-16225396%20; on the award, see https://news.berkeley.edu /2012/09/12/butler-wins-adorno-prize/.

Chapter 6

The Earth, Education, and Human Action

Thinking with Hannah Arendt about non-human nature is not instantly intuitive. By now we have seen that at the center of her reflections, be they more of a philosophical or a political character, are always human beings in their plurality. Although earth and nature indeed belong to the most intimate of human conditions and constitute the possibility of labor, she does not pay much attention to them in either *The Human Condition* or elsewhere. Arendt is interested in human action, in different aspects of the political in our lives. She describes the common world and its structures with the greatest excellence, comments on the political events of her times, and makes—often controversial—judgments, prompting academic and public debate. Nature—the earth, plants, and animals—seems to be, at best, at the margins of her attention. It would also be difficult to argue that she attributed any political significance to it.

However, the human world needs to be seen as an ever-changing web of relations, where human beings are embodied beings in a particular space. Not only does this space, earth, condition our being but also our lives have an impact on the earth, changing the earthly conditions of human life in a more or less conscious way. In modern times this influence has become more and more harmful; or perhaps we have become more effective in affecting the natural world through the growing impact of infrastructure and technologies. The term "Anthropocene" has been coined to describe exactly this: human interference in the earth has become so severe as to cause presumably irreversible changes in the planet's geology and climate, resulting in a crisis of global relevance.

In this chapter, we reflect on the environmental crisis and the political response to it. Our case study is the protest movement Fridays for Future, which opens a perspective not only to discuss Arendt's views on nature and the earth but also to link them to education and political subjectivity. Her appreciation of the natural world in the sense of the material basis of the human condition has increasingly been a subject of academic interest: her reflections are being debated in the context of the position of humans in the midst of an anthropogenic climate change. At the same time, her Aristotelian notion of a child as a not-yet-subject and her reflections about the role of education are being critically discussed both in an educational and in a political context. These debates invite us to rethink her notion of political subjectivity from new theoretical and practical perspectives. We thus begin by presenting Arendt as a thinker of the crisis, before we recall the meaning that she ascribes to the earth in *The Human Condition*, and discuss it through the lens of the concept of the Anthropocene. We then touch upon the role of thinking and judging in education to negotiate the political subjectivity of children (or more precisely: youth), a theme to which we return in Chapter 9, with reference to a related text from the 1950s, "Reflections on Little Rock." In the last part of this chapter, we refer to Fridays for Future, and especially its initiator Greta Thunberg, as an example—in the Arendt's sense—of political action reacting to a situation of crisis.

Thinking in the Midst of a Crisis

Arendt could very well be described as a thinker of the crisis, or perhaps of multiple crises, as this motive is ever present in her work, from the identity crisis in *Rahel Varnhagen* and her early Jewish writings, to *The Origins of Totalitarianism*, where she analyzes how totalitarian rule precludes even a possibility of a political space, to her multiple essay collections, where she critically and experimentally discusses the crises of her times—and the frequency with which she used the word "crisis" in the titles of her writings is perhaps the best evidence for her sensibility. We would argue that this is one of the reasons why academic and public interest in Arendt's writings is on the rise. It is because so many politically urgent challenges today call not for dogmatic but for critical and practical perspectives. Through mass media and online media, more people than ever seem to be informed about the entanglements in the world, or even in different worlds, since the earth, also in times of globalization, remains a ground for many lived spaces, which differ to a large extent in terms of economic sustainability, political freedom, or interpersonal practices. In other words, they differ in terms of the human condition, in Arendt's understanding (as mentioned in Chapter 1) of the human being as an infinitely conditioned being, conditioned by everything she encounters (HC 9).

As for Arendt a crisis is generally conditioned by a breach of tradition, (potential) political actors are faced with a situation of uncertainty and lack of commonly endorsed guidelines for action. At the same time, a crisis poses a great opportunity by giving them a vital impulse for free action. With the breach of tradition, its categories cease to provide guidelines for action. She illuminates this existential situation by telling a story of the lost treasure of revolution (GBPF 3–6), which can only be regained under conditions of political crisis. As discussed in Chapter 3 above, such revolutionary actors have no guidelines to follow and never know what results from their deeds and words, and often have no particular preparation for politics. Hence, the role of these unlikely political agents ends as soon as the crisis has been overcome. Revolution equips them with a treasure of spontaneous action, which they need to let go of upon their return to normality,[1] after the end of the state of political (and existential) emergency.

As Arendt notes, the modern age in general and the post-totalitarian world in particular might seem disorienting without a guiding thread of tradition and a normative reference to authority:

> To most people today this culture looks like a field of ruins which, far from being able to claim any authority, can hardly command their interest. This fact may be deplorable, but implicit in it is the great chance to look upon the past with eyes undistracted by any tradition, with a directness which has disappeared from Occidental reading and hearing ever since Roman civilization submitted to the authority of Greek thought. (TMA 28)

This chance is not only an occasion for reflecting on the past with eyes unclouded by tradition but also an opening for the future as a realm of political freedom of action. As such, it is a crisis.

This diagnosis is still relevant. To many, or maybe even to most people, our times are troubled times. Different kinds of crisis are screaming at us from the pages of newspapers every day. Not only the dramatic development of the Covid-19 pandemic since 2019 but also phenomena that gained public attention before that: the peak of forced migration in 2015, the rise of climate-related anxiety in 2018, the #BlackLivesMatter movement active since 2013 and exploding internationally in 2020, to name only the most broadcasted issues, all framed (with more or less merit) as a crisis. These particular situations elicited despair, suppression, or even aggressiveness in some, while in others they sparked an irresistible impetus to act.

121

Arendt on the Earth

In the very first paragraphs of *The Human Condition*, referring to the launching of the first artificial earth satellite in 1957, Arendt points to sentiments of future possibilities of leaving our planet for the conquest of space, echoing hopes that "Mankind (would) not remain bound to the earth forever" (HC 1). This moment, when amid the arms race during the Cold War the first successful attempt by human beings to reach out to the skies took place, provokes her reflection on the meaning of the earth for the *condition humaine*. The historical context of the moment is important, as the achievement is not an effect of an acting in concert within a free and constructive political space but rather a gesture of force under conditions of imminent war. Under the threat of an outburst of violence, it was an event that not only radically changed the scope of human worldliness but also questioned the necessity of the earthly character of human existence, beyond hitherto fictional visions of the conquest of space.

Arendt notes:

> the most radical change in the human condition we could imagine would be an emigration of men from the earth to some other planet. Such an event, no longer totally impossible, would imply that man would have to live under man-made conditions, radically different from those the earth offers him. (HC 10)

This indicates to what extent, when thinking about her scheme of human activities, everything that appears as labor is bound to the earthly condition of human life. If this earthly embeddedness ended or changed, we would be entirely dependent on the human-made artificial world for our existence.

Why should that be a problem? We might cite a number of fictional scenarios (both utopian and dystopian) that show an artificial world, completely detached from the natural earthly environment. This change, however, would be radical because

> the earth is the very quintessence of the human condition, and earthly nature, for all we know, may be unique in the universe in providing human beings with a habitat in which they can move and breathe without effort and without artifice. (HC 2)

This means that without the earth our entire worldliness would change. Work would substitute for labor, as no *natural* material basis would be given. Our bodies—maybe to a large extent not organic anymore but rather bionic—would need to be nursed and nourished through artificial means, entirely changing the life we know.

This, in itself, seems possible to imagine, though not realistic in any near future. And since Arendt herself did not share the sentiments expressed by the futurists of her day and did not take seriously the possibility of this particular tremendous change in the human condition, it is rather her more general reflections about the relationship between humans and nature that cast light on the relevance of her thought to understanding the world today in terms of the Anthropocene, where human impact on the earth and its climate has caused a devastating change to the planet.

Upon a closer look at reflections on the human condition in Arendt's writings, we discover a well-defined account of this relationship, indicating the severe impact of human activities on the earth in the modern age. For Arendt, it was primarily the atom bomb that posed a viable danger of destroying all organic life on earth (HC 149). Today we face an equally radical, but quite different scenario. It is not even a particular technology but the *event* of the Anthropocene itself that threatens the existence of life on earth (Hyvönen 2020: 244). Our future has grown very precarious throughout the last decades and—in spite of the hopes of 1950s dreamers—the state of space technology remains a great way off from securing us another home. Climate change-related anxiety has been increasing very fast. Arguably, everyone who critically observes scientists' responses to the proclaimed climate crisis will know that their diagnosis is virtually univocal. Without a radical change in our climate policies and practices, even if our generation does not face severe consequences of climate change, future generations will. In other words, the newcomers, coming into this world right now, children and youth, will bear this burden and are hence existentially and politically affected.

Action, in the sense of the Greek *archein* (to begin, to lead, to rule), has not only a creative but also a destructive potential (HC 189). As a human activity, it is shaped by natality, implying a radical uniqueness of every acting subject, and plurality, indicating a multiplicity of unique beings acting together and showing courage by stepping into the light of the public realm, where "not life, but the world is at stake" (WF 155). For this reason, action is neither sovereign nor foreseeable (HC 232). Its course and development depend on the free and spontaneous decisions of every involved agent and may support, oppose, undermine, reject, transform, or build upon other unique actions. Hence, "action, though it may have a definite beginning, never [. . .] has a predictable end" (HC 144). And although through work, which consists in building an artificial world of things, we inevitably exercise violence against nature (Hyvönen 2020: 247), it is beyond doubt that the capacity to act is the most dangerous of all human abilities and possibilities, and it is also beyond doubt that the self-created risks mankind faces today have never been faced before (CH 63).

It may be argued that "the Anthropocene [. . .] exposes in radical fashion the non-sovereign character of human action on which Arendt insisted throughout her work. We are not by any stretch of imagination in control of what we are doing" (Robinson 2018: 8). This results from the global interconnectedness of human behavior and actions, exponentiating the effect of the conditions of action, already rendering it *per se* unpredictable. Despite scientific evidence for the anthropogenic origins of climate change, environmental thinkers and activists face difficulties in actually establishing it as a fact, which is due to the fragility of truth and the prevalence of lying in politics (Hargis 2016: 481). As a result, neither political theory nor political practice is able to respond appropriately to this "urgent and life-threatening Emergency" (Gills and Morgan 2020: 885). Whether this is an expression of denialism or a failure to connect the dots, one thing is certain: "Thinking through the Anthropocene requires not explaining away the shock of the event, continuing our analyses as though nothing has happened. The Anthropocene ought to leave its mark on any given topic in political theory" (Hyvönen 2020: 244).

Arendt (HC 139) notes that not the Bible itself but the biblical tradition accounts for human beings relating to the earth as its masters, subduing the earth and claiming domination over other living creatures. This understanding, as she says, remains in a sense a cornerstone of our relationship to nature to this day. According to Arendt, however, the decisive factor shaping our distorted relation to the natural world was the world-alienation underlying the development of modern science. While pre-modern mathematics still reflected the structure of the world, modern sciences fully abstract from the living, earth-bound experience (HC 264–5). This "denial of human and embodied perspective [. . .] led to the toxic form of anthropocentrism that we associate with the Anthropocene" (Zerilli 2019b). But if we act into nature in all fundamental modes of our agency—work as constructing our objective world on the ground of the seemingly cyclical processes in the natural world; acting as beginning something new that might prove disastrous to the earth, which we seek to subdue, and at the same time an activity that remains absolutely out of our control; and in modern times also labor, not any longer as a natural cycle of production and consumption but rather as an ever-accelerating vicious circle of overproduction and overconsumption—are we, as human beings, doomed to do violence to the planet we inhabit?

From the perspective of *The Human Condition*, this seems to be the case: "*homo faber*, the creator of human artifice, has always been a destroyer of nature" (HC 139). Elsewhere, however, Arendt suggests a different meaning of making, which allows us to understand the human relation to nature through the original sense of culture as cultivation:

> The word "culture" derives from *colere*—to cultivate, to dwell, to take care, to tend and preserve—and it relates primarily to the intercourse of man with nature in the sense of cultivating and tending nature until it becomes fit for human habitation. As such, it indicates an attitude of loving care and stands in sharp contrast to all efforts to subject nature to the dominion of man. (CC 208)

Understanding our relationship to nature as loving care illuminates the relevance of the earth to human life, beyond both sheer survival and violent domination (Voice 2013: 186). Nature is not there simply to provide the means for us to sustain our lives, which would justify using and exploiting it as a source of human consumption. It does, however, provide us with resources to satisfy the necessities of biological life. Since the understanding of what is necessary and what is abundant has changed in the course of the modern age, as Arendt shows in *The Human Condition*, so has our attitude toward nature changed, and, most notably, our capabilities of using (and abusing) natural resources have grown enormously. The escalation of consumption comes at a price, as fulfilling our basic needs belongs to the realm of labor. If activities in this sphere dominate our lives, it happens at the cost of other human activities, first and foremost world-building through action and speech. This, however, leads to questioning our genuine humanity, as a "life without speech and without action [. . .] is literally dead to the world; it has ceased to be a human life because it is no longer lived among men" (HC 276). Treating the earth, and hence nature, not as a resource to be exploited but as a material condition of our common world has then a deeper sense than mere survival of the species. Beyond sustaining nature for its own sake, loving care as an existential partnership means that we also do this "for the sake of freeing our own capabilities for a fully human life" (Voice 2013: 187).

Based on this mutual relatedness, human beings are not above nature, as in a hierarchical order, and nature is not *outside* of us. If we were living in an entirely man-made world, we would only relate to our own creation, constituting a material, but not living (or at least not living without our maintenance) basis for our existence; a lifeless surrounding for the living humans, who then would indeed become the sole supreme living form due to the lack of competitors. Nature, however, has a life of its own, which forms a basis for the genuine relationship of loving care. It is something we did not create, which had already been there before we came, and provides an earthly home for us.

This normative account becomes relevant in the light of reactions to the "horrors of the Anthropocene" (Benjamin 2019), in spite of or maybe parallel to the scientifically based world-alienation. As we are not only embodied and natural but also cultural beings, the nature that we encounter is "always cultivated nature—nature being tended and being taken care of by one of nature's products called man. If nature is dead culture will die too, together with all the artifacts of our civilization" (Arendt in correspondence with McCarthy, quoted in Hyvöven 2020: 247). The existential concern about the disastrous state of the earth has become a public concern, much more so than ever before. Even if still not enough is being done, it seems that this is the moment in which science in a way "comes back to earth" and Arendtian politics may ally in responding to the anthropogenic climate catastrophe.

Thinking, Education, and Political Subjectivity

As we mentioned above, "crisis" is a prevalent notion in Arendt's writings. When referring to our times as times of crisis, we follow her claim that in the face of the precariousness of traditional ethical norms and political standards, thinking must be taken seriously as an initial move toward the formation of the political self. In this sense, not only the question of how one becomes a political subject but also the question of when one becomes one gains central relevance. In addressing these questions, we refer to Arendt's notion of education as introducing (children) into our common world (CE 192). We assume that both thinking and reflective judging, as practices to be continuously enacted, are part of this project and need to be

126

incorporated into earlier stages of education, in which the becoming of the political subject begins. To ground this claim, we discuss Arendt's view on the role of education in our common world, especially regarding the difference between children and adults, which she introduces in "The Crisis in Education." We then question the necessity and purposefulness of assuming a strict age limitation equated with adulthood as a necessary precondition for becoming a political subject, arguing that political competence is, like any competence, a question of practice. Here, we follow Arendt's primary intuition that the line between still being a child and already being an adult remains relative rather than her hesitant statement setting the point of transition at the time of college graduation. Opposing sharp divisions—based on artificial rather than natural age limits—that deny political agency and a political voice to young people, who are not yet entitled to voting rights, which is a common societal practice today, we argue that a continuous, common practice of exercising thinking and reflective judgment rests at the heart of education for politics. And thus education, in the sense of education for thinking and judging, proves to be much more than a limited, linear process reaching its end on graduation, and instead becomes an opening up to responsible and free political agency.

Arendt's aim in "The Crisis in Education," a critical reflection on the state of school education in the United States in the 1950s, is to illuminate the political relevance of education and how its shape and flow influence our common world. As usual when she discusses a problem that is seemingly beyond the realm of the political to make an actual event her case, she introduces herself as a layperson here, not a professional educator (CE 171). This gesture reminds one of her distancing from the traditional, or rather metaphysical, concept of thinking. She does not belong to the "circle of philosophers," as she decidedly states (WRLR 1). This statement brings to light her rigid distinction between philosophy and politics as different spaces of meaning, as discussed in Chapter 2. Arendt aligns herself with politics as the space where people appear to each other in their plurality to speak and act in concert. Two inner voices, which both represent the same person and inhabit the same body, provide an opening for the world, in its ethical and political aspect. Whoever does not engage in the practice of the dialogue with herself is unable to use her moral faculty—as in the well-known, though by now historically contested, example of Adolf Eichmann (PRD 30–1). In this sense, dialectical thinking is the very foundation for personal responsibility but also—arguably—for political subjectivity. One reason for this is that the acknowledgment of this kind of responsibility is a virtue that needs to accompany any political action resonating with Arendt's sole normative principle: care for the world (CC 222). The other reason is that expending and "enlarging" thinking is the condition for reflective judgment, to which Arendt also refers to as political thinking and which is a foundation of our argument throughout this book.

Political thinking engages not with two but with an indefinite multitude of voices and requires dialectical thinking as its source, as the latter contains plurality as if in a nutshell. Just as a plant grows from a seed, political thinking evolves from this dialogical practice. Arendt's reinterpretation of Kant discussed in Chapter 3 is described by Margaret Canovan (1990: 160) as "highly selective, not to say perverse," and serves as a foundation for her concept of judgment. In short, Arendtian political thinking employs Kant's aesthetic notion of "enlarged mentality" in political terms. When judging, we do not only consider our own point of view but also imagine thinking from the position of others. Arendt emphasizes that this imaginary community of thinking will not include everyone and will hence be limited: I think from where I am not. She also argues that the quality of our judgment grows with the variety of opinions we consider. In this way, the "validity of such judgments would be neither objective nor subjective, depending on personal whim, but intersubjective and representative" (SQMP 141). As we see, the practice of judging is very fragile and prone to mistakes, which is why it needs constant practicing and improvement for us to have a better understanding of the world, upon which we can act more responsibly with respect to care for the world.

For education, which should consist in introducing children into the world (CE 189) and thereby prepare them for acting, it is vital that the ability to think is given to everyone, although—for different reasons—not everyone will make use of it, while the ability to judge must be acquired through exercises. A number of scholars have come up with models of education for judgment. Among others, Stacy Smith argues that education preparing for participatory democratic politics must include practicing judgment in the sense of "practice as preparation," preceding the authentic action of adults as equals (Smith 2001: 69, 80). Morten Timmermann Korsgaard (2020) makes a case for the value of exemplary character of Arendtian judgment in education, and David Rodowick (2021) interprets judgment as a moral capacity and advocates a philosophical humanistic education. The topic is timely. On the doubt about the lack of an apparent connection between thinking, judging, and acting in Arendt that is present in some of these contributions, we propose that the moment of passage between political thinking as a faculty of the mind and political acting as *praxis* rests in Arendt's metaphor of the common world as a theater, and her statement that "the critic and the spectator is located in every actor" (Robaszkiewicz 2017: 144).

Authors proposing any form of education for thinking or judgment are always critical of Arendt's insistence on protecting children from the world and hence from any form of political activity, which denies children the status of a fully developed person. For Arendt, as children are, in the Aristotelian sense, human beings in the course of realization, parents need to assume twofold responsibility:

> Human parents [...] have not only summoned their children into life through conception and birth, they have simultaneously introduced them into a world. In education they assume responsibility for both, for the life and development of the child and for the continuance of the world. (CE 182)

In both aspects, parents look toward the future, without trying to determinate it:

> Education is the point at which we decide whether we love the world enough to assume responsibility for it and by the same token save it from that ruin which, except for renewal, except for the coming of the new and young, would be inevitable. And education, too, is where we decide whether we love our children enough not to expel them from our world and leave them to their own devices, nor to strike from their hands their chance of undertaking something new, something unforeseen by us, but to prepare them in advance for the task of renewing a common world. (CE 193)

Some forty years later Jean Bethke Elschtain (1995) argues that children's and young teenagers' participation in political activities might be an important step toward achieving this aim. But for Arendt such inclusion would amount to treating a newcomer as a *fait accompli*, hence a form of tyranny (CE 173). Arendt must have had her experience with totalitarian instrumentalization of children and youth in the Third Reich in mind when postulating the protection of children from the world and hence opposing their political engagement. But when, from this perspective, do human beings become political subjects capable of acting in public?

In *The Human Condition*, Arendt describes children as "newcomers," the bringers of the new and unexpected *par excellence* (HC 9), which coincides with her description of action. However, as we have seen, she objects against the premature exposition of children to the light of the public. Arendt (CE 192) introduces a distinction between children and adults and at the same time between education, which only children are subject to, and learning, possible for everyone, and between education, where obedience is a valid principle, and politics, where apparent obedience always amounts to support (PRD 47). Even though Arendt (CE 192) admits that "where the line between childhood and adulthood falls in each instance cannot be determined by a general rule; it changes often, in respect to age, from country to country, from one civilization to another, and also from individual to individual," she insists on determining such a line, somewhat hesitantly, as graduation from college—that would roughly be twenty or twenty-one years old. This differentiation should prevent both educating adults and treating children as if they were grown-ups capable of making political (or quasi-political) decisions, which would make them vulnerable and prone to manipulation. Arendt's objective is hence the protection of children from the world, but also the protection of the world from children and their revolutionary newness.

A good example of this attitude is her controversial and broadly discussed essay "Reflections on Little Rock" (1959), to which we will return in Chapter 9 in greater detail. Here, Arendt discusses what for her was the instrumentalization of children in the struggle against racial segregation and for equal rights of African Americans. In an attempt at deracializing public education in the Southern United States, nine African American youths (described by Arendt as children) were sent to a hitherto all-white public school. Dramatic photos showed them being attacked and shouted down by a white mob. Arendt was outraged. Yet we need to consider that the Little Rock Nine were adolescents aged fifteen to seventeen, so was it appropriate to refer to them as children and to question their political aptitude? Can we really doubt that human beings of that age are *per se* unable to think and develop their ability to judge? In her polemical piece, Arendt, handling what was from her perspective an abuse of children for addressing political problems that adults were unable to solve themselves for generations, asks critically: "Have we now come to the point where it is the children who are being asked to change or improve the world? And do we intend to have our political battles fought out in the school yards?" (RLR 50).

As the line of political "adulthood" depends on time and place, from today's perspective, at least in the case of one of the manifold crises of our world, the answer to this question seems to be: yes.

Treating the Crisis Like a Crisis

In 2018, a fifteen-year-old Swedish teenager, Greta Thunberg, decides to protest against the catastrophic results of the anthropogenic climate change. Her decision arises from profound distress but also from a need for action. She starts alone. Every Friday, she stands in front of the parliament building in Stockholm, holding a home-made sign saying "School Strike for Climate." She soon becomes a media sensation, in Sweden and beyond. Youth from other countries pick up the spirit and form their own strike groups. The now global grassroots movement that ensued from there has managed to raise environmental awareness to an extent unseen in the last decades, and has inspired many other protest actions.[2] The topic of climate change, even if present in the public debate at least since the 1960s, was not a central political and existential concern, often marginalized as eco-mania or rumor. One year after Greta Thunberg started her strike, an exemplary 2019 poll showed people in the United Kingdom identifying climate change as one of the three major challenges for the country, as important as health care and topped only by Brexit (Carrington 2019). In September 2019, UN Secretary-General António Guterres called the heads of government to bring plans, not words, to the climate action summit in New York (Taylor 2019). Shortly before this summit, on the day of the Global Climate Strike, countless people demonstrated their engagement all over the globe. Though temporarily overshadowed by the shock of Covid-19 and perhaps by other events, framed as crises, the climate crisis has now come back to the center of public attention, as it clearly poses a real menace to every living being on this planet.

A much-discussed issue is the relevance of digital communication for the School Strike for Climate. In the past decade, this factor has been emphasized with reference to multiple popular, public protest movements, including the Arab Spring, Gezi Park protests, Women's Black Marches of 2016 and 2017 in Poland, #BlackLivesMatter, and many more. It is said that digital communication plays a major role in establishing these actions and group organization, and that it is a central factor for the scope of protests, with the Arab Spring even having been called "a Facebook revolution" (e.g. Passini 2012;

Readon 2012). There are two things to be emphasized here, the first one being the development of the Internet as a platform for critical exchange.

Jeffrey Goldfarb, in his compelling 2006 study on Arendtian micropolitics, expresses great hopes concerning digital communication as a basis for acting in concert, ascribing a grand democratic potential to it, referring to the role the online platform MoveOn played in organizing protest gatherings against US war policy in 2004, energizing and empowering great numbers of people to join in. Goldfarb (2006: 87) quotes then MoveOn campaign manager Eli Pariser, who claims that: "You could say that MoveOn has a postmodern organizing model [. . .] it's opt-in, it's decentralized, you do it from your home." Hopes are, or perhaps one could already say were, high for the Internet to become a new, global, democratic, and free public space.

Five years later, Eli Pariser writes:

> To my preteen self, it seemed clear that the Internet was going to democratize the world, connecting us with better information and the power to act on it. The California futurists and techno-optimists [. . .] spoke with a clear-eyed certainty: an inevitable, irresistible revolution was just around the corner, one that would flatten society, unseat the elites, and usher in a kind of freewheeling global utopia. [. . .] For a time, it seemed that the Internet was going to entirely redemocratize society. [. . .] And yet the era of civic connection I dreamed about hasn't come. Democracy requires to see things from one another's point of view, but instead we're more and more enclosed in our own bubbles. Democracy requires a reliance on shared facts; instead we're being offered parallel but separate universes. (Pariser 2011: 3–5)

As disappointing as it is, we must acknowledge the irony of the development of Internet communication, as not only do the hopes of a free public space remain unfulfilled but also new antidemocratic, reactionary, and manipulative practices targeting—successfully—individual users to influence their political choices are on the rise. Furthermore, if we take a closer look at the events mentioned above, we have to admit that yes, electronic media played a role in spreading information and probably motivated many people to step out of their private realm to take action. However, the result—in every case—was actual gatherings of embodied political subjects in a certain place at a certain time. This shows that for now the virtual reality of the Internet mostly serves as a prelude to, or maybe a substitute for, material and tangible public realms, where actual people in their plurality come together to act in and speak about political matters. As Judith Butler

(2015: 8) points out, in critical gatherings, many of which concern various aspects of the precariousness of the assembling bodies, "it matters that bodies assemble, and that the political meanings enacted by demonstrations are not only those enacted by discourse" but by the appearance of embodied protesters in the space of protest. In this case, the vulnerability of the protesters lies in their young age, exposing them to disrespect, laughing down, disciplining, and silencing. At the same time, these gatherings are a site of creating power and so, in an educational context, can certainly be seen as sort of a rite of passage to fully-fledged political agency. The young age of the participants of the School Strike for Climate demonstrations also seems to be an advantage. As Butler (2015: 92) notes, in any embodied protest bodies are exposed and at risk, as they come "face-to-face with those they oppose, unprotected, injurable, persistent if not insurgent." While children's and youth's climate demonstrations certainly meet with a violent response, this violence lies in the symbolic realm. We are not aware of any direct physically violent counter-reaction to such a protest (at least not a public one), examples of which are too well known from other human rights, civil rights, feminist, antiracist, or economically motivated mass gatherings.

What has come to be known as Fridays for Future started with a concrete, embodied action, spread through virtual channels, only to rematerialize in street gatherings. Greta Thunberg and other young activists are facing a tremendous backlash, off- and online. They keep being scolded as tools in the hands of "cynical adults" who want to "spread fear" of climate catastrophe, believers in a "disturbed teen's climate dogma," Greta herself being "a schoolgirl puppet controlled by more sinister forces," and her mother being blamed for, literally, "pimping her child" (Maxwell and Miller 2019).

School strike is a risky form of protest. The underlying reason is the general tendency to downplay children—in the sense of people below the voting age—in politics, especially if they make an appearance in spheres beyond the institutional spaces designed for this aim. Skipping school exposed them not only to school retribution but also to accusations of simple opportunism. In the first reaction to the strike, young people taking part in Friday demonstrations were publicly accused by politicians in numerous countries of just looking for an excuse to cut class, and urged to advocate their cause in their free time, which was an apparently willful misjudgment of the strike. Also, to everyone who expresses an opinion that the participants of School Strike for Climate are solely interested in avoiding a school day, we would say: we do not know what your experience was, but we know considerably more fun ways to spend a day when you skip school than exposing yourself to the hatred of countless people who do not even know your name and demanding action in response to a crisis not so many want to acknowledge.

Since 2018, Greta Thunberg has become one of the most prominent climate activists worldwide. She is invited to many important political events. Her contributions are always very controversial, although she basically repeats the same message: if we do not radically change our way of treating the earth as if it were an unlimited resource at our greedy disposal, we ultimately endanger the existence of not only innumerable species but also our own. This message mirrors Arendt's principle of care for the world, and it is in line with the interpretation of her later writings as a gesture of acknowledging animals' plurality (Vasterling 2021). As animals, of course, are not the only living beings, we should also consider plants as potential subjects, as in the vegetal phenomenology proposed by Michael Marder (2013).

The initial act of Greta Thunberg resonates with Hannah Arendt's account of politics. She showed courage by stepping out into the public space. It was a spontaneous and free act coming from the decision of a responsible political subject. Based on her judgment, she started something new, unforeseen and unforeseeable. She gathered other people around her, people in their plurality, with their commonalities and differences. The School Strike for Climate was an act of civil disobedience, which created a space of power. Seen from this perspective, she represents, despite her young age, a superb example of a political subject.

Conclusion

Greta Thunberg is a girl in dark times, we could say, paraphrasing the title (*Men in Dark Times*) of Arendt's collection of portraits of women and men, who in times of crisis establish an "uncertain, flickering and often weak light that [. . .] will kindle under almost all circumstances" (MDT ix). She is a young political agent, who inspired an unprecedented rise of consciousness for her cause, and stepped up to Arendt's call for action when confronting a crisis:

> A crisis forces us back to the questions themselves and requires from us either new or old answers, but in any case direct judgments. A crisis

becomes a disaster only when we respond to it with preformed judgments, that is, with prejudices. Such an attitude not only sharpens the crisis but makes us forfeit the experience of reality and the opportunity for reflection it provides. (CC 171)

School Strike for Climate—today engaging young people in both school and university settings, adults of all ages, climate researchers, and activists—is a paramount example of Arendtian acting in concert, showing the importance of education for thinking and judgment, for who appears in the space of politics is not defined once and for all. With Arendt's account of the fragility of action in mind, we can say that even if the movement loses its impetus and the power wears off, what has been done will not be undone and the fabric of human actions is there for everyone to keep on weaving.

Notes

1. Arendt notes that events and acts appear rarely in human history compared with the everydayness of periods of perceived normality. She makes this remark in the course of a critique of social sciences with their statistical perspective on the world, obscuring the fact that the meaningfulness of human relationships is illuminated in such particular events, rather than in everyday behavior (HC 42).
2. As Reed and Weinman (2018: 5–7) reconstruct Arendt's understanding of action as a manifestation of our capacity to co-constitute a world through deeds and words: "To have agency is to have capacity to move and shake the world in alignment with the story one tells both about one's own actions and the way they appear in the world, to others," and such agency is enhanced by engaging and recruiting other humans into a given actor's enterprises. Agency, in this Arendtian line, is not the individual's ability to act, or a sort of sovereignty-over-self or autonomy; rather, it is the phenomenal result of action-in-concert and it takes the shape of an enterprise itself that brings people together.

Chapter 7

Social Justice and Feminist Agency

When in 1995 the volume of essays *Feminist Interpretations of Hannah Arendt* was published, the case became clear: feminists, too, could read Arendt and use her works and ideas for their reflections. This was not because there had not been feminist contributions to Arendt research (or Arendtian contributions to feminist research),[1] of which perhaps *Hannah Arendt and the Limits of Philosophy*, a book-length study of Arendt's storytelling by Lisa Disch (1994) deserves special attention, but because Bonnie Honig edited a volume whose topics ranged from Arendt's depreciation of the social to the feminist potential of her account of the public; from her figure of a conscious pariah to her controversial, to say the least, presentation of Africa and African Americans. It was the first collection of essays fully devoted to Arendt and feminism.

The reason for this volume's being a milestone in Arendt research was that her writings were seemingly inapt for linking with feminist thinking. For feminist theorists, she has been, and to a certain extent remains until today, either a riddle or a critical figure. The early feminist reception of her work was very negative, especially with respect to her distinction between the private and the public, since the central feminist claim—popularized first through the title of a 1970 essay by Carol Hanisch, "Personal is Political"—was that the private was precisely political. Arendt's, then seen as rigid, distinction between the public and the private was a red flag to feminists who did not spare her their criticism (Rich 1979: 211–12; O'Brien 1981: 100; Pitkin 1981: 338; Markus 1987: 76; cf. Young-Bruehl 1996: 307). This changed in the 1990s, when, according to the approach of "thinking with Arendt against Arendt" (Benhabib 1988), new generation of feminist scholars interpreted her works afresh and discovered multiple facets of her thought to be fruitful for feminist reflection. This includes a shift of focus from the role feminism plays in Arendt to the role Arendt plays in feminism (Honig 1995a: 3). In this way, the feminist reception of Arendt in the last three decades predominantly applies Arendt's concepts to current issues relevant to feminist debate

136

(e.g. Allen 1999b; Zerilli 2005a; Schott 2010; Borren 2013; Gardiner 2013; Kruks 2017; Robaszkiewicz 2018).

We start this chapter by reflecting upon Arendt's attitude toward feminism and her own experience of being a woman. We then move to what we see as the axis of what could be called "the Arendt problem" throughout the decades of feminist reception of her writings: her distinction between the private and the public, which runs against the feminist agenda. The critique of this distinction, and perhaps even opposition to it, was especially present in second wave feminism but is still central to the persistent feminist bias against Arendt today. We propose ways of transforming this contested idea so that it can be implemented within the feminist framework. In the last section of this chapter we suggest two spaces that Arendt outlines and which we see as apt for feminist thinking and acting.

Arendt and "the Woman Problem"

Let us start by looking at how Arendt situated herself as a woman and what personal experiences and convictions shaped this situation. As a starting point here we choose her notion of thinking. In Part I, we showed that Arendt saw her theoretical points, in the spirit of Socrates, more as proposals than as the deductive pursuit of philosophical truth or firm answers to questions previously posed. This gesture points toward her appreciation for the dynamic character of thinking, which always retains a possibility of rethinking, reassessment and revision. Both philosophical and the political thinking are activities that can strike different paths and by this token bring different outcomes. These outcomes may all remain valid as long as they do not deny facts and follow the principle of inner harmony: staying in tune with oneself. Like Socrates who prompts his interlocutors to think philosophically through his art of midwifery (PP 81), Arendt induces her readers to action through her exercises in political thinking.

Bracketing the results of her thinking is a serious theoretical gesture, which points to Arendt's affinity to phenomenology, among other inspirations to her thinking, and should not be mistaken for affected modesty. Arendt herself associates this "agnostic disposition" with her being a woman. When asked by Günther Gaus in their famous conversation if while working she would also think about the influence of her writings on her readers, she responded:

> When I am working, I am not interested in how my work might affect people. [. . .] What is important to me is the thought process itself. [. . .] You ask about the effects of my work on others. If I may wax ironical, that is a masculine question. Men always want to be terribly influential, but I see that as somewhat external. Do I imagine myself being influential? No. I want to understand. And if others understand—in the same sense that I have understood—that gives me a sense of satisfaction, like feeling at home. (WRLR 3)

This attitude, which prompts her to understand political phenomena and events, as opposed to approaching them with the arrogance and truth claim of a scientist assuming they can be grasped through an all-encompassing theory, is thus for Arendt a feminine virtue. What counts is thinking through and understanding itself, not certain knowledge, influence, or eminence among academic peers.

The above-cited passage is one of very few occasions when Arendt addresses her own condition of being a woman. The rarity of such remarks and their rather conservative tone led to skeptical, if not openly critical, reception of her writings on the part of feminist thinkers. Although she accomplished much as an intellectual, as a woman academic, and hence cannot be omitted from the history of women's emancipation, her nonchalant attitude toward herself being a woman is striking. In the interview quoted above, Arendt claims to be "old-fashioned" and thus to see some professions, specifically those requiring giving orders, as perilous to a woman who "wants to remain feminine" (WRLR 3); in 1959, when she was appointed the first female professor at Princeton University, she threatened to decline the position if the university persisted in emphasizing her gender in its press releases (Young-Bruehl 1982: 272). As Mary Dietz (1995: 19) argues, Arendt was reluctant to engage in the feminist movement, or what she called "the women problem" (Arendt 1932) generally, to the extent that she hardly ever even mentioned this topic.

And even though Arendt profited from the newly won freedoms, she did not rethink or reframe the status of women in her political framework. She remained largely blind to the feminist social and political agenda. One of the reasons might be her conviction of the fundamental equality of all human beings, which may be due to her seeing her origins in "the tradition of German philosophy" (Arendt 1978a: 246; cf. Dietz 1995: 18). And so, women for Arendt are primarily human beings among other human beings and their gender only matters in private. Her biographer, Elisabeth Young-Bruehl

(1996: 323), speculates that one of the reasons for her ignorance in this respect may be the fact that she has never been confronted with the necessity to reconcile the roles of an intellectual and a mother. Hence, while she hardly addressed being a woman—and a woman in the public sphere, as when she responded to the gender-related question of a *New York Times* journalist, "I am not disturbed at all about being a woman professor because I am quite used to being a woman" (Young-Bruehl 1996: 324)—the implications of being a Jew were theoretically more relevant and practically more tangible to her. Contrary to one of her feminist critics, Adrienne Rich, who, being half-Jewish herself, could write, "If asked to choose, I might have said [. . .]: I am a woman, not a Jew" (Rich 1993: 238), for Arendt her Jewishness was of social, and arguably political, relevance, while her being a woman was not. This difference in the intensity of experience might also be illustrated with reference to Arendt's contemporary, Simone de Beauvoir. While Beauvoir published her groundbreaking feminist study *The Second Sex* in the late 1940s, Arendt brought out *The Origins of Totalitarianism* at roughly the same time, and the books are even comparable in scope, as well as size.

Arendt and the "Social Question"

The central problem feminist scholars see in Arendt's writings until today is the way in which she frames the social. For her, not only is the social a hybrid space where political issues get privatized and private issues are drawn to the light of the public, but it also is the space which, in modern times, allowed for the emancipation of the subjugated, especially workers and women:

> The fact that the modern age emancipated the working classes and the women at nearly the same historical moment must certainly be counted among the characteristics of an age which no longer believes that bodily functions and material concerns should be hidden. It is all the more symptomatic of the nature of these phenomena that the few remnants of strict privacy even in our own civilization relate to "necessities" in the original sense of being necessitated by having a body. (HC 73)

Remarks like this, where the body and necessity are being connected by an unbreakable bond, and it is suggested that the working classes and women—specifically, their activities—have been brought out of their (hidden) place in the modern age, and are discursively being equated in their status with slaves, as chapter 8 of *The Human*

Condition might suggest, are appalling to feminist scholars. By banning certain issues from the range of political interest, Arendt seems to disrespectfully question all the things feminism is about: equality, empowerment of the powerless, appreciation for embodiment, and social justice.

Thinking with Arendt against Arendt—a gesture that has not gone out of fashion since feminists took an interest in Arendt in the early 1990s—Ayten Gündoğdu calls for an alternative interpretation of the depiction of the French Revolution in *On Revolution*, and by the same token, of the distinction between the political and the social. Gündoğdu argues that Arendt criticized the French revolutionaries not because they politicized poverty but because they failed to do so. She refers to the passages in which Arendt seems to suggest that the distinction between social and political issues is not firm, or negotiates conditions of possibility for certain social phenomena to appear in the public realm, and so gain political relevance. One such passage is her appreciation for the early labor movement (as opposed to the politics of trade unions), which forged a novel approach to politics, connecting questions of economic justice, social change, and democratic government (HC 216, 219; cf. Gündoğdu 2015: 56–9). Another was the discussion at the 1972 conference in Toronto where Arendt, confronted with questions about concrete examples of political issues, suggested that there was room for contextualization about which issues belong to the public realm, saying, "At all times people living together will have affairs that belong to the realm of the public—'are worthy to be talked about in the public.' What these matters are at any historical moment is probably utterly different" (Arendt 1979: 316; cf. Gündoğdu 2015: 64). Like Bonnie Honig (1995a), Rahel Jaeggi (2007), or Marieke Borren (2013) (to name just a few) before her, Gündoğdu (2015: 83) argues for the politicization of social issues to be possible, but adds that they are in need of translation, which would allow them to be recognized as "worthy to be talked about in the public": "politicizing of any social injustice involves a *translation* that can represent it as a shared problem that hinders equalization and freedom among a community of actors."

This mostly happens, we might say, in times of crisis, and it both requires and provokes political participation. In certain times and places, people have a feeling of being distant from the actual operations of power in the sense of institutionalized politics. This might happen when the democratic administrative framework functions properly and the quality of life is high enough not to provoke engagement or when people live in politically underprivileged spaces, explicitly discouraging them from such engagement. Arendt sees mass society as a kind of space that dampens people's public interest, spontaneous action, and, with its individualistic focus on the nuclear family, community relations. The model with which she contrasts this is the polis. Still, if we think of the ancient polis or of democratic societies today, action is only possible among equals. And then as now, our communities consist of those who belong, who are equals, and those who are, to different extents, seen and treated as unequal. As Arendt acknowledges, the Athenian democracy insisted on the equality of those who belong to the people and its institutions, all the while accepting as an absolute and necessary fact that most people neither were nor could be equal to the equals, and such '"unequals"—especially women, foreigners, and slaves—would secure means of existence for everyone, while the privileged could use their "leisure time" for political activity (HC 14; WA 105).

Today, even in republican democracies, these basic conditions of political action remain the same: acting is only possible between equals, and political equality is neither natural and self-evident nor universal. If one assumes, as Arendt does, that the experience of political freedom is *per se* worth striving for, it becomes a motivation for acting entirely in a political manner, in the sense of overcoming the routines of one's everydayness and, in Arendt's words, beginning something new. Now, if not every individual has equal access to this practice, we are dealing with an injustice concerning the most significant of human faculties. This injustice affects women today differently than in the time before suffrage was won, when even formal equality was a distant dream.[2] Nevertheless, the underrepresentation of women in what can broadly be described as areas of political participation is still very significant; women's rights concerning personal freedom and security, bodily integrity, equal pay, and property are denied, in jeopardy, or being negotiated in many places around the world. The injustice persists and needs to be addressed through thinking as well as political speech and action.

Another possibility of transforming Arendt's account of the social for feminist thinking and beyond would be to focus on social marginalization and, specifically, identity politics. Identity politics grew out of the protest movements of the second half of the twentieth century, and theorists like Iris Marion Young (1990), Axel Honneth (1994), or Charles Taylor (1994) influenced its shape. The main idea is to approach social and political marginalization and injustice as referring to specific social groups with shared identities. The normative core of such theories lies in the demand of the recognition of these groups' identities. After its rise in the early 1990s, identity politics seemed outdated. As Nancy Fraser (2007: 24) has cogently argued, this approach involves a twofold danger for any project in expanding agency, but especially feminist agency in the relevant sense: the overemphasis on the question of identity at the expense of social equality on the one hand; and the relocation of the active part from the marginalized to third parties, who execute the act of recognition, on the other hand.

Marieke Borren (2013: 198, 202) argues in this regard that Arendt's concept of political action offers an original approach to the problem of political marginalization of women. She shifts the emphasis of the feminist agenda from recognition of women in their group identity as women to the claim for the increase of the political participation of women as marginalized individuals. The focal point of the marginalization is now not the lack of social justice but the lack of political freedom in Arendt's sense. Thus, a static model of recognition is being replaced by a dynamic model of political participation, even if—as Arendt's account of action allows—it is outside of traditional political institutions. In this way, marginalization is eliminated not externally but from within, through the active commitment of the marginalized themselves, and this results from the common power of free action instead of from "being saved" through the charity of a third party. An apt example here could be the late nineteenth- and early twentieth-century struggle for suffrage, which, in virtually every society where women fought for the right to vote, has rather been won than granted.

As Borren (2013: 205) further stresses, Arendt's concept of power as empowerment allows emphasizing the advantages of such an approach: only the active participation of women in the public sphere provides them with the possibility of realizing their capacities as political beings and thus to experience political freedom. What is crucial, though, is that according to the human condition of plurality, even if every woman (setting aside the fragility of defining this notion) experienced her being a woman similarly in some respects, this would not result in any coherent "women's identity" because for any human being, gender is only one of multiple conditions shaping their lived experience. As Bonnie Honig (1995b: 150) notes, "Arendt would have been quite wary of any proclamation of homogeneity in 'women's experience' or in 'women's ways of knowing.'" In this sense, there is no "women's identity," and being a woman is not a political position. This is why all projects conceived as a "women's party," in the sense of institutionalized politics, are ephemeral. What seems to be a shared basis—being a woman or an identity common to all women—soon proves to eclipse quite different experiences and, decisively, political opinions (Robaszkiewicz 2018: 204–5). Of course, some elements of lived experience will be the same or very similar for all women inhabiting a certain space, as for example being subject to the same (oppressive) legal regulations for women who are citizens of the same state. To be sure, whether we then see these regulations as oppressive or not will be a question of our judgment and, in consequence, our political opinion.

In spite of this eligible critique, we argue that something can still be made of identity politics in our context, as some feminist theorists, like Lois McNay (2010) or Allison Weir (2008), turn in their newer writings to what they call "transformative identity politics," whose foundations have already been illuminated by Susan Bickford (1997). Her account of anti-anti-identity politics is opposed both to classical identity politics (we may add to Fraser's points of critique one more: identities are often given to individuals forming a group from the outside, as an instrument of control [Bickford 1997: 120]) and to critics of identity politics. She points to authors like Gloria Anzaldúa, María Lugones, Adrienne Rich, and Audre Lorde, among others, to develop a nuanced concept of identity as multidimensional and evolving from inside the group:

> I use the word "multidimensional" to indicate more than that identity is multiple, although multiplicity is part of it. The further point is that identity plays different kinds of political roles, is related to power in different ways. "Identity" thus has multidimensional effects in the world. (Bickford 1997: 119)

Such identity could bring together different dimensions of social positioning, embodiment, class, race, gender, or any other condition relevant for the groups' members, opening a possibility of defining identity not as a clear but a fuzzy notion, still providing a basis for common action. This understanding of identity may be read in connection with Arendt's plurality, bringing certain conditions—be they political, social, or private—that are common to the "us" of a group or a community together, and politicizing them so that they become a motivation for action.

Now, this section has focused on what we see as the central problem feminists have with Arendt's account of politics. But what (if anything) can Arendt's writings offer to contribute to feminist thinking and acting? In what follows, adding to what has already been said in this respect by other authors, we present two political spaces that Arendt outlines, and which can well accommodate feminist action.

Feminist Action

In what way can Arendt's account of politics be used in feminist thinking, even if we decide to think with Arendt against Arendt every now and then? Does such an account of feminist agency help us to reformulate and reinvigorate the productive critique of Arendt's thinking from a feminist perspective?

Let us return to Marieke Borren's claim that political participation was Arendt's central interest. For the question of the marginalization of women, this means two things: first, political and social equality is not achieved through an act of liberation from above or outside but through a continuous practice that allows the marginalized to experience political freedom. Second, the liberating power of politics can unfold in a broad spectrum of political attitudes, due to its unlimited content. The common world opens to everyone in a different way and this plurality of perspectives is indispensable for its existence. Hence, our answer to Pitkin, who objects that Arendt simply cannot clarify the content of "that endless palaver in the agora" (Pitkin 1981: 336), is that Arendt aims precisely at securing the contingency of political acting and speaking. The participatory freedom is realized in and through acting, regardless of the particular content of opinions and of pragmatic political goals.[3] Contrary to Habermas's (1977) interpretation of Arendt's theory of action in terms of deliberative democracy directed toward a social consensus, we argue that it is dissent that secures the continuous existence of the public and hence of the common world. Only in this way is the plurality of acting agents simultaneously presupposed and safeguarded. If today's feminism is challenged by an internal plurality of, often dissenting, discourses and attitudes, it is a good sign of its being politically alive. As we argue further in this chapter, plurality in this context is to be seen not only as a source of conflict but also as an opening for a worthwhile exchange.

Further, the expansion of women's political participation can only serve as a remedy for their marginalization if the problem of alleged elitism in Arendt's understanding of the public space and the domain of politics is opened up through new projects of increasing inclusiveness, including inclusiveness grounded in the kinds of material conditions Arendt was reluctant to see politicized. Generally, women can be prevented from political participation on two levels: a positive and a negative one. On the first level, there exist positive legal obstacles, as for example the denial of suffrage. On the second level, women are indirectly excluded from acting politically because they lack political competence due to their disadvantaged situation in society (Beauvoir 2011: 35). The first problem is to be solved through the inclusion of entire social groups: here, through the successful battle for women's suffrage. In the second case the means of inclusion must be individually implemented to enable a sustainable increase in political participation. The gain of suffrage is a single act (preceded historically in virtually every case by a long struggle), but it is only the continuous political participation of women that amounts to a genuine emancipatory achievement.

This aim can be accomplished only through reinforcing political competence, which involves both political thinking and acting. However, as Arendt (WF 155) underlines, one needs courage to step into the light of the public because there, sustaining not life, as in the private realm, but the world—the human in-between—is at stake. As political agents, even at the microscale of informal political encounters, we expose ourselves to others to involve them in acting in concert and hence refrain from the protective way of life we assume as living and fragile beings. When showing courage in stepping out of our safe space, we substantially transform care for the self into care for the world. This certainly is a challenge, and not every individual—especially if her position is inferior or precarious, as many women experience themselves in various societies today—is ready to take this step.

Arendt's exercises in political thinking might provide adequate means for reinforcement of political knowledge, supporting women in gathering their courage, intensifying and sustaining their political participation. As the quality of enlarged thinking depends on the diversity of perspectives that we take into consideration, the multiplicity of women's perspectives becomes relevant. This is because, in judging, considering marginalized voices is not only necessary but also decisive. As Donna Haraway (1988: 584) writes, "'subjugated' standpoints are preferred because they seem to promise more adequate, sustained, objective, transforming accounts of the world."

The marginalized see the world from a distance, which is the prerequisite of the position of the situated spectator, but it is often unattainable to the privileged, who occupy an established position in society. Perspectives and opinions which gain broad acceptance tend to display a certain homogeneity, which in some cases may even result in the suspension of political freedom and, when politics and history become automatic, in the petrification of societies and civilizations (WF 168). Privileging the previously marginalized helps us consider a greater variety of views and thus allows a better orientation in the common world in just the way Arendt argues:

> If someone wants to see and experience the world as it "really" is, he can do so only by understanding it as something that is shared by many people, lies between them, separates and links them, showing itself differently to each and comprehensible only to the extent that many people can talk *about* it and exchange their opinions and perspectives with one another, over against one another. Only in the freedom of our speaking with one another does the world, as that about which we speak, emerge in its objectivity and visibility from all sides. (IP 128–9)

Including marginalized voices does not predetermine or overdetermine what one is supposed to think but shows how to think politically, developing and improving one's political judgment; and the specific content of the political opinions held by those demarginalized political actors will depend upon their individual judgment. Such demarginalization and appreciation of unheard voices and unseen perspectives needs political practices and spaces in which these practices can be performed. In what follows, we examine two such spaces that Arendt outlines in her writings: councils and political friendship.

Feminist Spaces of Action

FEMINIST SPACE OF ACTION I: COUNCILS

Only once does Arendt suggest institutionalizing political action, and the institution she proposes proves to be just as ephemeral as the practice of acting itself. In *On Revolution*, she praises the councils that emerged in the course of many revolutions but which have been—due to their unstable character—misrepresented, or even forgotten in political history. In Arendt's view, councils offer a noteworthy, though never fully implemented, direct-democratic alternative to political parties, which only remotely represent the opinions of their voters and merely react to changes in the public mood (OR 249–55). Arendt's suggestion of councils as a suitable form of direct democratic institution confuses many of her readers, because it seems not only utopian but also very limited through the exclusion of the social question from its range of interests. But councils are for Arendt, similar to the polis, only a model of a public space, which could and should not be interpreted as a pragmatic solution. Councils serve as a good model because they capture the volatile nature of acting: they are a spontaneous, unexpected, unprompted phenomenon, and so an example *par excellence* of political action (Robaszkiewicz 2017).

In this context, Bonnie Honig (1995b: 150–1) reminds us of Arendt's appreciation of Rosa Luxemburg, especially of her unwillingness to belong. Luxemburg was a member of parties and associations but Arendt reads her biography as that of a radical politically conscious agent, through the lens of political excellence. Of course, Arendt mentions that being a woman was one of the factors that made Luxemburg an outsider (MDT 44–5). In the same breath, she diagnoses Luxemburg's distaste for the women's emancipation movement and points out that describing her as a self-conscious woman would indeed be a limitation of her political potential. Honig (1995b: 150) points to a similarity with Arendt's self-perception here, expressing "a certain respect for Arendt's refusal to be a joiner, for her wariness of identity politics and of membership in identity communities."

Such communities certainly included not only identities Arendt associated with natural and societal elements of the human condition but also political parties with a pre-established program and party discipline. In this respect, she (OR 164) depends on Luxemburg, who with "such amazing clearmindedness" pointed out that the programs were the major separating line between parties and councils, "for these programmes, no matter how revolutionary, were all 'ready-made formulas' which demanded not action but execution—'to be carried out energetically in practice.'" Arendt describes councils as spaces of spontaneous action, spaces of freedom, in which party membership plays no role, and whose aim is to transform the existing political order so that every member of society can participate in politics on an equal basis (OR 262–4). Arendt was drawn to councils as a mode of politics closest to her own account: councils were ephemeral like action itself, reminiscent of Arendt's account of the agora as a space for debate and action.

For her part, Arendt (HC 46) considers the lack of public spaces in which equality could manifest itself, spaces in which citizens could express their opinions and hence lead a public debate, as one of the main challenges of large democracies. As soon as these spaces exist, it is up to the citizens themselves to muster the courage to step out into the light of the public realm and act politically. She realizes that her model of councils has its limitations: only some will be willing to participate. The spaces of freedom are supposed to be open to everyone, but only some will claim them, and often not because of either determination or indifference but because of the very material conditions that Arendt seeks to exclude from political deliberation in her critique of "the rise of the social" (HC 38–49). The others, says Arendt (1969b: 233; OR 355), who have no interest in political participation, will have to accept the fact that decisions will be made without them. The question of structural political injustice is absent from her account: some citizens—for example, women or ethnic minorities—are marginalized and underprivileged based on cultural, legal, and political situations. Their access to political action can thus be severely limited. And so, this problem needs theorizing beyond these limits and it needs practice to display such spaces of freedom, as Arendt herself exemplifies through her model of councils, which she describes as "islands in a sea or as oases in a desert" (OR 275). The women's strike in Argentina, to which we refer in the conclusion to this chapter, is one such example.

Feminist Spaces of Action II: Political Friendship

Feminist authors and activists rarely use the concept of friendship to describe their relationships with other women outside of a personal context. It is rather solidarity, differently construed, that was (e.g. hooks 1986; Mohanty 1997; Allen 1999a) and still is the concept of choice, as in Verónica Gago's *Feminist International* (2020: 45): "Solidarity is our weapon." As a non-feminist, but an author inspired by Greek culture, Arendt chooses rather political friendship as her model of common action. *Philia politike* is a concept that can be traced back to Aristotle, who emphasized that friendship is necessary for life (NE VIII.1, 1155a5). The political mode of friendship presupposes mutual care and common interest on the part of fellow citizens (NE VIII.11, 1160a12), and so it becomes a condition of the common good of a political community, since it is aimed at the reciprocal advantage of all participants. It also aims at pursuing virtue, because it implies that friends wish each other well in an unbiased way (NE VIII.2, 1155b). Accordingly, friendship consists in the coexistence and communion of talking and thinking (NE IX.9, 1155b). It is this last, communicative aspect of *philia politike* that is crucial to its meaning in Arendt's concept of political judgment. Although she herself uses the term in only a few places, political friendship provides a very plausible model for the mutual relationship of the members of an Arendtian acting community and, at the same time, the normative basis of a speculative community of judgment.

Friendship appears at a basal level in Arendt already in the silent dialogue between I and myself. What Arendt values in the Socratic way of thinking is the "dialogue partners being friends" (LoM I 188). The one who is in disharmony with herself is in a much worse situation than if she had the whole world against her. Thus, the friendship that one cultivates with oneself is based on inner harmony. The plurality that is at the core of this dialogue is not a plurality of *doxai*: the world appears to one only in a way that one can reflect in the inner conversation. This is why the friendship between me and myself is not yet *philia politike* in the proper sense. Arendt describes the externalized dialogue between political friends as follows:

> The political element in friendship is that in the truthful dialogue each of the friends can understand the truth inherent in the other's opinion. More than his friend as a person, one friend understands how and in what specific articulateness the common world appears to the other, who as a person is forever unequal or different. [. . .] Socrates seems to have believed that the political function of the philosopher was to help establish this kind of common world [in which each citizen could show his opinion in its truthfulness and therefore understand his fellow citizens], built on the understanding of friendship, in which no rulership is needed. (PP 83–4)

Political friendship requires a plurality of perspectives on the common world, and what follows from it—a multiplicity of *doxai*. The dialectical character of plurality, based on the interplay between difference and sameness, also determines the nature of *philia politike*. Therefore, Arendt reads Aristotle speaking about the friend being another self through the lens of the Socratic tradition: that the self is a kind of friend (LoM I 189). Crucial here is the effort to understand the other perspective. Be it in a real conversation that accompanies action, be it in an imaginary dialogue of the extended way of thinking, the dialogue partners meet each other at eye level. The genuine will to understand the specific way in which the world opens up to another becomes the basic condition of life within a political community.

Arendt emphasizes the difference between intimate and political friendship. While the former takes place in the private sphere and in a sense resembles love, the latter takes place in the public sphere, between people acting together, and has little to do with intimacy. As Arendt states in a letter to Gershom Scholem:

> I have never in my life "loved" any people or collective—neither the German people, nor the French, nor the American, nor the working class or anything of that sort. I indeed love "only" my friends and the only kind of love I know of and believe in is the love of persons. (Arendt 2008: 466–7)

Love, Arendt argues, cannot survive exposure in public—it needs the protection of the private, based on the unity and lack of distance between lovers (HC 51–2). Similar to other emotions, it does not belong in the public space. Emotions abolish the distance between people, necessary to disclose oneself as a who, in similarity and difference to other people. This is why, by definition, emotions cannot be relevant in the public sphere, because the distance between actors acting in the political realm is the *sine qua non* of plurality and, therefore, of the political in general. When human emotions enter the public sphere, they are always instrumentalized, as in the case of fraternity—a kind of attraction that intimately develops between the oppressed in politically inconvenient times and is based on presupposed and predefined common humanity. Arendt (MDT 11–17), opposing Rousseau's notion of human nature based in egalitarian compassion, understands fraternity as an intimate feeling of togetherness that abstracts from all differences in view of a difficult situation and relies on the mutual compassion of people belonging to the oppressed group. Since it is peculiar to the "enslaved groups of people," it represents a response to worldlessness—the fact of being banished from the public sphere. In the feminist context, we could transfer this critique to the notion of sisterhood, as defined by Joanne Cutting-Gray (1993: 36) as "sympathetic sisterhood [. . .] based in naturalized gender difference, shared sympathy or shared suffering." This is certainly an interpretation of the term closer to Arendt's critical understanding of fraternity, but also diverging from the role it played in second wave feminists like Robin Morgan, *Sisterhood is Powerful* (1970), or Audre Lorde, *Sister Outsider* (1984), where sharing an oppression was primarily not a ground for compassion but an empowering incentive for resistance and action. Obviously, as fraternity, and in our case sisterhood, are based on what Arendt held for natural or social conditions, so her reading was different, which reminds us of the reflections on politicizing the social earlier in this chapter.

Arendt contrasted fraternity with *philia politike*, which is to be understood as a relationship based on the critical attitude between people who can enter into constructive polemics with each other. Her example is Lessing's *Nathan the Wise*, where this kind of friendship, as she argues, is a polemical relation. It is established between the different protagonists of the play, who, although they live in "dark times," through this intersubjective relationality open space for exchange, consensus, and dissent between different opinions and thus come out of the darkness to appear in the public space. The humanness here is realized in political fashion: in conversations with friends that are held for the sake of the common world, for what unites them—concern for the common world—is as important as what distinguishes them—*doxai* as ways in which the world opens up to each of them individually and uniquely (MDT 24–5). Through conversations between friends that foster expressing judgment and positioning in the world, mutual respect is expressed:

> Respect, not unlike the Aristotelian *philia politike*, is a kind of "friendship" without intimacy and without closeness; it is a regard for the person from the distance which the space of the world puts between us, and this regard is independent of qualities which we may admire or of achievements which we may highly esteem. (HC 243)

The distance created by such a communicative process is not only the condition of possibility of political plurality, but also makes political friendship a model for the community of judgment. The openness to the opinions of the others that is necessary for the enlarging of one's thinking, on the one hand results from the pursuit of the common good and, on the other hand, results in polemical pleasure, which are both parts of political friendship.

The feminist movement can be seen as a revolutionary space of political friendship. In this way, it conflates both spaces we outline above, which we see as having potential for feminist thinking and action. Not only today but from its very beginnings, feminism was not a dogmatic formation but rather a powerful movement which, while united in the aim of equality and freedom from patriarchal oppression, inhabited—as it still does—multiple perspectives, practical approaches, opinions, discussions, agreements and disagreements, and diverse assemblages. It may be exclusive or inclusive (Pearce et al. 2020; Koyama 2003), radical or liberal (MacKinnon 2007; Friedan 2010); it may draw its strength from the past or from (an even utopian) future (Hagengruber and Hutton 2021; Fielding 2017), from nature or technology (Mies and Shiva 1993; Haraway 1991, 2016). Feminists agree or disagree with each other in academia, in the media, and in the streets. As a critical position, feminism in its different guises is dynamic: opinions, alliances, and oppositions are not fundamentally set once and for all but, as political practices, are subject to further development, rethinking, and change. This makes the feminist movement a space of plurality *par excellence*, and prompts us to actually speak of feminisms, in the plural.

From the point of view of the Arendtian world, such versatility is desirable. The conditions of acting in the common world must always be renegotiated; judgments need to be in flux, even though they do serve us as guiding points in every moment. And these judgments and positions in their plurality are the source and at the same time a worldly manifestation of freedom. Without the confrontation of the different *doxai*—if we all agreed with each other—the public would become an "automatic process" in which all participants hold the same opinions, and the world would "petrify" (WF 167). For Arendt, consensus is not the aim of communication in the public space and it even proves destructive, as it entails unifying and hence tyrannical force. Thus, as mentioned above, Jürgen Habermas (1977) is right in emphasizing the communicative basis of action in Arendt, but he is mistaken in assuming that this communication is consensus-oriented. If Arendt's public space is co-constituted through political friendship, then it is neither, as Benhabib (1993: 102–3) states, "based on the power of persuasion and consensus," nor just, as Honig (1995b: 146) suggests, a "variety of (agonistic) spaces," but a space where both elements, consensus and dissent, converge in a dialectical fashion to remain alive (Allen 1999b: 102, 106).

Conclusion

Hannah Arendt was not a feminist. But the reception of her works by feminist thinkers, booming in the 1990s, proves that they do have great potential—be it controversial or constructive—for feminist theorizing. In this chapter we have shown how Arendt, while not being a feminist thinker or feminist herself, may still be seen as stimulating for feminist thinking. If one wanted to express it in a positive way, perhaps like Socrates: a gadfly irritating the people of Athens to motivate them to thinking and better understanding of the world and themselves. If Arendt was a feminist gadfly, she was a very unconscious one. It was only twenty years after her death that reading her works from a feminist perspective in any other way than critical became commonplace. Still, it remains thinking with Arendt against Arendt.

This does not change the fact that those of us who are familiar with this constructive take on Arendt see many events of feminist relevance today as Arendtian moments. One of those is the feminist strike in Latin America as described by Verónica Gago (2020). Gago and her *compañeras* from the Ni Una Menos collective came to mainstream media attention when in December 2020 a law legalizing free abortion up to the fourteenth week of pregnancy was passed in Argentina. This was the culmination of a decades-long struggle focusing on different issues of feminist relevance, varying from economic oppression to the wave of femicides flooding Latin America. In her book, Gago emphasizes the radically innovative character of the activism that developed in the process: the strike connected not only different groups of women but also other people who suffered from various forms of gender-based violence, particularly due to neoliberal practices of exploitation. Since many women cannot strike within the union framework, as they work illegally or from their homes, opening up the strike beyond any institutional framework (Gago 2020: 14) offered them a revolutionary possibility to raise their voices and transform themselves from victims into fighters, in a political sense (Gago 2020: 13). Driven by what Gago (2020: 2) calls "feminist *potencia*" (a desiring capacity, a force rendering what is perceived as possible), women and other feminized subjects protest against multiple forms of gender-related violence.

The strike, as described by Gago, seems to be a very Arendtian moment. It is an excellent example of free, plural, spontaneous, and concerted action. The informal political spaces emerging within the strike, even though not councils *sensu stricto*, are very close to them in their revolutionary spirit. Close friendship between engaged women and other activists has a definitely political character and is based in common action. And yet, Arendt is mentioned in Gago's book exactly once, in reference to Judith Butler's work. So why is

153

Arendt absent in Buenos Aires? We hope that this chapter has offered some clues in this respect.

Notes

1. The included bibliography comprises around fifty titles; some of them, however, do not focus on Arendt but rather refer to her among other theorists.
2. The last country to grant women the vote was Saudi Arabia, where women have had active and passive electoral rights in municipal elections since 2016 (El-Naggar 2016).
3. Patricia Owens (2012: 306) also comes to this conclusion, stating that for Arendt acting is a distinctive mode of being with others or concern for the public, understood as care for the world.

Chapter 8

Human Rights and Popular Sovereignty

We now turn our attention to two contemporary controversies that strike the general imagination as both pressing and necessary to consider in consultation with Arendt, namely claims concerning the rights of migrants, especially forced migrants, be they asylum seekers or refugees; and the populist impulse often unleashed within democratic societies in their wake. Arendt's work, especially *The Origins of Totalitarianism* and "We Refugees"—a very rich and reflective essay drawing on her own experience as a forced migrant—is generally considered canonical for anyone who wishes to confront issues surrounding the normative basis for what Seyla Benhabib (2004) calls "the rights of others," meaning what is owed politically by democratic states to those who are not their citizens but are within their sphere of influence, domestically or abroad. This is attested by the plethora of works available that address this issue while working closely with Arendt's mid-twentieth-century discussions of these issues; this chapter will primarily focus on Ayten Gündoğdu's (2015) recent reformulation and application of Arendt's arguments concerning statelessness and the international human rights regime that was just emerging when Arendt wrote *Origins*. Alongside this, many turn to Arendt today for an analysis of the populist tendencies that continuously reappear under conditions of popular sovereignty, especially as displayed in the electoral politics of the past decade and its controversial use of the plebiscite, most strikingly in the case of Brexit. Here, we cite in particular the work of Margaret Canovan (1981, 1999, 2002), which, having been written before the shocks that followed the breakdown of the mainstream consensus about the putative "end of history" and global hegemony of the liberal democratic order, seems to us the first resource to which we should turn to gain a perspective on the rise of populism and renewed (ethno) nationalism since the 2007–8 global economic crisis. Our central novel intervention in this chapter is to argue that Arendt's engagement with the issues of statelessness and human rights, on the one hand, and of populism and popular sovereignty, on the other, may be read more consistently together, expressly as regards their relevance for politics today.

Statelessness and the International Human Rights Regime

One central point in Arendt's work, also significant for her public participation, is her critique of human rights, as they were established by the United Nations in 1948, and her articulation of a defense of "the right to have rights" in order to guarantee the rights that any person on earth, regardless of whether or not they have legal status as nationals or resident aliens, can legitimately expect from the state in which they reside. In this section, we return to her argument and its relevance for what might well be the greatest crisis facing liberal democracies today as they aim to be true to both their commitment to open borders and societies and their commitment to democratic procedures through majoritarian decision making: the growing and seemingly unstoppable flow of migrants, often irregular migrants from the Global South into the democracies of the Global North. Most salient is the number of persons displaced by political instability in the Middle East and the Russian invasion of Ukraine, highlighting national boundaries within and at the borders of the European Union.

Arendt's main claim in the famous ninth chapter of *Origins*, entitled "The Decline of the Nation-State and the End of the Rights of Man," is that the history of defining, establishing, and protecting human rights was—from the very beginning—an exercise in the alignment of state power with emergent national identities. There was, Arendt argues, always a pretense and sometimes a genuine intention on the part of liberal states to extend the provision of the rights declared to belong to man and citizen to all people within the territorial sovereignty of those states, regardless of their nationality or lack thereof. However, as she memorably puts it, once the horrors of the First World War had unleashed a wave of displaced persons across the landmass of a devastated Europe, "The arrival of the stateless people brought an end to this illusion" (OT 276). Arendt shows, in other words, that the dream of universal human rights was exposed as a fantasy in the wake of the refugee crisis of the interwar period.

But what does the growing tide of displaced persons today suggest concerning the expectations that any person, irrespective of national origin and place of residence, may have of the state and/or of established international institutions with respect to hospitality and membership? In particular, how and why do these expectations come into conflict with the collective will formation of democratically constituted peoples? Still more pointedly, is there, for Arendt and *tout court*, an inevitable conflict between the rights of migrants and popular sovereignty? Our suggestion will be that—in the current state of affairs—these two norms are put in an almost unresolvable contest, for two reasons: first, human rights protections are based on either nationality or humanity, rather than personhood; second, these claims have a legal, rather than political, character. For both reasons, whatever their moral merit or legal validity, human rights constantly run the risk of lacking democratic political support and therefore legitimacy.

Following Gündoğdu (2015), we argue that the basis for demands for hospitality and membership ought to be political personhood, not humanity or nationality. Drawing on this, we further suggest that political personhood differs from humanity as the normative underpinning of claims to hospitality and to membership in two key respects. First, it picks out something distinctive about human beings not as a natural kind, whether taken as humankind or the human species, but in our power of participation in collective practices of meaning-making action, even if such participation has been disrupted or abrogated by recent events. Second, while the burden of defining legal personhood falls on the institutional actor, be it a state or an international body that has jurisdiction to recognize it, in the case of political personhood such a burden rests with the individual human being who acts or may act, and not on the institution that responds to such action.

Humanity and nationality, whether alone or together, are inadequate either to the task of establishing the legitimacy of this expectation or to the challenge of making that expectation enforceable (Weinman 2018: 129–34). For, surveying existing charters and conventions and their enforcement, it is clear that notwithstanding the increased attention it has received in the post–9/11 world, statelessness is not merely a pervasive problem that affects well over one in a thousand people worldwide, but also that it is a problem that is getting exponentially worse and promises only to intensify.

Not just the persistence of statelessness but also the lingering inability to define precisely who is stateless and thus merits the conferral of new national status point to what Alison Brysk and Gershon Shafir (2004) describe as "the citizenship gap." This gap, by which the authors mean the misfit between the universalist norms of possessing human rights and the particularist facts of possessing membership in a nation-state, is an increasingly prevalent problem under conditions of globalization and the "global war on terror," but the roots of this gap are much deeper. Shafir finds in Arendt's analysis

> the fundamental paradox of modern citizenship: since the sovereign nation-state was the primary enforcer of the "inalienable" and, therefore, universal human rights, individuals enjoyed rights not by virtue of their humanity but by virtue of their membership in [. . .] a particular, territorially based nation-state. (Shafir 2004: 23)

It is their membership within a nation and not their humanity, Benhabib (2004: 3) follows Arendt in asserting, that ascribes to individuals their putatively human rights, or more accurately, their "right to have rights."

The Irresistible(?) Tension between Migrants' Rights and Peoples' Will Formation

If, as Arendt and these contemporary authors working in her wake argue, there are these manifest shortcomings in the current approach based on the nation-state as the addressee for claims made by and concerning "the rights of others," which persons can in fact legitimately expect to receive hospitality and membership, and how? We hope to show that whatever amelioration can be found using the existing means of redress, the *aporia* Arendt identified in statelessness is no more a "puzzle" or "perplexity" concerning this tension; it is a genuine impasse. The only way to get through it well is somehow or other to disentangle the basis of the legitimate expectation for recognition of an individual's right from the basis of providing such recognition, the nation-state. Absent such disentanglement, we will forever find ourselves insisting on persons presenting themselves for recognition as nationals, so that a given national state can recognize them. The contemporary history Arendt recounted and our own contemporary history prove that this is doomed to fail as there simply are persons who are not nationals, and we cannot make the legitimacy of their expectations for recognition dependent on their having national status.[1]

Weinman (2018: 137–41) argued that systematic shortcomings remain in the capacity of existing human rights instruments to provide for the recognition of non-citizens' rights, and that promising proposals to address these shortcomings (like those of Weissbrodt

2008 and Gündoğdu 2015) require not merely new practical instruments in order to meet the normative demands of rights claimants but also a new normative framework to justify the legitimacy of the rights claims they make. Drawing on Arendt's thinking about plurality, here we call such personhood "political personhood" to stress its character as "an appearance in public" that constitutes the political in Arendt's sense, and to stress its salient differences from mere legal personhood. The *locus classicus* for Arendt's account of action as appearance in public, and as involving both acting and speaking, is Chapter 5 of *The Human Condition*.

Stateless persons expose the precariousness of even the most basic articulations of human rights as the challenges they face amount to the near impossibility of a viable existence. Since acting is only possible in the space of appearance, it is impossible to appear in that space if one is both formally and legally invisible. Membership in society, under such conditions, is profoundly difficult, if not impossible (Borren 2008). Facing stateless persons, we see the concrete expression of the systemic exclusion, pervasive but subtly hidden from view, that results from basing the right to have rights on a territorially sovereign state's recognition of an individual on that individual's status as a national of either that state or another such state. It is just this precariousness that Gündoğdu (2015: 21) calls attention to when arguing that "one of the most fundamental forms of rightlessness manifests itself today in the speechlessness of migrants," a plight that "suggests that one's speech is rendered meaningless or not taken into account" whenever a sovereign state finds that doing otherwise might be contrary to its interests and/or is not required by either its own laws or by the international agreements to which it is subject.

This abjection of the individual human being in the face of the state actor who effectively may alone grant human rights, analyzed so decisively by Arendt, is at the heart of many contemporary interventions on the fragility of the international system of human rights protections. A striking instance of this is a public comment on the ongoing "migrant crisis" in Germany and the European Union at large during summer 2015 by Omri Boehm (2015), who wrote that "in order to address the refugee crisis not only would Germany have to change, but so would political philosophy itself." The change that he and Gündoğdu, both following Arendt, envision here would not merely compel state actors such as the Federal Republic of Germany to recognize non-citizens in a radically different fashion than they do at present. Such a change would also entail that we acknowledge "the right to bear rights" as belonging to every person who has a claim to make on states, and non-state actors, as political persons. This is so regardless of whether or not such persons possess legal personality, and in particular their status as regards bearing a nationality. The violent exclusion of non-citizens from the status of those recognized by and before the law is disquieting because of the central focus of Arendt's analysis throughout Part II of *Origins*: the intertwined histories of ethnically homogenous nation-states and the spread of global European empires, phenomena through which citizens' rights and their protections came to be inscribed within national laws and international agreements. Gündoğdu provides a clear expression of Arendt's main conclusion about human rights guarantees as they currently exist: as

> the egalitarian dimensions of the nation-state were further undermined with the rise of imperialism and emergence of tribal or ethnic national-isms, it became even more difficult to invoke the Rights of Man to claim equal rights for those who were not nationals. (Gündoğdu 2015: 44)

Thus, both the formal structure of rights as something granted by the state and the specific history of those states point toward a fundamental challenge to the possibility of equal rights for all human beings on the basis of their shared humanity. Nor should we believe that merely by changing either the express content of existing rights instruments or the emphasis on state actors and the agreements that they reach among one another can we achieve the transformative change that Arendt and those who follow her are calling for. On the contrary, as Gündoğdu (2015: 44) concludes, "Arendt's critical inquiry suggests that, although some institutional structures are more promising in terms of offering effective guarantees for equal rights, no institutional form, including an international, postnational, or even cosmopolitan one, can be entirely free of these tensions." Which tensions exactly? Primarily, those between the legitimacy of an individual's expectation to equal protection of the law and the territorial sovereignty of a state or other institutional actor that claims responsibility for determining by its own grant who may or may not legitimately make a claim to that protection.

The sense of a right as something that is taken, rather than granted, is also integral to Gündoğdu (2015: 101), who points to the way in which Arendt's "theatrical understanding of personhood as an artificial mask created by law" is "very much in accord with her phenomenological approach to politics, which calls into question the metaphysical traditional that privileges 'being' and is suspect of 'appearances.'" For, as Gündoğdu (2015: 102) paraphrases Arendt's ultimate conclusion in Chapter 9 of *Origins*: "If personhood is an artifact, and not an inherently given essence—if there is no intrinsic overlap between humanness and personhood—then it is quite possible that not every human being is automatically recognized as a person." Such a lack of recognition is not only quite possible but, as we see in the face of the persistent presence of the stateless and their impaired political personhood and prospects for a fulfilled life, it is something like a constant fact of life, even under conditions of the rule of law and putative equal rights for all. For this reason, we simply cannot abide continuing with the status quo, where the subject to whom rights are granted and in whom equal personhood is recognized oscillates ambivalently between the essentialized "human being" and the historically determined "national citizen." We need to articulate a new normative and practical basis for the legitimate expectation of political and legal recognition of individuals as deserving of equal treatment.

Personhood and Peoplehood: An Inevitable Conflict?

As Arendt recognized, the traditional, metaphysical conception of the human is intimately paired both formally and historically with the national state as the party competent to recognize, simultaneously, the nationality and the humanity of the putative legal person who stands before the law. Thus, in order to address statelessness and the rights of others, we must at the same time and by means of the same normative and practical reformulation of the "Rights of Man" remove the emphasis on the essential individual and on the national state that is composed of such essential individuals, if we are to overcome the fundamental impasse at the heart of human rights as a concept and rights claims in practice.

Here we see why, again following Gündoğdu (2015: 165), it is necessary to take our "starting point not from a foundation derived through justificatory procedures but instead from *political practices of founding human rights*." Responding to the critique of foundationalism in Benhabib (2004), Gündoğdu (2015) echoes Arendt's response to Kant that, however important even inescapable institutions and legal orders are for the articulation and protection of equal civil and political rights, they will never be adequate for ensuring anything like equal access to the political realm as the space of appearance, insisting that we take "Arendt's call for a right to have rights" as the means by which we attend "to the political and ethical dilemmas that pervade new beginnings" (Gündoğdu 2015: 166). Politics, for Arendt and for the present analysis, is just the act of always beginning again from one's phenomenologically determined moment within the shared world of human natality: this ungrounded ground of the humanity we share "as men, not Man," with all its contradictions and lacking universalist grounding, holds the best promise for overcoming the violent politics of exclusion that the metaphysical tradition and universalist tradition of human rights perversely extends, even as it attempts to institutionalize the legal proscription of such exclusions.

Legal personhood—however grounded in essential metaphysics and/or historically situated national and international legal instruments—must give way to political personhood as the normative and practical basis of the legitimate expectation for recognition. But what, concretely, does this mean? What concrete political action does this entail? Gündoğdu (2015: 192–3) centrally stresses, among other instances, the political mobilization of the *sans-papiers* in France, who choose to occupy "public spaces that they are not entitled to inhabit" so as to "contest the immobility and invisibility imposed by the lack of legal status," and thus by "'taking' public sites, they come out of the shadows and establish a state where they can appear to others as subjects entitled to equal rights." In advancing this claim, she draws on the work of Bonnie Honig (2003: 98–101), who emphasizes "the importance of unauthorized practices of 'taking' for democratic politics." For the millions of undocumented migrants in France and across the European Union, as well as for the millions of undocumented migrants in the United States, the current international human rights regimes offer no substantial protections and so they remain in legal limbo and in perpetual precariousness.

For these reasons, lived reality stands in stark contrast to the legal prescriptions regarding national status and the equal rights of citizens and non-citizens within liberal democracies. Following Arendt's perceptive analysis of the fundamental aporia attendant on the embedding of the universalist frame of human rights within the particularist system of nation-states, our contention here is that the most promising way to address this misfit between the legal fiction of equality and the lived reality of precariousness is a redesign of both the normative basis and the practical mobilization of the legitimate expectation for hospitality and for membership, at least limited membership, for all persons living within democratic societies. Here, precisely, we see the power of a shift away from a framework based on the granting of rights to human beings-as-nationals—those recognized as legal persons—toward a framework based on the taking of rights as political persons.

Why does this intractable problem of statelessness press itself again in contemporary global politics in much the same way and with even more force than in the mid-twentieth century when Arendt discussed it? To answer this question, we must broaden the scope of analysis beyond "people on the move" and what is to be done about them, in order to examine an inherent instability within the notion of "the people" on whose behalf and in whose name states adjudicate the question of drawing and administering the crossing of national borders, both physical and figurative. The question of personhood, in other words, is inseparable from the question of peoplehood: there is no way to address, and redress, the *aporia* springing from the confusion of humanity and citizenship without first addressing the ambivalence that haunts "popular sovereignty," namely who is, and who are, "the people?" More precisely, does "popular" here describe the way in which sovereignty in a democratic polity resides in the hands of the *demos* (or *populus*)? Or does it rather denote that sovereignty in a democratic regime belongs to the leader or leaders who represent the collective, popular, will? This latter ambivalence, as Arendt notes and confronts time and again in her major works, amounts to a fundamental fissure between those mobilizations that are legitimate and democratic and those that are illegitimate and massive.

Democratic Sovereignty: Popular or Populist?

How can we tell the difference between legitimate popular sovereignty under the rule of law and an illegitimate mass-based, often ethnonationalist, sovereigntist regime? For Arendt, in her most sustained analysis of this question—her analysis of the "mob" and the "mass" in Chapters 5 and 10 of *Origins*—it is possible to pass such a judgment on the basis of what is mobilized when a movement attains "critical mass," specifically through its possession of a republican character or its lack thereof. In short, a movement can be either massive (populist, [ethno]nationalist) or republican, but it is never both. For this reason, the distinction between democratic and mass mobilizations brings clearly into focus the spectacular aspect of liberal democracy that its critics, such as Carl Schmitt (2005 [1922]) and those who follow in his wake, often miss through their myopic focus on its representative and institutional aspects. The question to be answered in this regard is this: Is one or another manifestation of "people power" a spontaneous self-expression of an artificially constituted people, bound to one another as members of a polity by, through, and under the rule of the law? Or is it a mass mobilization with tyrannical intent, a mob action expressing a totalitarian, or a figuratively or literally tribal, ideology? Margaret Canovan (2002) attempts to disentangle this thorny bramble of the people in distinction from the mob or the masses in her discussion of Arendt, focusing on how the republican significance of "the people" is constantly in tension with its massive significance.

Arendt's most consulted treatment of this dialectic is her descriptive and normative analysis of the French and American revolutions in *On Revolution*; in broad terms, her overarching claim is that the former was a failure because *le peuple* carried a massive significance in the winning interpretation, while the latter was a relative success because the people carried a republican significance in the winning interpretation.[2] As Canovan (2002: 404–9) demonstrates, Arendt's seemingly impossible simultaneous sympathy for "people power" and antipathy for "mass action" and/or "mob rule" needs to be explained by teasing out one consistent set of meanings for three key terms: mass, mob, and people. The basic argument is this. First, Arendt distinguishes "mob" from "people" by showing that while both the mob and people rest on being anchored in the class system, only the people is a class-based collectivity normatively oriented toward the public as such as the basis of solidarity. Next, the "mob" is to be distinguished from the "mass" by the different grounds of their worldlessness: while "mass worldlessness" rests on the complete absence of a world, a space of appearance, the worldlessness of the mob rests on its having lost its own place in a world that it still recognizes as existing. An alienated mass—of workers, for instance—lacks a world altogether and calls for the reconstruction of that missing world in a way fundamentally different from that of the mob (of "True Finns" or "Yellow Vests") calling for their country or their lives or their autonomy to be "given back" to them.

These two different forms of world-alienation bring into sharp focus what makes a people a people for Arendt, in essential differentiation from a mob, a mass, or a tribe. As Canovan (2002: 408–9) summarizes it, the "difference between the People and their

Others [mob, mass, or tribe] seems repeatedly to hinge on relation to the 'world' and relation to 'reality.' Non-Peoples are in some sense 'worldless,' whereas the People share a human world." This distinction is, at first blush, as clear as it is stark—and also problematic, for more than one reason, Eurocentrism, if not outright anti-Black racism, chief among these, as will be discussed in Chapter 9. But, as Canovan (2002: 409) notes, it remains unclear upon reflection how Arendt's theorization of the worldlessness of the mob, mass, or tribe in opposition to the "common world" of the people is meant to map onto specific groups of people appearing together within a specific geographical and temporal context. One can see this most pointedly in Arendt's often criticized attempt to demonstrate this difference by arguing that the failure of the French Revolution and success of the American one is best explained by the manner in which the Jacobin excesses of France's revolutionary moment undermined the possibility of forming what Lincoln would describe as "a government of the people, by the people, and for the people," which the American experiment avoided through its constitutional system of limited government and distributed powers. Salient critiques of Arendt's argument to this effect can be found in Asad (2003), Moyn (2008), and Scheuerman (1997).

With Arendt, we argue that a politics unapologetically grounded in the collective action of the people can still be something other than the mobilization of a body politic of "brothers" grounded on the exclusion of countless abject and savaged "others." This slippage from a republican politics growing out of the natality and plurality of a *demos* to a mass politics based on a monolithically defined *ethnos* concretizes Arendt's abstract claim that worldlessness, in particular the lack of a common world and hence a common sense based on living together in that common world (see Chapters 1 and 5 for more on these themes), undergirds the distinction between the massive and republican significations of the people as the bearers and agents of sovereignty under contemporary democratic conditions. In *Origins* and elsewhere, Arendt worries that democratic majorities might forget the intimate connection between politics and plurality while finding the promise of popular sovereignty in the rule of a unified and monolithic people that is identical with the majority, in terms of race, religion, or other identity markers.

This is immediately relevant for the recent resurgence of ethnonationalism because there is an intrinsic tendency toward the cultivation of (ethnic, cultural, racial, national) sameness, rather than political equality, within the body politic at the heart of what is called popular sovereignty. We can find this suggestion—in different forms—across Arendt's corpus: in her analysis of the aporia presented by the grounding of universal human rights in intrinsically particularist national citizenship (*Origins*, chapter 9); in her discussion of the "frailty" of the polis as a space of appearance that can only persist in contexts that are constituted in and constitutive of freedom, natality, and difference (*The Human Condition*, especially chapters 1 and 5); and in her reading of the tragedy of the Jacobins, and its legacy through the subsequent revolutions and revolutionary movements (*On Revolution*, especially chapter 2).

Siobhan Kattago (2017: 37) has recently observed that the renewed rise of ethnonationalism, often identified with populism, coincides with the renewed interest—both theoretical and, crucially, practical—in Carl Schmitt's jurisprudential and political-philosophical arguments concerning sovereignty and the primacy of the executive. The fascination with what could be called Schmitt's arch-sovereigntist approach to the constitution of public space and public life, as well as governance and law, emerges in this light as one symptom of a broader return to the politics of resentment: a reaction against the multilateralist and anti-nationalist wave of democratic institution-building in the wake of the 1989 revolutions. Kattago (2017: 42) quotes historian Timothy Garton Ash, who claims that what "'we are seeing in 2015,' [. . .] 'is Europe's reverse 1989'"; she thus calls our attention to the "irony of building walls" in Europe after the fall of the long-standing Berlin Wall. Kattago (2017: 42) underscores this claim by reminding readers of the further unfolding of this phenomenon: "the Slovakian President Robert Fico was ready to accept Christians only." Viktor Orbán achieved notoriety with his decision in the summer of 2015 to seal the Hungarian border with a razor-wire fence and his suggestion in September 2016 to deport refugees to camps housed either "on an island or in North Africa" (Kattago 2017: 42).

Digging beneath the surface of these events and decisions—and other leading indicators of the deeply entrenched successes of a renewed ethnonationalism, such as the destruction of the refugee camp in Calais and the related Brexit vote, the attacks on the independent judiciary in Poland, the rise of the AfD in Germany, and more—it is not hard to find a popular, if not populist, policy of intensifying the physical presence and efficacy of walls and fences, after three decades of policy meant to minimize the purpose and the presence not only of such boundary markers but even of political boundaries themselves. Why? As we have seen in this chapter, Arendt gives an account that transcends the particular efficient causes and aggravating factors of the current re-emergence of this populist and ethnonationalist impulse within democratic sovereignty, namely that whenever a popular movement takes on a massive character, resulting from and contributing to the worldlessness of those it unites against some common enemy of the people, its popular success will entail a rise in the populist construal of the popular sovereignty held to be the one and only true source of power in that polity.

Wendy Brown (2010: 47) both exemplifies and explains why so many have turned to Schmitt as a thinker for our time in her incisive discussion of Schmitt's analysis of sovereignty as a secularized theological concept, stressing the "co-constitutive relation of sovereignty, theology, and enclosure," by which she means the way in which a fence and/or wall quite literally and physically "founds and relates sacred space and sovereign power." This is why, as she observes, Schmitt uniquely advances the position that the capacity and competence of the sovereign to decide what is inside and what is outside is the fundamental constitutive moment. One crucial site of this "decision power" is of course the state of exception and the status of the constitution itself. At the most fundamental level, however, it is not the power to demarcate what is inside or outside the law in its normal administration; rather, the most primary decision power is that with which the sovereign and the state constitute one another together, and this is by marking off that territory that falls inside the sovereign's ambit from that which does not. And, along with that, determining who has access to the territory that both constitutes the state and makes it possible for the state to exercise its competence in the world.

As Brown (2010: 48) argues, this is the "theological aspect in late modern walling projects" and is one blatant, unmistakable sign of, and reaction against, "the decline of nation-state sovereignty." The wall-building project is indicative of a fundamental tension within liberal democracies insofar as they cast themselves as, and understand themselves to be, a site of popular sovereignty: since "sovereignty" is usually discussed as the alternative to the rule of law, sovereignty itself is taken to be "the state's power to act without regard for law or legitimacy" rather than as "the power of the demos to make laws for itself" (Brown 2010: 48). But what happens when, as is apparently the case all across the post-socialist space in central and eastern Europe—and not only there—democratic majorities call for and endorse politicians who provide policies that are grounded in a democratic sovereigntism that seeks to wall off, physically and legally, an ethnically defined demos from the rest of the world? For Arendt, and we join her in this conviction, the answer must come from a renewed connection between the political recognition of the personhood of human beings as human and the self-understanding of the people that is sovereign in and by that order as republican in Canovan's sense of Arendt's understanding of that term. Only such a renewed and politically underwritten connection, and not (as now) the legal recognition of human beings as residents or citizens of a particular constituted order, can ensure that all persons enjoy "the right to have rights."

The People's "Massive Significance"

Following the work of Peter E. Gordon (2007) and Samuel Moyn (2008), Yael Almog (2021) has recently called attention to the way in which Arendt's thinking about a common world and her attempt to preserve a plural politics constitutes both a form of German Jewish thought and "Weimar political theology" and a rejection of the main stream of that thinking as embodied in Schmitt and Walter Benjamin, especially the latter's "Theses on the Philosophy of History" and "Critique of Violence." It would take a longer work devoted to unpacking this theme and especially the unique place of Augustine as both an authority and a foil in Arendt's work—as it reaches across her corpus from her early *Love and Saint Augustine*, through the closing sentence of *Origins*, the continual return of early Christianity's reception and partial rejection of the classical concept of civic immortality in *The Human Condition*, and her two very different reflections on the reconstruction of Virgil's *Novus Ordo Saeclorum* in the early American republic in *On Revolution* and *The Life of the Mind*—to do justice to this sense of Arendt's work.

For the moment, however, and bearing in mind Brown's appropriation of Schmitt and the current politics of resentment that has taken hold in the United States and across Europe, the remainder of this chapter aims to show how Arendt's analysis of popular sovereignty teaches us about the spectacular mythologies of democracy. These mythologies somehow always center on the executive as a site of mediation between the "two bodies" of the people as an afterlife of the "two bodies" of the king in medieval and early modern political theology (Kantorowicz 2016 [1957]). Arendt's discussion of Robespierre's distinction between the "popular societies" (read: political parties) of Revolutionary France and the "one and indivisible popular society" that is the French people itself is especially illuminating in this regard (OR 243–47). Arendt (OR 244) argues that "this conflict between the government and the people, between those who were in power and those who had helped them into it, between the representatives and the represented, turned into the old conflict between rulers and ruled and was essentially a struggle for power," noting that "Robespierre himself, before he became head of government, used to denounce 'the conspiracy of the deputies of the people against the people' and 'the independence of its representatives' from those they represented, which he equated with oppression."

Whatever the consistencies of Robespierre's actions with his stated beliefs about the popular will and the division of sovereignty in government before and after the literal and figurative deposition of the king, what is clear to Arendt and relevant for the main thread of this chapter is how popular sovereignty must possess a warrant, whether or not it is divided and whether or not it is distributed in a system of representation. Such a warrant, as we saw in Canovan's analysis of Arendt's discussion of related issues in *Origins*, can be either massive or republican, but never both. In this sense, for Arendt, it is of vital importance that Robespierre and the Jacobins decided for the former in a conscious rejection of the latter. As we have tried to show in linking Arendt's acute analysis of the structural legal and political challenges presented by the global governance of migration with her discussion of mass mobilization, this particular Jacobin legacy has repercussions for politics under conditions of popular sovereignty that are relevant directly down to the practices of democratic politicians such as Viktor Orbán, no less than autocratic leaders such as Vladimir Putin or Recep Tayyip Erdoğan (Vormann and Weinman 2020: 20–3). A fuller discussion of Robespierre in particular and Jacobin policy in general, as Arendt understands it, and the way they influence contemporary politics would require a longer reflection on her analysis of the place of "the social question" in shaping popular sovereignty in Revolutionary France, the main subject matter of chapter 2 of *On Revolution*. This would, however, take us beyond the limits of our focus on popular sovereignty and its tensions with human rights protections in this chapter.

Arendt's reading of Robespierre as the execution (and executioner) in practice of Rousseau's theory of the *volonté générale* can be considered an episode in the wider project of reconstituting Arendt's political theology in general. That wider project would have to follow a path from the comparison of the French and American Revolutions Arendt pursues, through the various attempts to constitute popular sovereignty within the liberal order over the nineteenth and twentieth centuries and in the Soviet Union, and then again in the wake of the Second World War, and finally in the period since the end of the Cold War. While we cannot follow this trail in all its detail and with attention to each moment within it, we can see one important legacy of Arendt's analysis of the travails of popular sovereignty in the late eighteenth century by contrasting it with contemporary controversies.

From Robespierre to the Unified Executive and Orbanism

Arendt presents Robespierre as the original modern precedent of the unlimited executive as the agent of the undivided popular will, who serves as something of a foil to the American founders, meaning, for Arendt, primarily John Adams, Thomas Jefferson, and James Madison (OR 420). For all their differences, especially on the question of the utility or viciousness of political parties that so obsessed Robespierre, they are united in their opposition to the form of political partisanship advocated and implemented with such spectacular violence by Robespierre. Given this American counterweight, it is remarkable that the most robust example of executive power in contemporary liberal democracies, notwithstanding the president of the Republic in France, is the president that has emerged in the American Republic since, especially, the end of the Second World War. Following Brown's account of Schmitt's salience in thinking about popular sovereignty in our time, we look to and at this newly created office of the (unified) executive precisely as an office and not in terms of the current occupant of that office. In this light, it is necessary to ask: Why is the executive today, even when in fact the democratically elected holder of a constitutionally restricted office, cast as the strong sovereign and builder-of-walls, like Kings David and Solomon of ancient Israel?

Isaac Ariail Reed (2017) has argued in interpreting the phenomenon that is President Donald Trump as the second body of the American people, and following Jeffrey C. Alexander's (2010) work on Barack Obama's rise to power, that liberal political modernity is a particular instantiation, in practice, of the mythology of "the people."[3] Nothing is more important for this mythology, as Alexander (2006, 2010) argues, than the spectacle of national elections, especially the quadrennial festival that is the presidential election, which become one main locus for working out in detail the dynamic interrelation between the sacred and the profane, the civil and the anti-civil, often in the person of the presidential pretender himself—and it is always "himself" in this mythology, notwithstanding the nomination of Hillary Clinton (2016) and the election of Kamala Harris (2020) to the office of vice president.

Of course, there remains a complex difference between the king's two bodies as a way of representing power in state–society relations, and the people's two bodies as a part of the complex, interlocking systems of the modern globe. Filling the breach that remains in this hiatus with the values of popular sovereignty—when interpreted by democratic electorates and political leaders as democratic sovereigntism, that is, as the representation of the people's sovereignty in the person of the decisive executive—can take a wide array of forms. These forms and the policies in which they materialize might be based on an internationalist rule of law based policy; or a state–sovereigntist pure policy of pure decisionism and a politics of friendship and enmity; or any of a series of models that mediate or blend these two. In this light, it appears, one would do well to understand what is popular and what is populist in democratic sovereigntism, without collapsing popular sovereignty into populism (as self-avowed populists often do) or defining populism as a defamation or denial of "true" popular sovereignty, as populism's most fervent critics—such as Jan-Werner Müller (2016: 6)—often do.

The so-called refugee crisis and where it leaves the concept, if not the practice, of solidarity as a basis for political mobilization in Europe and the expanded European Union thirty years on from the revolutions of 1989 presses upon us anew the worry that democratic majorities are motivated by a massive, rather than republican, sense of popular sovereignty. Writing in this vein, Siobhan Kattago (2017: 37, 40) argues that in the widely noted success of nationalist far-right movements across the globe, "today's disenchantment" with the EU and with the "liberal order" "is deeper than disappointment with representative government" and is in fact indicative of a politics of resentment that shifts "political debate from solidarity and community to fear of foreigners and disenchantment with politics in general." This shift, in light of Canovan's account of Arendt, may not be so much to do with short- or medium-term trends in post-1989 politics and its shortcomings; rather, it may be an expression of the permanent possibility for popular sovereignty to take on a massive, rather than republican, significance for the majority or at least the sufficiently great number of voters. Thus, citizens of these democratic nation-states might well persist in electing governments that will not accede to the view of the governing elites of the traditional EU powers.

As Kattago (2019: 25) argues elsewhere in a reflection on the contemporary salience of the analysis of the aporia of human rights in *Origins*, the ethnonationalist right's success might well be predicated on the very structure of liberal modernity, where to be a citizen and to be a rights-bearing person are considered identical in principle, but where in practice this means that if you are not a national citizen—if you are stateless or otherwise have no recognized or recognizable nationality—you are rightless and utterly abject. What is the possible alternative to this scenario? What could form the basis of solidarity neither grounded in ethnicity and exclusion, nor floating in the ethereal inclusion of the market where (à la Marx) all that is solid melts into air?

Conclusion

If the Arendtian views espoused by Canovan, Gündoğdu, and Kattago, among others, are correct, then the conditions of a properly popular popular sovereignty, not grounded on the politics of exclusion, would involve a self-consciously mobilized people that interprets its relationship to its elected leadership as one of delegation for the sake of preserving a space of appearance for a politics based on what Arendt describes as plurality. A corollary follows upon this conclusion: we ought not hold, with Foucault (2010) and the American revolutionaries of 1776, that modern democratic societies succeeded in "replacing sovereignty with governance" and ask to what effect it did so. Rather, with Arendt and moving beyond the resources her written works provide, we must raise and at least begin to answer, two questions about the performative character of democratic sovereignty, hedged between power and authority, as she struggled to reconceptualize this pair of related social phenomena.

First, how did the conditions for successfully performing sovereignty change when they came to include the requirement to perform "the people"? Following the analysis of two very different recent campaigns for the US presidency grounded in the personal charisma of the candidate offered by Reed, writing about Donald Trump, and Alexander, describing Barack Obama, we have argued that an essential aspect of this shift rests in the would-be representative of the people successfully performing in public as the second body of the people, itself the object of an interpretation shared by the would-be elected official and the electorate to which the "power of the people" will be delegated and from which act of delegation the authority of the president derives in deed as well as in principle.

Second, how does sovereignty intersect with other forms of modern power (e.g. financial capitalism)? Following Brown's appropriation of Schmitt, we hope to have shown that while sovereignty is often positioned by both policymakers and theorists as being in a zero-sum game with financial capitalism—where, if it is possible to provide each with a fictive agency, capitalism always and only wants open borders and the free flow of labor and capital, and sovereignty always and only (or mostly) wants closed borders and strong physical and legal impediments to those flows—the reality is far more complex. We have found that savvy political actors in the Visegrád countries in particular have been able to couple a sovereigntist commitment to the enduring meaning of the borders, both physical and spiritual, that surround and protect "the autonomy of the people" with capitalist commitments to trade and security agreements. Might this be the newest development of a popular sovereignty with a massive significance, that successfully counters the republican vision of popular sovereignty in a unified federation of Europe envisioned by Jürgen Habermas (1997) and others?

Notes

1. The reader interested in more on this with reference to Arendt's treatment of statelessness and the right to have rights might consult Benhabib (2004), Menke (2014), and Waldron (2000).
2. Canovan (2002: 403), following Bernstein (1996: 61, 111, 126–33), observes that even while Arendt was amply aware of the ways in which "informal and powerful" mobilization can do tremendous harm, in the form of mob behavior or mass mobilization, the term "'the People' was an honorific term in her vocabulary," and perhaps one can reasonably call her politics themselves "populist," insofar as "she often seems sympathetic to informal political action."
3. Alexander's central focus is the mythical connection between electorates and presidential candidates, who emerge onto the cultural scene via heroic narratives, often managed by campaign staff and public relations

Chapter 9

Thinking With and Against Arendt about Race, Racism, and Anti-racism

Parallel to the growing academic and public popularity of Hannah Arendt's writings in recent year, doubts about and open critique of her pronouncements concerning race have been on the rise, prompted especially by events around the #BlackLivesMatter movement. Priya Basil (2021) laments—with a hint of anachronism—about her disappointing rereading of Arendt as a racist; Ayşa Çubukçu (2020) points to the discrepancy in her treatment of 1960s rebel movements, praising (white) student revolt while condemning "black violence"; the *Jerusalem Post* (Frantzman 2016) calls Arendt a "white supremacist." At the same time, local initiatives in Berlin and Leipzig advocate for renaming streets and squares dedicated to her. In his recent reconstruction of Arendt's body of work for a general readership, Arendt scholar and pragmatist philosopher Richard J. Bernstein (2018) makes two main claims concerning what we will call "the good, the bad, and the ugly" legacies of Arendt's thinking concerning race, scientific racism, and anti-racist activism relevant for contemporary political life that we wish to emphasize and extend in this chapter. Here, we review the continuing scholarly and popular controversies about what Arendt wrote concerning race and discrimination, chiefly in Volume II of *The Origins of Totalitarianism* and in her essay "Reflections on Little Rock," which we have briefly summarized above, in Chapter 6.

Before we descend into those details, let us flag that, like Bernstein (2018: 52), we agree with Danielle S. Allen (2004) and Kathryn T. Gines (2014),[1] among others, that Arendt did not understand "the depth and political consequences (even according to her *own* concept of politics) of vicious discrimination against Blacks in America." Indeed, as was already clear at the time Bernstein wrote a few very eventful years ago, current political events make clear that race continues to be a major fault line when it comes to the interweaving of social equality and political equality that so troubled Arendt in her diagnosis of "the rise of the social," but Arendt herself misses this in her treatment of race-based discrimination in America. All the same, Bernstein (2018: 52) continues, "if we think with Arendt against Arendt, then we discover resources in her writings for confronting the perniciousness of racism today." Or, as Franco Palazzi aptly notes, it is worthwhile to

> offer an alternative to both the decades-long systemic underrepresenta-
> tion of Arendt's writings on race (often dismissed as negligible accidents
> in an otherwise bright intellectual production) and a more recent, icono-
> clastic tendency which sometimes seems aimed at (rightly) stigmatizing
> her prejudices, but little more. (Palazzi 2017: 395)

We agree, and might stress further that Arendt actually offers resources for contemporary anti-racist thinking that we would not find elsewhere. To retrieve them, we need to enter into dialogue with her, even if we find the judgments she herself made when thinking in public about these matters in the 1950s wrongheaded. We will discuss those judgments in detail shortly. But first, let us clarify what resources in particular Arendt has to offer that justify the claim that "thinking with Arendt against Arendt" is not just a pithy phrase but also good *praxis* that can actually advance our understanding of the obstinacy of race-based discrimination. In the case in point, this entails recovering how and why her own exercise went so badly wrong and how we might do better today embracing Arendt's model of exercising political thinking through imagining the possible, and not actual, perspectives and opinions of others.

For, it is the strength of Arendt's honest assessment of judgment's inextricable connection to opinions, themselves always evolving and limited by the imaginative power of the would-be judge, that at the same time exposes the frailty of her account of responsibility, in particular as she mobilizes that concept with respect to the school desegregation debate at the heart of "Reflections," which she frames there—following the conventional language of the time—as "the Negro question." When, for instance, Gines (2014: 129) concludes that "Arendt's representation of the Negro question as a Negro problem rather than a white problem is an indication of her poor judgment," she makes the point that the poverty of Arendt's judg-ment is a function of how Arendt "does not adequately imagine nor represent the standpoint of African Americans or Africans [. . .] because her image of Black people is always already distorted and partial." What is crucial, and frankly painful for readers of

Arendt like ourselves who recognize her thinking as an irreplaceable resource for their own, is that she, as Allen (2005), Gines
(2014), and Palazzi (2017), for example, show in great detail, wrote
"Reflections" without a proper or thorough knowledge of the facts
about what exactly happened in Little Rock and why it happened in
this particular way, perhaps carried away by a political emotion. She
confused the names of the Black school girls depicted in press photos,
misunderstood the absence of the Little Rock Nine's parents, and
apparently had no knowledge about the history of school segregation
in the South, only installed after 1877; and this list is far from being
complete. We could then conclude that through her uninformed
judgment, Arendt failed to live up to her own account of "enlarged
mentality." Starting from this point, this chapter hopes both to
uncover more fully the reasons for Arendt's poor judgment in questions of race that she makes in "Reflections" and *Origins* but also
uncover the meaning of her writings (especially *Origins*) to critical
thinking about race and racism, and in the same breath to ask: What
is the ultimate salience of Arendt's own understanding of judgment?

Returning to Arendt on Race with Sixty Years of Hindsight

Holding in mind this presentation of the stakes in thinking "with
Arendt against Arendt" about the tensions between the exercise of
judgment and Arendt's practice of conducting exercises in political
thinking, which is necessary for the survival of the political in her
sense of public life, let us now see what brought Arendt to express
her judgments of race and politics in the manner she did, what those
views actually were, and why and how they have proven so controversial. As a guide, we will follow Roger Berkowitz's (2020) account of
her "Reflections" and its contemporary salience.[2] Both his summary
of Arendt's commentary and his response to the controversy about it
up to the present day are helpful to give us an overview.

Berkowitz (2020: 141–2) contends, after summarizing some of
the central arguments about "Reflections" offered by Gines (2014),
Owens (2017), Norton (1995), and Burroughs (2015), that the most
revealing critique might still be that of Ralph Ellison (1965: 343–4),
who argued that when Arendt wrote that "black parents should
fight their political battles and not send their children to do so" she
showed that she "has absolutely no conception of what goes on in
the minds of Negro parents when they send their kids through those
lines of hostile people," and how Black parents have no choice but

to initiate them into the racist world where a child "is expected to face the terror and contain his fear and anger *precisely* because he is a Negro American." Arendt, Berkowitz (2020: 142) continues, "found Ellison's response persuasive," acknowledging in a private letter to Ellison, now available through the Library of Congress archive of her papers, that

> her original criticism of the NAACP for using black children to fight adult political causes misunderstood the "ideal of sacrifice" so important in the black community. [Arendt wrote:] "You are entirely right; it is precisely this 'ideal of sacrifice' which I didn't understand; and since my starting point was a consideration of the situation of Negro kids in forcibly integrated schools, the failure to understand caused me indeed to go into an entirely wrong direction." (Berkowitz 2020: 142)

Berkowitz (2020: 142) insists, however, that Arendt scholars (Seyla Benhabib 1993, Elisabeth Young-Bruehl 1982, and Jill Locke 2013 are his examples) are wrong when they "argue that Arendt's letter to Ellison is an admission that she has abandoned her essay"; for the truth is that "while Arendt admits she was wrong in her characterization of black parents, she never retreats from her principled criticism of forced integration." We must not simply wash our hands of the matter and close the case on "Reflections" by concluding that Arendt abandoned her rejection of National Guard enforced desegregation. Rather, with the benefit of six decades of hindsight, Berkowitz (2020: 142) finds that it is our task to come to terms with how Arendt both "fully opposed legal segregation and Jim Crow," holding it to be "absolutely necessary to abolish the Jim Crow laws enforcing segregation," while also judging it wrong "to force desegregation on Southern whites who were vehemently opposed to integration," because "discrimination in the social sphere may be the result of unjust prejudices, but it is also a basic right."

Coming to terms with how one person can hold both these views might not be easy, especially because we tend to frame our worldly reality as a rational system, where such contradictions should not take place. In this context, Arendt might be the theorist to illuminate not only the fact that our world is endlessly complex, but also that (ostensible) contradictions are a part of it. This and her lack of broader knowledge about the circumstances of the Little Rock events are of course not an excuse for her misled judgment, in the latter case quite the opposite. Two points, however, should be mentioned for a better understanding of the complexity of the interpretation and critical discussion around the essay, especially in the context of judgment. First, Arendt was speaking from the background of her ontology of the common world, and second, her focus was primarily on children being put in the role of political actors in the particular case of school desegregation.

As for the first remark, according to her framework from *The Human Condition* (which was published roughly at the same time as "Reflections"), she distinguishes between the political and the social and sees school as being a social institution and hence a kind of club where people can associate according to their taste. However, as we argue in Chapter 1, what appears as political is dependent on particular worldly conditions, such as time and place; every human activity or concern can be politicized under favorable circumstances. We must disagree with Arendt's placing school in the realm of the social. There are numerous historical examples—beyond the desegregation of schools in the US South in the 1950s—of (often clandestinely) school being a locus of political resistance and struggle for protection of cultural identity, rights of minorities, and women's rights, to name just a few. bell hooks (1994), for example, was a schoolgirl herself at the time of school desegregation in the US South and her experience was quite contrary to Arendt's intuition: while before integration school was a place of radical self-reinvention for the students and the education of Black children was a political commitment for the teachers, desegregation brought depoliticization of school education, racism, and the dullness of knowledge only being about information: "For black children education was no longer about the practice of freedom" (hooks 1994: 3). Perhaps the most striking fact in this context is that this was the case for Arendt herself, who in the age of fifteen felt offended by her teacher and led her classmates to boycott the teacher's classes. As a result, she was expelled from school (Young-Bruehl 1982: 34). Why did she insist that school is a social matter, then?

This can be explained in light of the second point: in "Reflections," Arendt focuses on the protection of children. She is consistent in emphasizing this necessity, not only in "Reflections" but also every time she comes to speak about children. Indeed, it was the media coverage and especially the picture of Elizabeth Eckford trying to enter the school, surrounded by a vicious mob, obviously harassing her, that shocked Arendt and prompted her to write the essay, a political reaction to what deeply moved her.[3] In "The Crisis in Education," which we discuss more broadly in Chapter 6, she describes children as newcomers, according to her concept of natality. Children, she argues, as "human beings in process of becoming but not yet complete," need to be protected from the world instead of being "forced to expose themselves to the light of a public existence" (CE 183). This view not only fits into her phenomenological anthropology but, we would argue, has to do with her own experience with and observations of the National Socialist regime, which instrumentalized children, stripping them of their potentiality for the new and changing them through relentless ideologizing into little soldiers of the cause. We also find it interesting that Arendt speaks about the protection of the New and protecting it from a premature initiation, but as Allen (2005: 36) explains, the children at the heart of these events were no newcomers but rather experienced in their condition of Blackness in a society predominantly ruled by white people. All this might shed some light on Arendt's insistence on protecting children from the public, though the question of who qualifies as a child and who no longer does remains open.

Arendt was judging as herself, in the sense of trying to take as many perspectives as possible into consideration, but not stepping into someone else's shoes. Hannah Arendt as the author of *The Human Condition* is not another persona than Hannah Arendt as the author of "Reflections." We can see what results in this particular case as an expression of crass ignorance or as the best possible judgment from a very underinformed standpoint, from which, to state the obvious, she failed to engage with the perspective of the main actors in this event: Black people themselves, whose rights were at stake. Her engagement in representative thinking[4] was clearly faulty, and according to her critics, such as Gines (2014: 124), "she ignores the standpoint of the oppressed" and thereby "occupies and represents the standpoints of those already present in the public realm, the oppressors." Whichever interpretation we choose, what results is anything but the best practice example of reflective judgment.

All the same, we agree with Berkowitz, who on the substantial point about school desegregation persists somewhat in Arendt's vein:

> To simply claim that prejudices are wrong and to integrate schools *as if* the prejudices underlying segregation could be wished away, is to deny the power of prejudice in human life. It is not an accident that 65 years after the beginning of school desegregation, American schools are nearly as segregated as they were before. (Berkowitz 2020: 147)

Berkowitz (2020: 147) further argues on the wider point of what this episode teaches us about Arendt's argument against the use of state power to overturn private or social prejudices in the social realm that while "Arendt's assumption that how one raises one's children inclusive of where one sends them to school is a private matter is controversial and possibly wrong, [. . .] any principled judgment about school desegregation must distinguish between the need for political equality, the social discrimination, and private uniqueness"; for if "we are to guard and preserve plurality, we must also find ways to protect the right of parents to educate their children as they wish." Whatever we make of Arendt's central claim about the use of federal power (and armed force, let us bear in mind) in order to prevent the state enforcement of a prejudice that was seen as warranted and in order by the local authorities and the democratic majority of the citizens of Little Rock, Arkansas, we cannot simply hide behind the obvious wrongness of her particular judgments when confronting the wider questions surrounding the intertwinement of social issues and political action in this case.

Arendt's thinking about race and race-based discrimination, oppression, and exploitation, both in *Origins* and in "Reflections," is an attempt at representational thinking, however misguided from today's perspective. It is true and very important that Arendt held views about the ideology of race, scientific racism, and the human self that are mutually incompatible, as we will now explore by working through the specific claims of *Origins* that have proven positively influential on postcolonial theory and genocide studies ("the good"), alongside those that have been discredited ("the bad") and those that have been decried ("the ugly"). But, as Berkowitz (2020) and Bernstein (2018) have recently joined Benhabib (1996) and Young-Bruehl (1982) in arguing, we must not end with that pronouncement. Rather, we must be intrepid in carrying out *with* Arendt the practice of representational thinking *against* Arendt's own judgments in the 1950s in order to examine the ongoing blind spots we have as democratic citizens committed to both strict equality in public life alongside plurality and privacy as no less important basic rights.

Here it is crucial to recall what Benhabib (1988: 45) points to as a striking feature of Arendt's thinking about Eichmann as a negative exemplar of moral judgment; for Arendt, "one of the most perplexing characteristics of Eichmann" was that "he was 'at home' with himself." On this basis, Benhabib reminds us of Arendt's dissatisfaction with the notion of conscience as a harmony of the self, a theme with which Arendt engaged, one could say struggled, in many of her works, especially in the last decade of her life. Benhabib herself does not bring this observation to bear on the disconnect she and many other thinkers influenced by Arendt find in trying to come to terms with "Reflections." If we do take this observation in this light, however, we see that Arendt is somehow "at home" with the vilest Wilhelmine prejudices of her Konigsberg upbringing (her pejorative descriptions of *Ostjuden*, from her earliest Jewish writings, through *Eichmann* and beyond could serve as an example), even as she is also the author of those aspects of *Origins* that make her an important resource for thinking about scientific racism, imperialism, and antisemitism today. Again, Arendt was judging as herself, from her particular conditioned standpoint, and obviously made a wrong judgment. What makes it even more difficult is that human beings are not always in harmony all the time. In fact, we are in disharmony most of the time, especially when engaging in representative thinking. But when we do finally express a judgment, we need to be in harmony with ourselves insofar as we must take responsibility for expressing this particular judgment and (potentially) acting upon it. Was Arendt in disharmony when making her judgments in "Reflections" or did she think they were the best possible judgments?

The "Good": of The Origins of Totalitarianism *and its* Continuing Value for Postcolonial Thought

When it comes to controversies concerning Arendt's thinking about Africa, Africans, and African Americans, time has generally been kinder to *The Origins of Totalitarianism* than to "Reflections on Little Rock," perhaps because *Origins* is the primary text to which we turn for Arendt's thinking about three phenomena that she was decades ahead of scholarship in thinking together: antisemitism, imperialism, and totalitarianism. Her overarching thesis in linking these three historical formations was so novel and counterintuitive, and so compelling even if not (at least entirely) correct, that it is small wonder that even those least inclined to give Arendt the benefit of the doubt on any matter grant that *Origins* has done much to shape the discourse about race thinking, bureaucratic modernity, and the horrors of totalitarian terror. In short, as Arendt summed up in her preface to the first edition, written in the summer of 1950:

Antisemitism (not merely the hatred of Jews), imperialism (not merely conquest), totalitarianism (not merely dictatorship)—one after the other, one more brutally than the other, have demonstrated that human dignity needs a new guarantee which can be found only in a new political principle, in a new law of earth, whose validity this time must comprehend the whole of humanity while its power must remain strictly limited, rooted in and controlled by newly defined territorial entities. (OT ix)

To be sure, there are numerous critiques of the Eurocentric and/or anti-Black racist thinking it is commonly claimed is to be found in this work, which we refer to in the following two sections of this chapter. The relatively positive response to *Origins* when it comes to matters of race, in comparison to the more or less universal condemnation with which "Reflections" is met, can be explained by the fact that the former text offers insights Arendt had, decades before the mainstream of scholarly research arrived at them. This is so, as even her sharpest critics acknowledge with respect to *Origins*, notwithstanding some marginal claims that do little more than put on view the prejudices of Arendt's *Bildung* in the German Empire of the first two decades of the twentieth century, at least until the time of publishing *Origins*, and perhaps until overseeing its revised editions (in 1958 and 1967, respectively) or even later than that.

What are these insights? Any account of the positive lasting legacy of *Origins* as a resource for thinking about anti-Black racism as integral to the politics of nineteenth- and twentieth-century modernity must center on Arendt's so-called boomerang theory concerning the volatile mix of scientific racism and modern bureaucratic state institutions analyzed in parts two and three of the book, and most especially in chapter 7 ("Race and Bureaucracy"). Arendt's profoundly novel, even revolutionary, intuition is that there is a substantial ideological and institutional continuity between European imperialist rule in Africa and across the globe between (especially) the 1880s and the 1910s, on the one hand, and the rise of totalitarian regimes and their programs of state-organized mass murder in the 1930s and 1940s, on the other. Put starkly, Arendt asserts that the Nazi genocide and Stalinist purges and pogroms took the shape they did in large part because of a process that began with the bureaucratic administration of peoples based on the ideology of race.

Arendt (OT 207) argues that race and bureaucracy were the "two main political devices of imperialist rule," isolating this pair because race was "an escape into irresponsibility where nothing human could any longer exist" and bureaucracy was "the result of a responsibility that no man can bear for his fellow-man and no people for another people." Time and again in this volume (in Chapters 4, 5, and 6, especially) we have seen how responsibility is not just a core concept for Arendt but also, on her account, an integral feature of a functioning civil society. It is, therefore, in keeping with her unique perspective on the world and a sign of the novelty of her approach to the Shoah that she links it with Imperialism, while also linking the National Socialism and Soviet regimes, specifically through the destruction of any individual capacity for judging and acting responsibly. Only a Hannah Arendt, of whom there is and was only one, would come up with such an argument, where the cultural conditions surrounding an individual's power of judgment and ability and willingness to exercise it are argued to have so much force in global politics. To whatever extent they own this, the critics and commentators cited in this chapter are in this conversation with and against Arendt because of this unique and irreplaceable kernel of her thinking about race and politics: you simply cannot find this elsewhere.

So, what is Arendt's singular insight, whatever its salience and value? For Arendt (OT 207), race "was discovered in South Africa" and "was originally the barely conscious reaction to tribes of whose humanity European man was ashamed and frightened"; "bureaucracy," meanwhile, was discovered "in Algeria, Egypt, and India" and "was a consequence of the administration by which Europeans had tried to rule foreign peoples whom they felt to be hopelessly their inferiors and at the same time in need of their special protection." Already in this overview of her argument we see the ways in which, as readers such as Patricia Owens (2017) note, Arendt might well be complicit in some of the racist prejudices of the Europeans whose imperialist actions she excoriates in this passage. We might, for instance, have a lingering concern that perhaps she, too, sees the Africans whom the imperialist Europeans saw as (at best) "hopelessly inferior" in at least somewhat the same light. This worry is at least partly substantiated by other claims in *Origins* discussed in the next section.

Leaving aside for the moment what are surely undertones of Arendt's Eurocentrism, what is crucial for understanding the boomerang effect of imperialism is how Arendt (OT 221) argues that having "discovered what a 'lovely virtue' a white skin can be in Africa" through the project of colonial imperialism in Africa, Europeans exported these lessons globally and reimported them back home; for instance, in the way "the British Intelligence Services (especially after the first World War) began to attract England's best sons, who preferred serving mysterious forces all over the world to serving the common good of their country." Once this occurred, Arendt (OT 221) concludes, "the stage seemed to set for all possible horrors." In other words, colonial imperialist rule in Africa introduced all the key features required for the ideological and institutional "advance" that was totalitarian government and its state-sanctioned mass murder of non-combatant civilians, up to and including the physical and ideo-logical infrastructure of the extermination camps—the clear refer-ence to "all possible horrors"—to see the light of day.

It merits noting that historian A. Dirk Moses (2011: 73) argues that such presentations of Arendt's so-called boomerang theory mistake Arendt's position, holding that she was actually "advancing an alternative continuity argument in the service of a broader agenda about *discontinuity* between what she called 'the Western tradition' and totalitarianism." It would take us afield from the focus of this chapter to descend into this debate in detail, but we ought to take at least long enough to note, as Michael Rothberg (2009: 37–8) has argued, that "Arendt is ahead of her time in grasping the specificity of what would become known as the Holocaust as well as in linking the genocide to colonialism," even if, in his view, *Origins* "demands a double reading" that recognizes "the unprecedented insights that Arendt brings to understanding modern history" but also "how those insights are interlaced with forms of blindness about race and colonialism that might be typical of Europeans of the era." The degree to which Arendt concurred with or differed from "what was typical" of her milieu is the subject of extended discussion by Richard King (2012: 5), who argues that hierarchical race-thinking emerged "much earlier and much more decisively than [Arendt] allowed" and that she resists this conclusion because of her own complicity in Eurocentric prejudices about the putative ahistorical character of African people and peoples.

Interpreters will likely continue to debate the extent to which Arendt's undeniable Eurocentrism militates against her far-sightedness concerning the roots of totalitarianism in imperialism. What cannot be denied is that, as Pascal Grosse (2006: 37) notes, *Origins* is a "constitutive book for postcolonial studies." Still more strikingly, perhaps, Paul Gilroy (2005: 17) concludes that Arendt "correctly identified the understanding of the state-formation process generated by the study of colonial government" in striking contrast "with the orthodoxies that have emerged from narrower histories of

Europe, conceived as a wholly innocent and essentially self-contained entity." Christopher Lee, calling attention to this conclusion, finds that crossing Arendt studies with postcolonial studies shows that her

> counter-history of power [. . .] combined with the intellectual model she presented through the political urgency of her work, her self-reflection on her own identity, and her active attempts to reconcile her experiences with her philosophical views constitute the main reasons for her enduring legacy. (Lee 2011: 110–11)

It would appear that Arendt's judgment of questions of race in the broader context of twentieth-century politics and modern European and global history were very different in the degree of their truthfulness. This is especially curious if we bear in mind that the revised manuscript of *Origins* as we know it was finished within months of her writing "Reflections." Can Arendt's thinking and writing about race really be "so good and so bad" at the same time? Strangely, perhaps, this seems to be the case, for reasons we address in the next section.

The "Bad" and the "Ugly": Misrecognition of Black People and the Social/Political Distinction

Shiraz Dossa (1980) finds an "ethnocentric strain" in Arendt's characterizations of Africans that echoed rather than distanced itself from the mentality of the white Europeans who conquered central and southern Africa, arguing that in passages such as those from the "Race and Bureaucracy" chapter quoted above, Arendt presents the African as a "natural man" and thus the "inhumanity" of Black people "as self-evident." Kathryn Gines (2014: 92) argues that "Arendt's attempt to criticize the race thinking and racism used to justify imperialism is weakened by her inability to distance herself from a very racist (even essentialist) characterization of African people." Stipulating for the moment that it is not plausible that, however much Arendt may have carried her Wilhelmine Empire prejudices with her during her American sojourn, the author of the "Race and Bureaucracy" chapter of *Origins* was motivated by express anti-Black bias, we must ask: Why? Why would Arendt be motivated to not just to "miss" the operative power of the "ideal of sacrifice" in the African American community (as she writes to Ellison after hearing his critique) but also as Gines (2014: 25) notes, to write in *On Violence* dismissively of the Black Power movement?

The deeper answer here is that Arendt is not thinking about race in these moments of her work, but rather one of her central themes: the absolute necessity of a hard and fast distinction between matters that are truly political and those that are—and *ought to be*—"merely" social. We have seen this commitment as it arises in numerous places in Arendt's oeuvre, and the controversies surrounding it are now familiar to the reader of, especially, Chapter 1 (where the version of these issues in *The Human Condition* is discussed) and Chapter 8 (where the *On Revolution* version is foregrounded).

But there is an added dimension to this debatable and core feature of Arendt's manner of thinking politics, where Arendt simply and irrefutably leads herself astray by refusing to see anti-Black racism as inherently political in the American context, as Robert Bernasconi has studied carefully over the past three decades. Bernasconi (1996: 15) argues that while reasonable people will continue to debate the ways in which Arendt "gave to the distinction between the social and the political a normative status," what is not debatable is the manner in which in *On Revolution* this distinction "led her to applaud the American Revolution, among other things, for ignoring the social and economic cost paid by those who did not share in the prosperity they helped to produce for others." In other words, while Arendt did not directly support the views of white racists who gave social prejudices a legal warrant, her underlying commitment to a view of politics that is free of concerns wedded to the reproduction of society in the bodily processes of labor and work leads her astray.

How so? As Bernasconi (1996: 18) notes, this commitment entails that she ignores the ways in which the "distinction between the political and the social" she defends for her own reasons "served the interests of the White population at the expense of not only the social, but also inevitably the political, interests of the Black population, in actual fact and without Arendt's intent." Bernasconi (1996: 19) concludes that this is an especially unfortunate mistake on her part because "Arendt's impatience with economic and social issues is extraordinary in the light of the fact that on her own view the precondition of politics is liberation from necessity." Here, too, we see the value of thinking with Arendt against Arendt: it is because we, like Bernasconi, agree with her unique account of freedom that we must reject her argument about the particular application of the distinction between the social and the political in the case of US politics in the era of the Civil Rights Movement and the disestablishment of the legal enshrinement of racial discrimination commonly called "Jim Crow."

Arendt's writings from the 1950s and 1960s have no answer when it comes to the unique manner in which social and economic inequality intersect with political inequality in the American experience. As we saw with Bernstein at the outset of the chapter, it seems that in this case Arendt's deeply felt as well as reasoned antipathy for the subsumption of politics into social and economic administration and for the preservation of the public as the space of appearance of political equals blinds her to the unique ways in which political agency is denied to Black Americans in particular. But can we even expect something of the best version of her work, given that we are even further from a definitive answer to these questions today? Social revolution is and has always been the fundamental fear of white supremacist ideology in the United States, right down to the January 6, 2021 attack on the United States Congress. Arendt herself, on this point, fails to fully acknowledge the deep-rooted, explicitly political depths of the "social problem" of racism in America, in an attempt to safeguard the distinction between the social and political, while demoting racism to the sphere of social preference.

For Gines (2014: 65–6), the problem is truly much deeper than just the school desegregation issue discussed in "Reflections"; for Arendt, as she states, is simply wrong in her analysis of the institution of slavery in the American context (in *On Revolution*), which was "not intended to be a temporary institution" and was always "a racialized institution" in the sense of part two of *Origins*. Arendt is perhaps reticent to recognize this, not just because it reflects badly on her generally positive picture of "the American experiment" but also because it is in tension with her preferred chronology of the long arc of "Race-Thinking Before Racism" (the title of chapter 6 of *Origins*), where she argues that "Racism has been the powerful ideology of imperialistic policies since the turn of our century" (OT 158). Gines, like King above, asks: Why only since the turn of the twentieth century? Was not the foundation of the United States of America also implicated in racism? How could it not be when the institution of slavery was undeniably integral to the project, so much so that slavery was even explicitly written into the US Constitution, even if James Madison (who, along with John Adams and even more than Thomas Jefferson and others, is one of the clear heroes of Arendt's account of the American Revolution) tried very hard to prevent any express references thereto in the document?

Even more disconcerting, as Gines (2014: 123) discusses in her conclusion, is that unlike in *Origins*, where Arendt connected the atrocities perpetrated by Europeans in, chiefly, Africa and later in the subcontinent and South Pacific during the last quarter of the nineteenth century to the atrocities perpetrated by Nazi Germany and the Soviet Union in the second quarter of the twentieth century, when Arendt turned to "the Negro question" in *On Violence*, she not only insisted on seeing the "Negro question as a Negro problem, not a white problem," but worse still, ignores "that anti-Black racism (like Jew hatred) is political." As readers of Arendt and as citizens trying to think politics in late modernity and under conditions of global capitalism, we can and surely will continue to have principled debates about matters related to the social/political distinction so dear to Arendt, such as the following. Which, if any, "merely" social problems ought not to be politicized—and we know they could through the work of, among others, Borren (2008), Gündoğdu (2015), and Loidolt (2018), which we discuss in Chapter 1? How, if at all, should we preserve some space of privacy, free of public administration—suddenly very heated again in the United States, where the Supreme Court seems ready to remove the five-decades-old precedent holding that the Constitution contains something like an implied right to privacy? And, how, if at all, might we best ensure that legally enshrined redistributive efforts by the state ultimate contribute to the political equality of its members?

We may or may not take the positions that Arendt does on these points, and that is natural enough in the light of her practice of thinking politics. What cannot be abided as we do so, as Gines (2014: 11) claims and we agree, is ignoring that Arendt's "attitudes and ideals about politics and what counts as political in the explicitly Jewish context are not always consonant with her broader theoretical framework concerning what is political, especially when it comes to Africans and African Americans." It is important to remember in this regard that unlike with antisemitism, which Arendt studied carefully and systematically in part one of *Origins*, we can find in her corpus no sustained analysis of anti-Black racism in America. The closest one comes, as discussed briefly above, in the analysis of slavery in *On Revolution*, where Arendt's claims are (at best) highly debatable and perhaps ought more justly to be described as self-serving for her larger historiographical and political theoretical aim of broadly vindicating the actions of the revolutionaries in Colonial America while castigating those of the revolutionaries in France (as

189

discussed in detail in Chapter 8). As Patricia Owens (2017: 403) argues, "Arendt's anti-black racism is rooted in her consistent refusal to analyse the colonial and imperial origins of racial conflict in the United States given the unique role of the American republic in her vision for a new post-totalitarian politics."

Are Gines (2014) and Owens (2017) being unfair to Arendt here? We think not. Arendt's presentation of the American Revolution in *On Revolution* is of a piece with her refusal to recognize the deep resonance between her own practice of solidaristic action in civil society as a Jew and on behalf of other Jews—"If one is attacked as a Jew, one must defend oneself as a Jew. Not as a German, not as a world-citizen, not as an upholder of the Rights of Man, or whatever" (WRLR 12)—and the activism of Black Americans struggling both to eradicate the enduring legacies of slavery and at the same time to make the white majority in the United States itself recognize how deeply interwoven are the constitutional order and the legally enforced inferiority of Black and other non-white Americans. As Gines concludes her chapter on this issue:

> slavery is not only a social issue and a crime, it is also an institution that is at the core of the foundation of U.S. society and government. How do we reconcile the fact that American rebels were able to engage in a revolution that emphasized freedom and new beginnings while simultaneously maintaining a racialized system of slavery? Arendt understands that this poses a dilemma [. . .] but offers no solution. (Gines 2014: 76)

This matters, not only as we come to terms with Arendt's influential, if controversial, comparative reading of the American and French revolutions, but also and even more importantly because it gets at a deep vein both in the history of political thought and in the practice of politics in the liberal, republican, constitutional tradition. Namely, what Gines (2014: 64) calls "the dialectical relationship between freedom and slavery"; this dialectic manifests sharply in the United States context because

> the foundation of political freedom by the founding fathers was possible precisely because it could be juxtaposed with the institution of slavery [. . .] freedom had all the more significance in the United States because it stood in such drastic contrast to slavery. This is a central aspect of the relationship between slavery and freedom in America that Arendt misses. (Gines 2014: 64)

In this regard, first of all, we must attend here to the crucial if narrow issue of Arendt's (in)ability to recognize the political agency of Black

Americans as a minority mobilizing itself, very much along the lines of how she herself participated in solidaristic mobilizations in her youth and early adulthood (Villa 2021: 2–3). Beyond this, there is the degree to which we ought to esteem the American Experiment; many readers, specialists or not, Americans or not, are given pause by just how favorably Arendt viewed the United States, both historically and as her adopted home in the 1950s and 1960s. Both these points are important enough in their own right, but even more important, perhaps, is the following concern: can Arendt's conception of freedom *tout court*, the absolute beating heart of her whole body of political thought, ever escape the dialectical entanglement that the historically situated theory and practice of freedom shares with slavery? Not only in the context of the American Revolution, or in the US Constitution as "a living document," but over the entire course of what she calls "the tradition," beginning with Plato and ending with Marx (TMA 17).

To this we add a recent insight from Linda Zerilli (2019a: 1324), who points to an overlap between the rule/action binary at the heart of *The Human Condition* and a racialized/anti-racist politics, one which is too rarely recognized in the intense debates about Arendt's position on race and politics. Her point is that rule, which is "inherently racialized," entails a politics dead to the "vicissitudes of human action" because a democratic people understood as an *ethnos* and a democracy as autochthonous emerges directly from the denial of the spontaneous, plural, and unpredictable character of action. As Zerilli (2019a: 1325) notes, the "idea of politics as a form of rule [attempts] to solve [the] problem of the vicissitudes of action," not necessarily only in domination but also in the very forms of legally enshrined inferiority at stake in "Reflections."

One way to interpret this remark is to read Arendt's action in an elitist, and potentially racist, vein: the white elite need servants, sweatshop workers, Global South food producers, and slaves to enjoy their public appearance and political agency. Another way is to assume that the natural condition is something we share as human beings, and as human beings we all could enter the public realm and act together, in consensus and dissent.

The fact that both access to and engagement in the public realm are so unequally distributed is indisputably the result of socio-economic inequalities, broadly construed, which—beyond doubt—is Arendt's greatest blind spot. For, as Marieke Borren (2013: 111) reminds us, "it is impossible to participate in political action on an empty stomach." Similarly, Arendt does not deny agency to Black people in "Reflections." It is true though, on a critical note, that she misjudged the gravity of their oppression and very much comes across as a white, originally European person, explaining both to the US government how to organize desegregation in the face of (legalized) discriminatory practices, to which she herself was not subject, and to the Black activists how they should fight their oppressors. Sharing publicly the judgments included in "Reflections" in this particular historical and political moment—even if she notes that, as a Jew, she "take[s her] sympathy for the cause of the Negroes as for all oppressed and underprivileged peoples for granted" (RLR 46)—was definitely paternalistic; whether it makes her a racist remains dependent on the definition of racism we assume.

Conclusion: Further Exercises Are All We Have

Bearing in mind all that we have learned in reconstituting "the good, the bad, and the ugly" to be found in the content of Arendt's claims about race and racism in *Origins* and "Reflections," we now hope to see what fruit, precisely, can be gleaned from thinking with Arendt—specifically, her claims about judgment as a part of democratic life—and against Arendt—specifically, her judgments about race in American politics and society and the interlinked legacies of colonialism, imperialism, and anti-Black racism. Our procedure in this chapter in particular, and this volume in general, makes clear Arendt's keenest and most lasting observation: the political, which is what makes us human at all, entails an ongoing practice of exercises in political thinking. This practice inevitably involves discarding certain judgments in favor of others informed through widening our imaginary community of judgment, and adding new—as diverse as possible—perspectives to them in order to make them more representative. Through such exercises, including critical reflection of all perspectives in our reach, we might hope to make our judgments more "truthful."

Just how far can one go in reconstructing a democratic commitment to the improvement of judgment through an enlarged mentality that grows by representing in one's imagination ever more possible judgments by absent others? This question, we note by way of inconclusive conclusion, is an abstract and generalized version of one of the central salient critiques Gines (2014) offers concerning Arendt's position in "Reflections." Namely, aside from any idiosyncratic or personal failures on Arendt's part, Gines sees a flaw in a democratic theory of judgment grounded in an individual, whose perspective (however enlarged) always remains partial and implicated in the circumstances. Most saliently, as regards the theme of this chapter, the would-be judge can and will only be able to occupy the decision space of someone whose life is shaped by the social, cultural, and economic features of their lived experience, as exemplified by Arendt, who—from Gines's perspective—proved herself incapable of seeing the motivations of Black Americans facing legally warranted social and economic, as well as political, inequality.

At this point we need to go back to what we said about judging (in Chapter 3), but before doing this, let us briefly take a closer look at the kind of theorizing Arendt practiced and which is at the heart of the critical reception of her writings. In an epistolary essay "What and How We Learned from Hannah Arendt," Elisabeth Young-Bruehl and Jerome Kohn (2001), both her former students, reflect upon Arendt as an academic teacher. At one point Kohn writes:

> I wanted to ask you if you think Arendt had or held to a theory of anything—of totalitarianism or politics, or of action or revolution, or of society or culture or education, or of authority or religion or history, or of human freedom, or of the distinct temporal dimensions of the activities of the human mind? Those are certainly among topics that engaged her but did she formulate anything that could be called a "theory" of them [. . .]? That she theorized them is obvious, but the distinction between theorizing, "thinking," and theory that can be stated as its outcome seems to me to have been crucial for her. (Young-Bruehl and Kohn 2001: 229)

To this, Young-Bruehl answers:

> I agree with you that she had no such thing as a theory of education and that she did not really make theories of anything. There is no Arendtian theory or any Arendtism. But she did have characteristic ways of thinking [. . .] and she had characteristic ways of judging. (Young-Bruehl and Kohn 2001: 234)

If we acknowledge that, for Arendt, theorizing was an attempt to think about and understand the phenomena of the world and that her judging was more a practice than a theory, we notice that what Gines sees as a flaw in Arendt's democratic theory of judgment—namely that a judging subject depends in her judgment on her lived experience and situatedness in the world—is precisely the point and the chief virtue of Arendt's account. Arendt's aim seems not to have been to display a theory of judgment for others to implement but to describe a lived experience of judging as political thinking and explore ways in which we can make it better.

Or, of course, fail in the attempt to do so. The core of this experience is uncertainty. There is literally no human being in the world who always makes the right judgment. This is our worldly experience, even if we design ethical, religious, or rational devices to help us bear this uneasy feeling that although we, time and again, form our opinions and guide our actions through our best judgment, in any particular present moment we never know if our judgment is "right," and if the future will confirm its truthfulness. Referring to a historical example, also relevant to Arendt's biography—namely to Jews who stayed in Germany in the mid-1930s, even in the face of persecution already taking place at that time—for Arendt (WRLR 5) emigration was an obvious choice: "I thought immediately that Jews could not stay. I did not intend to run around Germany as a second-class citizen [. . .]. I thought that things would just get worse and worse." We now know that those who stayed, perhaps hoping for an improvement of the situation, made a wrong judgment. But how could they know better? If we think, for example, in the face of a crisis of democracy in many countries worldwide, or of being in a region on the verge of war, how, under such circumstances ("dark times" or not), do we recognize this moment when hope is lost and judge rightly? How do we know? We do not, of course. Thus, we judge, as best we can.

If we understand Arendt less as a "theorist" and more as a thinking practitioner, this influences the framing of the questions around Arendt and race in the specific context of assessing the relevance of Arendt's thinking for contemporary debates about race and politics, to a central recurring feature of Arendt's body of work. Here, as elsewhere, we see why the essayistic form of her writing and the experimental form of her thinking suit one another so well, and yet also, and for the same reasons, continue to place history, freedom, and equality as Arendt understands each into productive tension with one another as the ground of judgment.

Does this mean that Arendt's judgments in *Origins* and "Reflections" should not be declared wrong? Of course not. We, as her readers, are to judge. Was Arendt Eurocentric? Definitely yes. Did she have a blind spot when it comes to the historical, social, and political standing of Black Americans? Certainly—one only needs to look at the first paragraphs of "Reflections" (RLR 46), where she claims colonialism to have been "the one great crime in which

America was never involved." Was she a racist? We do not think so. In her treatment of (Black) slavery, her description of Africa—in which, to be sure, she largely depends on Joseph Conrad's novel *The Heart of Darkness*, which was also, as Tuija Parvikko (2015) reminds us, a reference for Edward Said in *Orientalism*—and her misjudgment of the motivation for Black activism, she certainly proved to be insensitive to the problems of Black oppression, shuffling them, as she did with "the woman question," into the realm of the social, which was not of her concern. It is up to every theorist and every reader today to pass judgment on Arendt's judgments in respect to race and racism. When we do so, we must decide whether to disqualify her writings altogether or, as has happened with feminist theory, to think with Arendt against Arendt and be inspired by the richness of her thinking, which is, as Kohn (Young-Bruehl and Kohn 2001: 229) notes, rooted in the experience of the common world—not a theory but actual being in the world and thinking in an intimate connection to experience.

Notes

1. We follow Kathryn Sophia Belle's preference that we cite this work by the name under which it was published while also acknowledging that she changed her name in 2017.
2. Originally composed for the *Hannah Arendt und das 20. Jahrhundert* exhibition, displayed at the German Historical Museum in Berlin from March through October 2020.
3. At this point, Arendt's spontaneity of acting comes to mind but, to be fair, this cannot be the reason for the shortcomings in her judgment, as the essay was waiting for publication for more than a year, but Arendt—although broadly advised against it—decided to publish it unchanged (RLR 45–6).
4. Which, as discussed in Chapter 3, is the making-present through one's imagination of the possible judgments of those who are not present at the time one exercises judgment, and is the chief means by which the "enlarged mentality" of a thinking subject, but also a good democratic citizen, can be forged and improved.

The Hidden Treasure of
Hannah Arendt's Philosophy

Reading Arendt's writings as exercises in political thinking, as opposed to reading them through a scholarly political theory or political science lens, exposes the enlightening potential and their practical power of Arendt's political-philosophical project. As a political theorist she always keeps one goal in mind: to understand the common world and the political phenomena that are crystallized therein. This understanding is a foundation for any informed judgment. As the public sphere is a space that the persons acting in it share with one another, an element of plurality is always included in their activities. In the world, opinions must coexist in their diversity and neither action nor the power that derives therefrom can ever be understood as a matter of the individual. At the same time, political actors require the unifying power of the common world, without which their differences could only be expressed in parallel discourses instead of in public dialogue.

Political life therefore requires both the plurality of actors involved, with their diverse opinions and perspectives, and the common world as a space that connects them. Neither of these foundations is, in Arendt's eyes, unconditionally guaranteed. Plurality is endangered not only by phenomena such as totalitarian rule, which oppresses individuality through coercion and indoctrination (OT 438), but also by the seemingly much less malign rise of mass society, in which everyone thinks and acts alike (HC 58). For its part, the common world, the space of appearance, is threatened due to the alienation of the individual inhabitants of the world: from themselves, from their activities, and from one another. Public discourse and political thinking dissolve into myriad individualistic perspectives that articulate a series of solipsistic worlds; which is to say: both totalitarian states and mass democracies give rise to a world in which there is no world in common.

Arendt relates this individualism and relativism to a tendency in twentieth-century social science to forgo clear distinctions and

196

to define terms in a largely arbitrarily manner. She sees in this a danger not only for the possibilities of communication in the political realm but also for the constitution of the common world. Arendt (WA 95–6) notices that we more and more grant social and political scholars the "curious right" to ignore these distinctions and to "define one's terms," giving the examples of "tyranny," "authority," and "totalitarianism," as if such ill-defined terms "have simply lost their common meaning" and as if, perhaps in that process, "we have ceased to live in a common world where the words we have in common possess an unquestionable meaningfulness." The result is that "we assure ourselves that we still understand each other," by which "we do not mean that together we understand a world common to us all [but only rather a] process of argumentation in its sheer formality" (WA 95–6). Such an arbitrary definition of terms in the social sciences would be only of academic concern were it not for the fact that social scientific debates of phenomena such as tyranny, totalitarianism, or authority do not simply end in isolated scholarly discourses that lack any shared basis for judgment. In addition to this, and more pernicious, is the resulting permutation of the "ivory tower" problem, where solipsistic scholarly argumentation of individual theories remains logical and exact but cannot be understood as a world-building practice with any significance for those concerned. Such scholarship contributes nothing to an understanding that could be shared in the public sphere and, as a purely formal game, brings about nothing new.

For this reason, Arendt argues that the ability to act politically, which in principle is given to every human being by virtue of their birth, is constrained by the conditions of modern life, with professionalization and its compartmentalization as one key element of that constraint. In order to be able to act responsibly, as we have seen in Chapters 4 and 5 particularly, human beings require a practical capacity for worldly reflexivity that enables every political actor to open up the shared world in their unique way. Such reflexivity is facilitated by the ability to think politically, if only that ability is actually practiced, such that reflective judgment is actually exercised in public. This, for Arendt, is both the means and the end of her own "exercises in political thinking," which help political actors to understand the common world and to communicate in it in a common political language. In a very real way, these exercises are not (or not limited to) the printed product of thinking politically in *Between Past and Future*; rather, they are the ongoing practice of reflection in which we engage together with her as we read, accept, reject, and modify her judgments in conversation with those essays, and others.

Understanding Arendt's thinking (about) politics not as a body of arguments to be found in her collected works but as *ongoing* "exercises in political thinking," we have argued in this book that her judgments—even, or especially, where they seem today to have been mistaken—retain their potential to reshape conversations about contemporary politics in ways that have been neglected or under-developed. In all of her works, Arendt refers to the experiences of a particular time, her own or those of others. This, for us as authors writing from our own time perspective, makes at least some of her conclusions and recommendations appear anachronistic or worse, and reasonably provokes questions concerning the relevance of her thinking, as discussed in especially Chapters 7 and 9. Recasting Arendt's work as exercises in political thinking displays the true relevance of her writings, not in this or that specific finding—about propaganda in mass societies, or about individual responsibility under dictatorships, say—but in the constant insistence on the two key features identified above: the plurality of opinions and the unity of the common world in which those opinions can be expressed, exchanged, and heard. Reading Arendt's writings as exercises shares the emphasis she placed on their propaedeutic and political function as an invitation to further debate, relativizing the content of, especially, her most controversial or (to our judgment) wrongheaded conclusions.

The experiences to which Arendt refers are, to be sure, different from the experience of today's inhabitants of the world. All the same, it is vital to acknowledge that the common world changes with every generation of political actors appearing in it, and Arendt knew this well. For this reason, as she also adumbrates, political thinking must change in order to correspond to the current conditions of the world. Because Arendt's exercises are flexible in this way, they become the hidden treasure of her political philosophy that makes them fruitful for today's reader. The path of thinking must be retread by every generation; Arendt offers invaluable assistance in this task through her exercises in political thinking, which serve as a part of an education in how we might travel this path on our own, initiating us in responsible political practice, in full knowledge that we will err at times, as she did.

Our goal in introducing Arendt as a crucial figure in the constellation of *Thinking Politics* has been twofold. First, to embed the concept of exercises in political thinking in the broader context of Arendt's work to examine the role it plays as the basis of her model of judgment and political action. This was the work of Part I, where we defined Arendt's exercises in political thinking as a model for reflective judgment, and at the same time both a propaedeutic basis and necessary capacity for responsible political action. First, we explored Arendt's unique of understanding of action: how words and deeds co-constitute the space of appearance that both constitutes and institutes politics as freedom (Chapter 1). Next, while the separation between the practical and the theoretical way of life is a fact of tradition, today, after the breach of tradition, the relationship between thinking and acting needs to be determined anew. In the opening between thought and action, Arendt reveals a mode in which thinking is not only useful for active life but even indispensable for its best practice (Chapter 2). Concluding Part I, we saw that in politics, we cannot rely on the authority of the past or appeal to general rules. What, then, we asked with Arendt, should we do, finding that reflective judgment must stand in for any firm orientation in political practices? Following Arendt's challenging interpretation of Kant's account of judgment, we found that while judging is a faculty of the mind, the judging subject is neither singular, on her own, like in metaphysical thinking, nor engaged in the duality of an inner dialogue, and that for this reason judgment involves plurality, which not only conditions our mental activity but also refers to our lived experience in the world. This, we saw, is why political thinking involves engaging in exercises, judging in public (Chapter 3).

Having explored how Arendt understood the exercises in political thinking in Part I, we then moved on to engage in such exercises and to apply her method in the face of contemporary political challenges, which was the work of Part II. Here, we read Arendt's writings as such exercises themselves, searching in them not for some determinate theoretical answer to the questions of political life and thought but rather for invitations to the reader to talk about possible perspectives and possible solutions to these questions, or as Arendt wanted it: to understand, whether regarding personal responsibility under dictatorship, in the case of Heidegger (Chapter 4) or Eichmann (Chapter 5); or how to face a crisis, be it the gradually unfolding climate crisis (Chapter 6) or the fast burning political turmoil engendered by the so-called migrant crisis of the 2010s (Chapter 8); or, again, regarding the political salience of identity categories related to gender and sex (Chapter 7) or race (Chapter 9).

As we learn from Arendt's practice rather than any theory, political thinking is an experience that, like any experience, can only be acquired and expanded through practice. Unlike in the case of action, which can be exercised by every human being by virtue of birth, the ability to judge requires development and continious improvement. And since the common world as a political space that people share with one another in its plurality is by definition subject to constant change and development, the potential exercise of political judgment is never fully actualized. The wealth of perspectives that can be taken into account has to be expanded again and again and varies depending on the question the person making the judgment aims to address. Political thinking is therefore not a competence acquired once and for all but rather has to be grasped in its shifting dynamics. As we argued at the outset and try to exemplify throughout Part II, the original subtitle of Arendt's essay collection called *Between Past and Future*, "Eight Exercises in Political Thought," should read rather "Eight Exercises in Political Thinking." Only when it is thus phrased do we best see the dynamic character of the judging practice as a practice.

The essayistic manner of Arendt's thinking and her distinctive literary voice are expressed in all of her writings and emanate from her most deeply held principle: the commitment to plurality. The questions she asks are examined from different perspectives, while the search for a final "true" answer is bracketed in advance. Again and again, Arendt emphasizes that her reflection does not claim to be complete, general, or universal or universalizable. The goal is pointedly *not* the formulation of a fixed theory but rather understanding: an actualized thinking about the common world and its affairs, which can (and must) be taken up repeatedly in order to account for even more new perspectives. To read Arendt conscientiously is itself both akin to practicing political thinking as she expresses it and actually constitutive for such political thinking. Her readers are introduced to the practice of judgment through Arendt's exemplary selected political questions (questions that attracted her own interest, we might add) and through this experience gain the competence of critical reflection, which is of decisive importance for making judgments in factual political practice.

We have not aimed in this work to answer questions of the practical applicability of Arendt's exercises in political thinking in a general and programmatic manner, as if we were to ask: What is Arendt's "method" for doing political theory? Nor have we tried to vindicate any of her exercises in political thinking in particular, as if we were to ask: Is Arendt's theory of the source of totalitarianism correct? Rather, our aim was to invite our readers to rethink some of Arendt's concepts from today's perspective as well as to illuminate a new way of reading her works, which, we hope, inspires engagement in and with the world we share. Specifically, we hope to have shown, Arendt's exercises can function as an essential element of political education (broadly construed) today, the aims of which are, among other things, to strengthen democratic competence, develop political solidarity, increase intercultural communication and the willingness to engage in political activities outside of the usual power structures and at the local level.

By examining more closely Arendt's concept of exercises in political thinking, our work understands itself as an opening for further research into the practical applicability of her political thinking. In this sense, we hope most of all to initiate a dialogue in the Arendtian spirit, and not to persuade anyone of any particular conclusion concerning what we believe her own conclusions were or what we believe ought to be concluded concerning those conclusions.

Bibliography

Works by Hannah Arendt

Arendt, Hannah. 1932. "Rezension über Alice Rühle-Gerstel: Das Frauenproblem in der Gegenwart. Eine psychologische Bilanz." *Gesellschaft* 10 (2): 177–9.

Arendt, Hannah. 1943. "We Refugees." *Menorah Journal* 31: 69–77.

Arendt, Hannah. 1953. "A Reply to Eric Voegelin: The Origins of Totalitarianism (A Review)." *The Review of Politics* 15 (1): 76–84.

Arendt, Hannah. 1959. "Reflections on Little Rock." *Dissent* 6: 45–56.

Arendt, Hannah. 1969a. *On Violence.* New York: Harcourt Brace.

Arendt, Hannah. 1969b. "Thoughts on Politics and Revolution." In *Crises of the Republic,* 211–45. New York: Harcourt Brace.

Arendt, Hannah. 1970. *Men in Dark Times.* New York: Harcourt Brace.

Arendt, Hannah. 1973. *The Origins of Totalitarianism.* New York: Harcourt Brace.

Arendt, Hannah. 1978a. *The Jew as Pariah: Jewish Identity and Politics in the Modern Age.* New York: Grove.

Arendt, Hannah. 1978b. *The Life of the Mind One: Thinking.* New York: Harvest.

Arendt, Hannah. 1978c. *The Life of the Mind Two: Willing.* New York: Harvest.

Arendt, Hannah. 1979. "On Hannah Arendt." In *Hannah Arendt: The Recovery of the Public World,* edited by M. A. Hill, 301–39. New York: St. Martin's Press.

Arendt, Hannah. 1990a. *On Revolution.* London: Penguin Classics.

Arendt, Hannah. 1990b. "Philosophy and Politics." *Social Research* 57 (1): 73–103.

Arendt, Hannah. 1992. *Lectures on Kant's Political Philosophy.* Chicago: University of Chicago Press.

Arendt, Hannah. 1998. *The Human Condition.* Chicago: Chicago University Press.

Arendt, Hannah. 2000. *Rahel Varnhagen: The Life of a Jewess.* Baltimore and London: John Hopkins University Press.

Arendt, Hannah. 2002. *Denktagebuch.* Munich and Zurich: Piper.

Arendt, Hannah. 2003a. "Personal Responsibility Under Dictatorship." In *Responsibility and Judgment,* 17–48. New York: Schocken Books.

Arendt, Hannah. 2003b. "Some Questions of Moral Philosophy." In *Responsibility and Judgment*, 49–146. New York: Schocken Books.

Arendt, Hannah. 2005a. "Introduction *into* Politics." In *The Promise of Politics*, 93–200. New York: Schocken Books.

Arendt, Hannah. 2005b. "Understanding and Politics." In *Essays in Understanding 1930 – 1954*, 307–327. New York: Schocken Books.

Arendt, Hannah. 2005c. "What is Existential Philosophy?" In *Essays in Understanding 1930–1954*, 163–87. New York: Schocken Books.

Arendt, Hannah. 2005d. "What Remains? The Language Remains. A Conversation with Günter Gaus." In *Essays in Understanding 1930–1954*, 1–23. New York: Schocken Books.

Arendt, Hannah. 2006a. "The Concept of History: Ancient and Modern." In *Between Past and Future: Eight Exercises in Political Thought*, 41–90. New York: Penguin Classics.

Arendt, Hannah. 2006b. "The Crisis in Culture: Its Social and Its Political Significance." In *Between Past and Future: Eight Exercises in Political Thought*, 194–222. New York: Penguin Classics.

Arendt, Hannah. 2006c. "The Crisis in Education." In *Between Past and Future: Eight Exercises in Political Thought*, 170–93. New York: Penguin Classics.

Arendt, Hannah. 2006d. *Eichmann in Jerusalem: A Report on the Banality of Evil*. New York: Penguin Classics.

Arendt, Hannah. 2006e. "The Gap Between Past and Future." In *Between Past and Future: Eight Exercises in Political Thought*, 3–15. New York: Penguin Classics.

Arendt, Hannah. 2006f. "Tradition and the Modern Age." In *Between Past and Future: Eight Exercises in Political Thought*, 17–40. New York: Penguin Classics.

Arendt, Hannah. 2006g. "Truth and Politics." In *Between Past and Future: Eight Exercises in Political Thought*, 223–59. New York: Penguin Classics.

Arendt, Hannah. 2006h. *Vom Leben des Geistes*. Munich and Zurich: Piper.

Arendt, Hannah. 2006i. "What is Authority?" In *Between Past and Future: Eight Exercises in Political Thought*, 91–141. New York: Penguin Classics.

Arendt, Hannah. 2006j. "What is Freedom?" In *Between Past and Future: Eight Exercises in Political Thought*, 142–69. New York: Penguin Classics.

Arendt, Hannah. 2007. *Vita activa*. Munich and Zurich: Piper.

Arendt, Hannah. 2008. *The Jewish Writings*. New York: Schocken Books.

Arendt, Hannah. 2018. "Heidegger at Eighty." In *Thinking Without a Banister*, 419–31. New York: Schocken Books.

Arendt, Hannah and Heinrich Blücher. 2000. *Within Four Walls: The*

Correspondence Between Hannah Arendt and Heinrich Blucher, 1936–1968, edited by Lotte Köhler. Boston: Houghton Mifflin Harcourt.

Arendt, Hannah and Martin Heidegger. 2004. *Letters 1925–1975*, edited by Ursula Ludz. Orlando: Harcourt.

Arendt, Hannah and Karl Jaspers. 1993. *Correspondence 1926–1969*. Boston: Houghton Mifflin Harcourt.

Arendt, Hannah and Mary McCarthy. 1995. *Between Friends: The Correspondence of Hannah Arendt and Mary McCarthy 1949–1975*, edited by Carol Brightman. New York: Harcourt, Brace, Jovanovich.

Other Works

Alexander, Jeffrey C. 2006. *The Civil Sphere*. New York: Oxford University Press.

Alexander, Jeffrey C. 2010. *The Performance of Politics*. New York: Oxford University Press.

Allen, Amy. 1999a. *The Power of Feminist Theory: Domination, Resistance, Solidarity*. New York: Routledge.

Allen, Amy. 1999b. "Solidarity after Identity Politics: Hannah Arendt and the Power of Feminist Theory." *Philosophy and Social Criticism* 25 (1): 97–118.

Allen, Danielle S. 2004. *Talking to Strangers: Anxieties of Citizenship since Brown v. Board of Education*. Chicago: University of Chicago Press.

Allen, Danielle S. 2005. "Invisible Citizens: On Exclusion and Domination in Ralph Ellison and Hannah Arendt." In *Nomos XLVI: Political Exclusion and Domination*, edited by M. Williams and S. Macedo, 28–76. New York: New York University Press.

Almog, Yael. 2021. "Hannah Arendt's Political Theology." Critical Theory for Political Theology 2.0, *Political Theology Network*, May 25. https://politicaltheology.com/hannah-arendt/.

Anonymous. 1966. "Mitternacht einer Weltmacht. " *Der Spiegel*, February 7, 110–13. http://ww.spiegel.de/spiegel/print/d-46265617.html.

Aristotle. *Nicomachean Ethics*, cited according to Bekker pagination.

Asad, Talal. 2003. *Formations of the Secular Christianity, Islam, Modernity*. Stanford, CA: Stanford University Press.

Aschheim, Steven E., ed. 2001. *Arendt in Jerusalem*. Berkeley: University of California Press.

Assy, Bethania. 2005. "Hannah Arendt's Doxa Glorifying Judgment and Exemplarity—A Potentially Public Space." *Veritas* 50 (1): 1–21.

Barbour, Charles. 2014. "The Republican and the Communist: Arendt Reading Marx (Reading Arendt)." In *(Mis)readings of Marx in Continental Philosophy*, edited by Jernej Habjan and Jessica Whyte, 51–66. New York: Palgrave Macmillan.

Bar On, Bat-Ami. 2002. *The Subject of Violence: Arendtean Exercises in Understanding*. Lanham, MD: Rowman & Littlefield.

Bartky, Sandra. 2002. *Sympathy and Solidarity: And Other Essays*. Lanham, MD: Rowman & Littlefield.

Basil, Priya. 2021. "Gegen mich andenken. War die deutsche Philosophin Hannah Arendt rassistisch?" *Die Wochenzeitung*, May 6. https://www.woz.ch/-b7f0.

Beauvoir, Simone de. 2011. *The Second Sex*. New York: Vintage Books.

Beiner, Ronald. 1992. "Interpretive Essay." In *Hannah Arendt: Lectures on Kant's Political Philosophy*. Chicago: University of Chicago Press.

Benhabib, Seyla. 1988. "Judgment and the Moral Foundations of Politics in Arendt's Thought." *Political Theory* 16 (1): 29–51.

Benhabib, Seyla. 1990. "Hannah Arendt and the Redemptive Power of Narrative." *Social Research* 57 (1): 167–96.

Benhabib, Seyla. 1992. *Situating the Self: Gender, Community and Postmodernism in Contemporary Ethics*. Cambridge: Polity Press.

Benhabib, Seyla. 1993. "Feminist Theory and Hannah Arendt's Concept of Public Space." *History of the Human Sciences* 6 (2): 97–114.

Benhabib, Seyla. 1996. *The Reluctant Modernism of Hannah Arendt*. London: Sage.

Benhabib, Seyla. 2004. *The Rights of Others: Aliens, Residents, and Citizens*. Cambridge: Cambridge University Press.

Benhabib, Seyla. 2017. "Whose Trial? Adolf Eichmann's or Hannah Arendt's? The Eichmann Controversy Revisited." In *The Trial That Never Ends: Hannah Arendt's "Eichmann in Jerusalem" in Retrospect*, edited by Richard J. Golsan and Sarah M. Misemer, 209–28. Toronto: University of Toronto Press.

Benhabib, Seyla. 2018. *Exile, Statelessness, and Migration*. Princeton, NJ: Princeton University Press.

Benjamin, Lucy. 2019. *Upon Which Notion of the Earth Do Our Judgments Build Worlds?* Syndicate Symposium on *A Democratic Theory of Judgment* by Linda Zerilli. https://syndicate.network/symposia/philosophy/a-democratic-theory-of-judgment/.

Berkowitz, Roger. 2011. "The Power of Non-reconciliation—Arendt's Judgment of Adolf Eichmann." *HannahArendt.net* 1/2 (6): 1–11. https://www.hannaharendt.net/index.php/han/article/view/11/55.

Berkowitz, Roger. 2017. "Reconciling Oneself to the Impossibility of Reconciliation: Judgment and Worldliness in Hannah Arendt's Politics." In *Artifacts of Thinking: Reading Hannah Arendt's Denktagebuch*, edited by Roger Berkowitz and Ian Storey, 9–36. New York: Fordham University Press.

Berkowitz, Roger. 2020. "Zur Kritik an Hannah Arendts 'Reflections on Little Rock.'" In *Hannah Arendt und das 20. Jahrhundert*, edited by Dorlis Blume, Monika Boll, and Raphael Gross, 139–47. Munich: Piper.

Berkowitz, Roger and Ian Storey. 2017. *Artifacts of Thinking: Reading Hannah Arendt's Denktagebuch*. New York: Fordham University Press.

Bernasconi, Robert. 1996. "The Double Face of the Political and the Social: Hannah Arendt and America's Racial Division." *Research in Phenomenology* 26: 3–24.

Bernasconi, Robert. 2011. "Proto-racism: Carolina in Locke's Mind." In *Racism and Modernity*, edited by Iris Wigger and Sabine Ritter, 68–82. Berlin: LIT.

Bernstein, Richard J. 1986. *Philosophical Profiles*. Cambridge: Polity Press.

Bernstein, Richard J. 1996. *Hannah Arendt and the Jewish Question*. Cambridge: Polity Press.

Bernstein, Richard J. 2018. *Why Read Hannah Arendt Now*. Cambridge: Polity Press.

Bethke Elshtain, Jean. 1995. "Political Children." In *Feminist Interpretations of Hannah Arendt*, edited by Bonnie Honig, 263–83. University Park, PA: Pennsylvania State University Press.

Bickford, Susan. 1997. "Anti-Anti-Identity Politics: Feminism, Democracy, and the Complexities of Citizenship." *Hypatia* 12 (4): 111–31.

Bilsky, Leora. 2004. *Transformative Justice: Israeli Identity on Trial*. Ann Arbor, MI: University of Michigan Press.

Bilsky, Leora. 2010. "The Eichmann Trial and the Legacy of Jurisdiction." In *Politics in Dark Times: Encounters with Hannah Arendt*, edited by Seyla Benhabib, 198–218. Cambridge: Cambridge University Press.

Boehm, Omri. 2015. "Can Refugees Have Human Rights?" *New York Times*, October 19. https://opinionator.blogs.nytimes.com/2015/10/19 /could-refugees-have-human-rights/.

Borren, Marieke. 2008. "Towards an Arendtian Politics of In/visibility, On Stateless Refugees and Undocumented Aliens." *Ethical Perspectives* 15 (2): 213–37.

Borren, Marieke. 2010. *Amor Mundi: Hannah Arendt's Political Phenomenology of World*. Amsterdam: F & N.

Borren, Marieke. 2013. "Feminism as Revolutionary Practice: From Justice and the Politics of Recognition to Freedom." *Hypatia* 28 (1): 197–214.

Bot, Michael. 2013. "Irony as an Antidote to Thoughtlessness." *Amor Mundi*, July 10. https://hac.bard.edu/amor-mundi/irony-as-an-antidote -to-thoughtlessness-2013-10-07.

Brown, Wendy. 2010. *Walled States, Waning Sovereignty*. Cambridge, MA: Zone Books.

Brunkhorst, Hauke. 2000. "Equality and Elitism in Arendt." In *The Cambridge Companion to Hannah Arendt*, edited by Dana Villa, 178–98. Cambridge: Cambridge University Press.

Brysk, Alison and Gershon Shafir, eds. 2004. *People Out of Place: Globalization, Human Rights and the Citizenship Gap*. New York and London: Routledge.

Burroughs, Michael D. 2015. "Hannah Arendt, 'Reflections on Little Rock,' and White Ignorance." *Critical Philosophy of Race* 3 (1): 52–78.

Butler, Judith. 2005. *Giving an Account of Oneself.* New York: Fordham University Press.

Butler, Judith. 2011. "Hannah Arendt's Challenge to Adolf Eichmann." *The Guardian*, August 29. https://www.theguardian.com/commentisfree/2011/aug/29/hannah-arendt-adolf-eichmann-banality-of-evil.

Butler, Judith. 2012. *Parting Ways: Jewishness and the Critique of Zionism.* New York: Columbia University Press.

Butler, Judith. 2015. *Notes Toward a Performative Theory of Assembly.* Cambridge, MA: Harvard University Press.

Canovan, Margaret. 1981. *Populism.* New York: Harcourt Brace Jovanovich.

Canovan, Margaret. 1990. "Socrates or Heidegger? Hannah Arendt's Reflections on Philosophy and Politics." *Social Research* 57 (1): 135–65.

Canovan, Margaret. 1995. *Hannah Arendt: A Reinterpretation of Her Political Thought.* Cambridge: Cambridge University Press.

Canovan, Margaret. 1999. "Trust the People! Populism and the Two Faces of Democracy." *Political Studies Association* 47 (1): 2–16.

Canovan, Margaret. 2002. "The People, the Masses, and the Mobilization of Power: The Paradox of Hannah Arendt's 'Populism.'" *Social Research* 69 (2): 403–22.

Carrington, Damian. 2019. "Public Concern Over Environment Reaches Record High in UK." *The Guardian online*, June 5. https://www.theguardian.com/environment/2019/jun/05/greta-thunberg-effect-public-concern-over-environment-reaches-record-high.

Clarke, James. 1993. "Social Justice and Political Freedom: Revisiting Hannah Arendt's Conception of Need." *Philosophy and Social Criticism* 19 (3–4): 333–47.

Çubukçu, Ayşa. 2020. "Of Rebels and Disobedients: Reflections on Arendt, Race, Lawbreaking." *Law and Critique* 32 (1): 33–50.

Cutting-Gray, Joanne. 1993. "Hannah Arendt, Feminism, and the Politics of Alterity: 'What Will We Lose If We Win?'" *Hypatia* 8 (1): 35–54.

Dekel, Irit and Esra Özyürek. 2021. "What Do We Talk About When We Talk About Antisemitism in Germany?" *Journal of Genocide Research* 23 (3): 392–9.

Descartes, René. 1641. "Meditations." https://www.sacred-texts.com/phi/desc/med.txt.

Di Cesare, Donatella. 2018. *Heidegger and the Jews: The Black Notebooks.* Cambridge, UK and Medford, MA: Polity Press.

Dietz, Mary G. 1991. "Hannah Arendt and the Feminist Politics." In *Hannah Arendt: Critical Essays*, edited by Lewis P. Hinchman and Sandra K. Hinchman, 231–55. New York: State University of New York Press.

Dietz, Mary G. 1995. "Feminist Receptions of Hannah Arendt." In

Feminist Interpretations of Hannah Arendt, edited by Bonnie Honig, 17–50. University Park, PA: Pennsylvania State University Press.

Disch, Lisa. 1994. *Hannah Arendt and the Limits of Philosophy.* Ithaca, NY and London: Cornell University Press.

Dolan, Frederick M. 2000. "Arendt on Philosophy and Politics." In *The Cambridge Companion to Hannah Arendt*, edited by Dana Villa, 261–76. Cambridge: Cambridge University Press.

Dossa, Shiraz. 1980. "Human Status and Politics: Hannah Arendt on the Holocaust." *Canadian Journal of Political Science/Revue canadienne de science politique* 13 (2): 309–23.

Ellison, Ralph. 1965. "Leadership from the Periphery." In *Who Speaks for the Negro?*, edited by Robert Penn Warren. Toronto: Random House.

El-Naggar, Mona. 2016. "Saudi Women Vote for the First Time. What Did That Look Like?" *New York Times*, October 18. https://www.nytimes.com/2016/10/17/ insider/saudi-women-vote-for-the-first-time-what-did-that-look-like.html.

Euben, Peter. 2000. "Arendt's Hellenism." In *The Cambridge Companion to Hannah Arendt*, edited by Dana Villa. Cambridge: Cambridge University Press.

Evans, Richard J. 2005. *The Third Reich in Power.* London and New York: Penguin.

Faye, Emmanuel. 2009. *Heidegger: Die Einführung des Nationalsozialismus in die Philosophie.* Berlin: Matthes und Seitz.

Faye, Emmanuel. 2011. *Heidegger: The Introduction of Nazism into Philosophy.* New Haven, CT: Yale University Press.

Fielding, Helen A. 2017. "A Feminist Phenomenology Manifesto." In *Feminist Phenomenology Futures*, edited by Helen A. Fieding and Dorothea E. Olkowski, vii–xxii. Bloomington: Indiana University Press.

Forst, Rainer. 2007. "Zur Aktualität der politischen Theorie Hannah Arendts." In Heinrich Böll Foundation, *Hannah Arendt: Verborgene Tradition—unzeitgemäße Aktualität?* Berlin: Akademie.

Foucault, Michel. 1983. "Afterword: The Subject and Power." In *Beyond Structuralism and Hermeneutics*, edited by Hubert Dreyfus and Paul Rabinow, 208–26. Chicago: University of Chicago Press.

Foucault, Michel. 2010. *The Birth of Biopolitics: Lectures at the Collège de France (1978–1979).* New York: Palgrave Macmillan.

Frantzman, Seth J. 2016. "Hannah Arendt, White Supremacist." *The Jerusalem Post*, June 6. https://www.jpost.com/opinion/hannah-arendt-white-supremacist-456007.

Fraser, Nancy. 2007. "Feminist Politics in the Age of Recognition: A Two-Dimensional Approach to Gender Justice." *Studies in Social Justice* 1 (1): 23–35.

Friedan, Betty. 2010. *The Feminine Mystique.* London: Penguin.

Gago, Verónica. 2020. *Feminist International: How to Change Everything.* London and New York: Verso.

Gardiner, Rita A. 2013. *Thinking with Arendt: Authenticity, Gender and Leadership.* University of Western Ontario, Electronic Thesis and Dissertation Repository. Paper 1468. http://ir.lib.uwo.ca/etd/1468.

Gills, Barry and Jamie Morgan 2020. "Global Climate Emergency: After COP24, Climate Science, Urgency, and the Threat to Humanity." *Globalizations* 6: 885–902.

Gilroy, Paul. 2005. *Postcolonial Melancholia.* New York: Columbia University Press.

Gines, Kathryn T. 2014. *Arendt and the Negro Question.* Bloomington: Indiana University Press.

Goldfarb, Jeffrey C. 2006. *The Politics of Small Things: The Power of the Powerless in Dark Times.* Chicago: University of Chicago Press.

Goldstein, Jürgen. 2012. *Perspektiven des politischen Denkens: Sechs Portraits.* Weilerswist: Velbrück Wissenschaft.

Golsan, Richard J. and Sarah Misemer, eds. 2017. *The Trial That Never Ends: Hannah Arendt's "Eichmann in Jerusalem" in Retrospect.* Toronto: University of Toronto Press.

Gordon, Mordechai, ed. 2001. *Hannah Arendt and Education: Renewing Our Common World.* Boulder, CO: Westview Press.

Gordon, Peter E. 2007. "The Concept of the Apolitical: German Jewish Thought and Weimar Political Theology." *Social Research* 74 (3): 855–78.

Grosse, Pascal. 2006. "From Colonialism to National Socialism to Postcolonialism: Hannah Arendt's 'The Origins of Totalitarianism.'" *Postcolonial Studies* 9 (1): 35–52.

Grunenberg, Antonia. 2006. *Hannah Arendt und Martin Heidegger: Geschichte einer Liebe.* Munich and Zurich: Piper.

Gündoğdu, Ayten. 2015. *Rightlessness in the Age of Rights.* Oxford and New York: Oxford University Press.

Guyer, Paul and Allen W. Wood, trs. and eds. 1998. *The Cambridge Edition of the Works of Immanuel Kant: Critique of Pure Reason.* New York: Cambridge University Press.

Habermas, Jürgen. 1977. "Hannah Arendt's Communications Concept of Power." *Social Research* 44 (1): 3–24.

Habermas, Jürgen. 1981. *Philosophisch-politische Profile.* Frankfurt am Main: Suhrkamp.

Habermas, Jürgen. 1988. "Martin Heidegger? Nazi, sicher ein Nazi!" In *Die Heidegger Kontroverse*, edited by Jürg Altwegg, 172–5. Frankfurt am Main: Athenäum.

Habermas, Jurgen. 1990. *Philosophical Discourse of Modernity.* Cambridge: Polity Press.

Habermas, Jürgen. 1997. *A Berlin Republic: Writings on Germany.* Lincoln: University of Nebraska Press.

Hagengruber, Ruth and Sarah Hutton, eds. 2021. *Women Philosophers from the Renaissance to the Enlightenment*. London: Routledge.

Haraway, Donna. 1988. "Situated Knowledges: The Science Question in Feminism and the Privilege of Partial Perspective." *Feminist Studies* 14 (3): 575–99.

Haraway, Donna. 1991. *Simians, Cyborgs, and Women: The Reinvention of Nature*. New York: Routledge.

Haraway, Donna. 2016. *Staying with the Trouble: Making Kin in the Chthulucene*. Durham, NC: Duke University Press.

Hargis, Jill. 2016. "Hannah Arendt's Turn to the Self and Environmental Responses to Climate Change Paralysis." *Environmental Politics* 25 (3): 475–93.

Hayden, Patrick. 2014. *Hannah Arendt: Key Concepts*. London and New York: Routledge.

Heidegger, Gertrud, ed. 2010. *Martin Heidegger: Letters to His Wife 1915–1970*, Cambridge: Polity Press.

Heidegger, Hermann. 2009. "'Die Selbstbehauptung der deutschen Universität.' Bemerkungen zur Rektoratsrede." *Heidegger Jahrbuch* 5: 361–6.

Heidegger, Martin. 1985. "The Self-Assertion of the German University." *The Review of Metaphysics* 38 (3): 467–502.

Heidegger, Martin. 1994. "Bremer und Freiburger Vorträge." *Gesamtausgabe* 79. Frankfurt am Main: Klostermann.

Heidegger, Martin. 2000. "Meine Beseitigung (1946)." *Gesamtausgabe* 16. Frankfurt am Main: Klostermann.

Heidegger, Martin and Karl Jaspers. 1990. *Briefwechsel 1920–1963*, edited by Walter Biemel and Hans Saner. Frankfurt am Main: Klostermann.

Herzog, Annabel. 2000. "Illuminating Inheritance. Benjamin's Influence on Arendt's Political Storytelling." *Philosophy and Social Criticism* 26 (5): 1–27.

Herzog, Annabel. 2001. "The Poetic Nature of Political Disclosure: Hannah Arendt's Storytelling." *Clio* 30 (2): 169–95.

Heuer, Wolfgang. 2012. "Narrativität und Bildlichkeit des politischen Handelns." In *Politische Existenz und republikanische Ordnung: Zum Staatsverständnis von Hannah Arendt*, edited by Karl-Heinz Breier and Alexander Gantschow, 253–78. Baden-Baden: Nomos.

Hill, Samantha. 2021. *Hannah Arendt (Critical Lives)*. London: Reaktion Books.

Hinchman Lewis P. and Sandra K. Hinchman, eds. 1994. *Hannah Arendt: Critical Essays*. Albany: State University of New York Press.

Honig, Bonnie. 1988. "Arendt, Identity, and Difference." *Political Theory* 16 (1): 77–98.

Honig, Bonnie. 1995a. "Introduction: The Arendt Question in Feminism."

Feminist Interpretations of Hannah Arendt, edited by Bonnie Honig, 1–16. University Park, PA: Pennsylvania State University Press.

Honig, Bonnie. 1995b. "Toward an Agonistic Feminism: Hannah Arendt and the Politics of Identity." In *Feminist Interpretations of Hannah Arendt*, edited by Bonnie Honig, 135–66. University Park, PA: Pennsylvania State University Press.

Honig, Bonnie. 2003. *Democracy and the Foreigner*. Princeton, NJ: Princeton University Press.

Honig, Bonnie. 2017. *Public Things: Democracy in Disrepair*. New York: Fordham University Press.

Honneth, Axel. 1994. *Kampf um Anerkennung: Zur moralischen Grammatik sozialer Konflikte*. Frankfurt am Main: Suhrkamp.

hooks, bell. 1986. "Sisterhood: Political Solidarity Between Women." *Feminist Review* 23: 125–38.

hooks, bell. 1994. *Teaching to Transgress: Education as the Practice of Freedom*. New York and London: Routledge.

Hyvönen, Ari-Elmeri. 2020. "Labor as Action: The Human Condition in the Anthropocene." *Research in Phenomenology* 50 (2): 240–60.

Hyvönen, Ari-Elmeri. 2021. "Genealogy of Experiential Frames: Methodological Notes on Arendt." *Genealogy* 5 (42): 1–14.

Jaeggi, Rahel. 2007. "Die in Dunkeln sieht man nicht: Hannah Arendts Theorie der Politisierung." In *Hannah Arendt: Verborgene Tradition—unzeitgemäße Aktualität?*, edited by Stefanie Rosenmüller, 241–50. Berlin: Akademie.

Jaspers, Karl. 1919. *Psychologie der Weltanschauungen*. Berlin: Piper.

Jaspers, Karl. 1977. *Philosophische Autobiographie*. Munich: Piper.

Jaspers, Karl. 2008. *Philosophie II: Existenzerhellung*. Berlin and Heidelberg: Springer.

Jonas, Hans. 2008. *Memoires*. Waltham, MA: Brandeis University Press.

Jones, Kathleen B. 1993. *Compassionate Authority: Democracy and the Representation of Women*. New York and London: Routledge.

Kant, Immanuel. 1991a. *Kant: Political Writings* (Cambridge Texts in the History of Political Thought), 2nd. ed., edited by H. S. Reiss. Cambridge and New York: Cambridge University Press.

Kant, Immanuel. 1991b. "Toward Perpetual Peace." In *Kant: Political Writings* (Cambridge Texts in the History of Political Thought), 2nd. ed., edited by H. S. Reiss. Cambridge and New York: Cambridge University Press.

Kant, Immanuel. 2011. *Träume eines Geistersehers, erläutert durch Träume der Metaphysik*. Project Gutenberg. https://www.gutenberg.org/ebooks/36076.

Kant, Immanuel. 2012. "An answer to the question: What is enlightenment?" In *Kant, Practical Philosophy. The Cambridge Edition of the*

Works of Immanuel Kant. Edited by Mary J. Gregor, 11–22. Cambridge: Cambridge University Press.

Kantorowicz, Ernst. 2016. *The King's Two Bodies*. Princeton, NJ: Princeton University Press.

Kattago, Siobhan. 2017. "The End of the European Honeymoon? Refugees, Resentment and the Clash of Solidarities." *Anthropological Journal of European Cultures* 26 (1): 35–52.

Kattago, Siobhan. 2019. "Statelessness, Refugees and Hospitality: Reading Arendt and Kant in the Twenty-First Century." *New German Critique* 46 (1): 15–27.

King, Richard H. 2012. "On Race and Culture: Arendt and Her Contemporaries." In *Politics in Dark Times: Encounters with Hannah Arendt*, edited by Seyla Benhabib, 113–34. New York: Cambridge University Press.

Knott, Marie Luise, ed. 2017. *The Correspondence of Hannah Arendt and Gershom Scholem*. Chicago: University of Chicago Press.

Knowles, Adam. 2019. *Heidegger's Fascist Affinities: A Politics of Silence*. Stanford, CA: Stanford University Press.

Kohn, Jerome. 1990. "Thinking/Acting." *Social Research* 57 (1): 105–34.

Koivusalo, Markku. 2010. "Hannah Arendt's Angels and Demons: Ten Spiritual Exercises." In *Hannah Arendt: Practice, Thought and Judgment*, edited by Mika Ojakangas, 105–50. Helsinki: Helsinki Collegium for Advanced Studies.

Korsgaard, Morten Timmermann. 2020. "Visiting Exemplars. An Arendtian Exploration of Educational Judgement." *Ethics and Education* 15 (2): 247–59.

Koyama, Emi. 2003. "Transfeminist Manifesto." In *Catching a Wave: Reclaiming Feminism for the 21st Century*, edited by Rory Dicker and Alison Piepmeier, 244–59. Boston: Northeastern University Press.

Kruks, Sonia. 2017. "Hannah Arendt, Gender, and Political Judgment: A Phenomenological Critique." In *Rethinking Feminist Phenomenology*, edited by Sarah Cohen Shabot and Christinia Landry, 121–36. Lanham, MD: Rowman & Littlefield.

Kunath, Robert. 2021. "Anti-plurality and Genocide: Hannah Arendt's Understanding of Holocaust Perpetrators and Contemporary Holocaust Research." In *Hannah Arendt: Challenges of Plurality*, edited by Maria Robaszkiewicz and Tobias Matzner, 159–74. Cham: Springer.

Lechte, John. 2018. "Rethinking Arendt's Theory of Necessity: Humanness as 'Way of Life', or: the Ordinary as Extraordinary." *Theory, Culture & Society* 35 (1): 3–22.

Lederman, Shmuel. 2019. *Hannah Arendt and Participatory Democracy: A People's Utopia*. London: Palgrave Macmillan.

Lee, Christopher J. 2011. "Locating Hannah Arendt within Postcolonial Thought: A Prospectus." *College Literature* 38 (1): 95–114.

Locke, Jill. 2013. "Little Rock's Social Question: Reading Arendt on School Desegregation and Social Climbing." *Political Theory* 41 (4): 533–61.

Locke, John. 1796. *Two Treatises of Government*. Glasgow: W. Paton, for R. Smith, Bookseller, Paisley, and D. Boag.

Locke, John. 1836. *An Essay Concerning Human Understanding*. London: Tegg and Son.

Locke, John. 1998. *An Essay Concerning Human Understanding*. London: Penguin Classics.

Loidolt, Sophie. 2018. *Phenomenology of Plurality: Hannah Arendt on Political Subjectivity*. London and New York: Routledge.

Lorde, Audre. 1984. *Sister Outsider: Essays and Speeches*. Berkeley: Crossing Press.

Ludz, Ursula. 2007. "Arendt's Observations and Thought on Ethical Questions." *Social Research* 74 (3): 797–810.

MacKinnon, Catherine A. 2007. *Are Women Human?: And Other International Dialogues*. Cambridge, MA and London: Harvard University Press.

McNay, Lois. 2010. "Feminism and Post-identity Politics: The Problem of Agency" *Constellations* 17 (4): 512–25.

Marcuse, Herbert. 2005. Correspondence with Martin Heidegger 1947–8. https://www.marcuse.org/herbert/pubs/40spubs/47MarcuseHeidegger.htm#mh2.

Marder, Michael. 2013. *Plant-Thinking: A Philosophy of Vegetal Life*. New York: Columbia University Press.

Markus, Maria. 1987. "The 'Anti-feminism' of Hannah Arendt." *Thesis Eleven* 17: 76–87.

Marshall, David. 2010. "The Polis and Its Analogues in the Thought of Hannah Arendt." *Modern Intellectual History* 7 (1): 123–49.

Martin, Berndt. 1989. *Martin Heidegger und das "Dritte Reich": Ein Kompendium*. Darmstadt: WBG.

Maslin, Kimberly. 2013. "The Gender-Neutral Feminism of Hannah Arendt." *Hypatia* 28 (3): 585–601.

Maxwell, Gordon and Toby Miller. 2019. "Why Are So Many Adults So Frightened of Greta Thunberg?" *Psychology Today*, September 8. https://www.psychologytoday.com/sg/blog/greening-the-media/201909/why-are-so-many-adults-so-frightened-greta-thunberg.

Menke, Christoph. 2014. "Dignity as the Right to Have Rights: Human Dignity in Hannah Arendt." In *The Cambridge Handbook of Human Dignity: Interdisciplinary Perspectives*, edited by Marcus Düwell, Jens Braarvig, Roger Brownsword, and Dietmar Mieth, 332–42. Cambridge: Cambridge University Press.

Mies, Maria and Vandana Shiva. 1993. *Ecofeminism*. Atlantic Highlands, NJ: Zed Books.

Millett, Kate. 1969. *Sexual Politics*. New York: Ballantine Books.

Mohanty, Chandra T. 1997. "Women Workers and Capitalist Scripts: Ideologies of Domination, Common Interests, and the Politics of Solidarity." In *Feminist Genealogies, Colonial Legacies, Democratic Futures*, edited by M. Jacqui Alexander and Chandra Talpade Mohanty, 3–29. New York: Routledge.

Morgan, Robin, ed. 1970. *Sisterhood is Powerful*. New York: Random House.

Moses, A. Dirk. 2011. "Hannah Arendt, Imperialisms, and the Holocaust." In *German Colonialism: Race, the Holocaust, and Postwar Germany*, edited by Volker Langbehn and Mohamad Salama, 72–92. New York: Columbia University Press.

Moyn, Samuel. 2008. "Hannah Arendt on the Secular." *New German Critique* 105: 71–96.

Müller, Jan-Werner. 2016. *Populism*. Philadelphia: University of Pennsylvania Press.

Neiman, Susan. 2001. "Theodicy in Jerusalem." In *Arendt in Jerusalem*, edited by Steven E. Aschheim, 65–90. Berkeley: University of California Press.

Neiman, Susan. 2010. "Banality Reconsidered." In *Politics in Dark Times: Encounters with Hannah Arendt*, edited by Seyla Benhabib, 205–315. New York: Cambridge University Press.

Norton, Anne. 1995. "Heart of Darkness: Africa and African Americans in the Writings of Hannah Arendt." In *Feminist Interpretations of Hannah Arendt*, edited by Bonnie Honig, 247–62. Philadelphia: Pennsylvania State University Press.

Ober, Josiah. 1996. *The Athenian Revolution*. Princeton, NJ: Princeton University Press.

O'Brien, Mary. 1981. *The Politics of Reproduction*. Boston: Routledge.

Owens, Patricia. 2012. "Not Life but the World is at Stake: Hannah Arendt on Citizenship in the Age of the Social." *Citizenship Studies* 16 (2): 297–307.

Owens, Patricia. 2017. "Racism in the Theory Canon: Hannah Arendt and 'the One Great Crime in Which America Was Never Involved.'" *Millennium: Journal of International Studies* 45 (3): 403–24.

Palazzi, Franco. 2017. "'Reflections on Little Rock' and Reflective Judgment." *Philosophical Papers* 46 (3): 389–441.

Parekh, Serena. 2013. "Reconciling with Heidegger: Friendship, Disappointment and Love in the Wake of the Controversy." *Philosophy and Social Criticism* 39 (9): 885–92.

Pariser, Eli. 2011. *The Filter Bubble: What the Internet is Hiding from You*. London: Viking.

Parvikko, Tuija. 2015. "Heart of Darkness. Rereading Hannah Arendt's Critique of Colonialism and Race-Thinking with Edward W. Said." In *The Politics of World Politics*, edited by Paul-Erik Korvela, Kari Palonen, and Anna Björk, 247–63. Jyväskylä: SoPhi, University of Jyväskylä. https://jyx.jyu.fi/bitstream/handle/123456789/46807/978-951-39-6284-5.pdf.

Parvikko, Tuija. 2021. *Arendt, Eichmann and the Politics of the Past*. Helsinki: University of Helsinki Press.

Passerin d'Entrèves, Maurizio and Seyla Benhabib, eds. 1997. *Habermas and the Unfinished Project of Modernity: Critical Essays on The Philosophical Discourse of Modernity*. Cambridge, MA: MIT Press.

Passini, Stefano. 2012. "The Facebook and Twitter Revolutions: Active Participation in the 21st Century." *Human Affairs* 22 (3): 301–12.

Pearce, Ruth, Sonja Erikainen, and Ben Vincent. 2020. "TERF Wars: An Introduction." *The Sociological Review Monographs* 68 (4): 677–98.

Pitkin, Hanna Fenichel. 1981. "Justice: On Relating Private and Public." *Political Theory* 9 (3): 327–52.

Pitkin, Hanna Fenichel. 1995. "Conformism, Housekeeping and the Attack on the Blob: The Origins of Hannah Arendt's Concept of the Social." In *Feminist Interpretations of Hannah Arendt*, edited by Bonnie Honig, 51–81. University Park, PA: Pennsylvania State University Press.

Pitkin, Hanna Fenichel. 1998. *The Attack of the Blob: Hannah Arendt's Concept of the Social*. Chicago: University of Chicago Press.

Plato. *The Apology of Socrates*, cited according to Stephanus pagination.

Plato. *Gorgias*, cited according to Stephanus pagination.

Plato. *Seventh Letter*, cited according to Stephanus pagination.

Plato. *Theaetetus*, cited according to Stephanus pagination.

Pluhar, Werner, tr. 1987. *Kant: Critique of Judgment*. Indianapolis: Hackett.

Rawls, John. 1971. *A Theory of Justice*. Cambridge, MA: Harvard University Press.

Readon, Sarah. 2012. "Was the Arab Spring Really a Facebook Revolution?" *New Scientist*, April 3. https://www.newscientist.com/article/mg21428596-400-was-the-arab-spring-really-a-facebook-revolution/.

Reed, Isaac Ariail. 2017. "Chains of Power and Their Representations." *Sociological Theory* 35 (2): 87–117.

Reed, Isaac Ariail and Michael Weinman. 2018. "Agency, Power, Modernity: A Manifesto for Social Theory." *European Journal of Cultural and Political Sociology* 6 (1): 6–50.

Rich, Adrienne. 1979. *On Lies, Secrets and Silence: Selected Prose 1966–1978*. New York: W. W. Norton.

Rich, Adrienne. 1993. "Split at the Root: An Essay on Jewish Identity." In *Adrienne Rich's Poetry and Prose*, edited by Barbara Charlesworth Gelpi and Albert Gelpi, 224–39. New York: W. W. Norton.

Robaszkiewicz, Maria. 2017. *Übungen im politischen Denken: Hannah Arendts Schriften als Einleitung der politischen Praxis*. Wiesbaden: Springer.

Robaszkiewicz, Maria. 2018. "Women as *zoa politika*, or: Why There Could Never Be a Women's Party. An Arendtian-Inspired Phenomenology of a Female Political Subject." In *Women Phenomenologists on Social Ontology*, edited by Ruth Hagengruber and Sebastian Luft, 195–206. Cham: Springer.

Robaszkiewicz, Maria. 2021. "From the Darkness to the Light: Hannah Arendt's Phenomenology of Migration." In *Hannah Arendt: Challenges of Plurality*, edited by Maria Robaszkiewicz and Tobias Matzner, 107–25. Cham: Springer.

Robinson, Benjamin Lewis. 2018. "Between Future and Past: An Exercise in Political Ecology." *HannahArendt.net* 9 (1), 1–12. https://www.hanna harendt.net/index.php/han/article/view/406/534.

Rodowick, David. 2021. *An Education in Judgment: Hannah Arendt and the Humanities*. Chicago: Chicago University Press.

Rosenthal, Abigail. 2011. "Defining Evil Away: Arendt's Forgiveness." *Philosophy* 86 (2): 155–74.

Rothberg, Michael. 2009. *Multidirectional Memory: Remembering the Holocaust in the Age of Decolonization*. Stanford, CA: Stanford University Press.

Scheuerman, William E. 1997. "Revolutions and Constitutions: Hannah Arendt's Challenge to Carl Schmitt." *Canadian Journal of Law & Jurisprudence* 10 (1): 141–61.

Schmitt, Carl. 1988. *The Crisis of Parliamentary Democracy*. Cambridge, MA: MIT Press.

Schmitt, Carl. 2005. *Political Theology*. Chicago: University of Chicago Press.

Schoonheim, Liesbeth. 2020. "The 'rightful place in man's enduring chronicle': Arendt's Benjaminian Historiography." *History of European Ideas* 46 (6): 844–61.

Schott, Robin May. 2010. "Natality and Destruction: Arendtian Reflections on War Rape." In *Birth, Death, and Femininity: Philosophies of Embodiment*, edited by Robin May Schott, 49–69. Bloomington: Indiana University Press.

Shafir, Gershon. 2004. "Citizenship and Human Rights in an Era of Globalization." In *People Out of Place: Globalization, Human Rights and the Citizenship Gap*, edited by Alison Brysk and Gershon Shafir, 11–28. New York and London: Routledge.

Smith, Stacy. 2001. "Education for Judgment: An Arendtian Oxymoron?" In *Hannah Arendt and Education: Renewing Our Common World*, edited by Mordechai Gordon, 67–91. Boulder, CO: Westview Press.

Sobczynski, Adam and Alexander Camman. 2016. "Ein moralisches Desaster." *Die Zeit*, October 12.

Stangneth, Bettina. 2014. *Eichmann Before Jerusalem: The Unexamined Life of a Mass Murderer*. New York: Vintage.

Sternberger, Dolf. 1977. "The Sunken City: Hannah Arendt's Idea of Politics." *Social Research* 44 (1): 132–46.

Taminiaux, Jacques. 1997. *The Thracian Maid and the Professional Thinker: Arendt and Heidegger.* Albany: SUNY Press.

Taminiaux, Jacques. 2000. "Athens and Rome." In *The Cambridge Companion to Hannah Arendt,* edited by Dana Villa, 165–77. Cambridge: Cambridge University Press.

Taylor, Charles. 1994. *Multiculturalism and "The Politics of Recognition."* Princeton, NJ: Princeton University Press.

Taylor, Matthew. 2019. "Climate Crisis Seen as 'Most Important Issue' by Public, Poll Shows." *The Guardian online,* September 18. https://www.theguardian.com/environment/2019/sep/18/climate-crisis-seen-as-most-important-issue-by-public-poll-shows.

Trawny, Peter. 2016. *Heidegger and the Myth of a Jewish World Conspiracy.* Chicago: Chicago University Press.

Tsao, Roy. 2002. "Arendt Against Athens: Rereading *The Human Condition.*" *Political Theory* 30 (1): 97–123.

Vasterling, Veronica. 2007. "Cognitive Theory and Phenomenology in Arendt's and Nussbaum's Work on Narrative." *Human Studies* 30 (2): 79–95.

Vasterling, Veronica. 2021. "The Human-Animal Distinction in Relation to World and Plurality." *HannahArendt.net* 11 (1): 115–32. https://hannaharendt.net/index.php/han/article/view/461/661.

Villa, Dana. 1996. *Arendt and Heidegger: The Fate of the Political.* Princeton, NJ: Princeton University Press.

Villa, Dana. 2021. *Arendt* (Routledge Philosophers). New York: Routledge.

Voegelin, Eric. 1953. "The Origins of Totalitarianism." In *The Review of Politics,* 15 (1): 68–76.

Voice, Paul. 2013. "Consuming the World: Hannah Arendt on Politics and the Environment." *Journal of International Political Theory* 9 (2): 178–93.

Vormann, Boris and Michael Weinman. 2020. *The Emergence of Illiberalism: Understanding a Global Phenomenon.* New York: Routledge.

Vowinckel, Annette. 2001. *Geschichtsbegriff und Historisches Denken bei Hannah Arendt.* Cologne: Böhlau.

Vowinckel, Annette. 2004. *Hannah Arendt: Zwischen deutscher Philosophie und jüdischer Politik.* Berlin: Lukas.

Waldron, Jeremy. 2000. "Arendt's Constitutional Politics." In *The Cambridge Companion to Hannah Arendt,* edited by Dana Villa, 201–19. Cambridge: Cambridge University Press.

Walsh, Philip. 2015. *Arendt Contra Sociology: Theory, Society and Its Science.* New York: Routledge.

Weber, Max, 2014. "Politics as a Vocation." *Moulin Digital Editions.*

https://ia802609.us.archive.org/35/items/weber_max_1864_1920_polit
ics_as_a_vocation/weber_max_1864_1920_politics_as_a_vocation.pdf.

Weinman, Michael. 2018. "Arendt and the Legitimate Expectation for Hospitality and Membership Today." *Moral Philosophy and Politics* 5 (1): 127–49.

Weinthal, Benjamin. 2012. "Berlin Jewish Museum Event Calls for Israel Boycott." *Jerusalem Post*, September 16. https://www.jpost.com/jewish -world/jewish-features/berlin-jewish-museum-event-calls-for-israel-boy cott.

Weir, Allison. 2008. "Global Feminism and Transformative Identity Politics." *Hypatia* 23 (4): 110–33.

Weissbrodt, David S. 2008. *The Human Rights of Non-citizens*. Oxford: Oxford University Press.

Wilkinson, Lynn R. 2004. "Hannah Arendt on Isak Dinesen: Between Storytelling and Theory." *Comparative Literature* 56 (1): 77–98.

Wolin, Sheldon. 1983. "Hannah Arendt: Democracy and the Political." *Salmagundi* 60: 3–19.

Worth, Sarah E. 2008. "Storytelling and Narrative Knowing: An Examination of the Epistemic Benefits of Well-Told Stories." *The Journal of Aesthetic Education* 42 (2): 42–56.

Young, Iris Marion. 1990. *Justice and the Politics of Difference*. Princeton, NJ: Princeton University Press.

Young, Iris Marion. 1997. "Asymmetrical Reciprocity: On Moral Respect, Wonder, and Enlarged Thought." *Constellations* 3 (3): 340–63.

Young-Bruehl, Elisabeth. 1982. *For Love of the World*. New Haven, CT: Yale University Press.

Young-Bruehl, Elisabeth. 1996. "Hannah Arendt Among Feminists" In *Hannah Arendt: Twenty Years Later*, edited by Larry May and Jerome Kohn, 307–24. Cambridge, MA: MIT Press.

Young-Bruehl, Elisabeth and Jerome Kohn. 2001. "What and How We Learned from Hannah Arendt: An Exchange of Letters." In *Hannah Arendt and Education: Renewing Our Common World*, edited by Mordechai Gordon, 225–56. Boulder, CO: Westview Press.

Zaborowski, Holger. 2010. *Eine Frage von Irre und Schuld: Martin Heidegger und der Nationalsozialismus*. Frankfurt am Main: Fischer.

Zerilli, Linda. 2005a. *Feminism and the Abyss of Freedom*. Chicago: University of Chicago Press.

Zerilli, Linda. 2005b. "'We Feel Our Freedom': Imagination and Judgment in the Thought of Hannah Arendt." *Political Theory* 33 (2): 158–88.

Zerilli, Linda. 2016. *A Democratic Theory of Judgment*. Chicago: University of Chicago Press.

Zerilli, Linda. 2019a. "Racial Regimes, Comparative Politics, and the Problem of Judgment." *Ethnic and Racial Studies* 42 (8): 1321–6.

Zerilli, Linda. 2019b. "A Reply to Lucy Benjamin." Syndicate Symposium

on *A Democratic Theory of Judgment* by Linda Zerilli. https://syndicate
.network/symposia/philosophy/a-democratic-theory-of-judgment/.

Zertal, Idith. 2010. *Israel's Holocaust and the Politics of Nationhood.*
Cambridge: Cambridge University Press.

Zielinski, Luisa. 2016. "In His Own Words." *The Paris Review*, October
18. https://www.theparisreview.org/blog/2016/10/18/in-his-own-words/.

Index

220